"Every new parent and professional who should read *Raising a Secure Child*. It is that good. Biringen has distilled many years of experience as a researcher, clinician, and parent into every page of this well-written book. She knows what she is talking about. She describes the complex subject of attachment between parent and child in a way that is useful for the clinician as well as for the parent. I rarely come across a work that is so useful in my work as a child psychiatrist."

—Gerald E. Nelson, M.D., child psychiatrist,
author of *Good Discipline, Good Kids* and *One Minute Scolding*

"What Dr. Spock did for children's physical health, Dr. Biringen does for mental health. A must read for all adults who relate to children and want them to have emotional intelligence. Learn new skills for emotional availability between parents and children, which are also 'life skills' that will help individuals in all their relationships."

—Lawrence D. Martel, Ph.D.,
author of *The 7 Secrets of Learning Revealed* and *School Success*

Most Perigee Books are available at special quantity discounts for bulk purchases for sales promotions, premiums, fund-raising or educational use. Special books, or book excerpts, can also be created to fit specific needs.

For details, write: Special Markets, The Berkley Publishing Group, 375 Hudson Street, New York, New York 10014.

RAISING A
SECURE CHILD

*Creating an
Emotional Connection
Between You
and Your Child*

Zeynep Biringen, Ph.D.

A Perigee Book

A Perigee Book
Published by The Berkley Publishing Group
A division of Penguin Group (USA) Inc.
375 Hudson Street
New York, New York 10014

Perigee trade paperback edition: July 2004

Visit our website at www.penguin.com

Library of Congress Cataloging-in-Publication Data

Biringen, Zeynep.
Raising a secure child : creating an emotional connection between you and your child /
Zeynep Biringen.—1st Perigee ed.
p. cm.
Includes bibliographical references.
ISBN 0-399-52994-2
1. Parent and child. 2. Child rearing. 3. Security (Psychology) in children. I. Title.

HQ755.85.B553 2004
649'.1—dc22
2004044487

Printed in the United States of America

10 9 8 7 6 5 4 3 2 1

Dedication

This book is based on sixteen years of scientific research on the construct of emotional availability, conducted by me and my colleagues, first at the University of California at Berkeley while I was a doctoral student and later as a MacArthur Postdoctoral Fellow, working with Robert Emde, Inge Bretherton, and Joseph Campos. I am indebted to Dr. Robert Emde and Dr. JoAnn Robinson for collaborating with me in the refinement of the Emotional Availability Scales, and to Dr. Emde for continued interest, inspiration, enthusiasm, and support in this area. Most of all, his creative spark on the topic of emotional expressions and emotional exchange has helped me remain focused on this area. I also thank my international colleagues in Australia (Drs. Frances Gibson, Cathy McMahon, and Judy Ungerer); in Germany (Drs. Andreas Wiefel and Gabriele Oepen); in Israel (Drs. Avi Sagi, David Oppenheim, Yair Ziv, and Ora Aviezar), who have helped me further train professionals to use the system of emotional availability described in this book; and numerous other colleagues in Belgium, Japan, and England, who have used the system and provided feedback. I would like to thank Dr. Ann Easterbrooks for collaborations and disseminations of this work on emotional availability to the scientific community.

I thank Drs. Mary Main and Inge Bretherton for inspiration and intellectual exchange in the area of infant-parent and child-parent attachment. I have learned more from these exchanges than I can describe in words. It is no wonder that my own research has focused on the integration of emotions and attachment.

I thank the MacArthur Foundation, the National Science Foundation, Sixma Xi Scientific Research Society, and Colorado State University for support of the research presented here.

I thank my students and colleagues at Colorado State University, including but not limited to Wendi Grigg, Jamie Damon, Ellen Coker, Barbara Kase, Jen Krafchick, Dave Brown, Jen Mone, Shauna Skillern, and Ron and Bonnie Bend, for ongoing intellectual exchange on this topic and for reviewing parts or all of this book and/or of the video we have produced on emotional availability in relation to "school readiness." I am grateful for their suggestions and insights. I extend special thanks to the Pikes Peak Mental Health Center of Colorado Springs, Colorado, for sharing with me their work on "attachment disorders," and many aspects of the work presented on adopted children draws from their expertise. I thank my colleagues Drs. Karen Barrett, Debbie Fidler, and Lorraine Kubicek, for insightful discussions on emotional availability in families where a child has special needs, and Dr. Robert Pianta, for consulting on my National Science Foundation project and providing important feedback on this concept at the scientific level.

I am indebted to Vicki St. George, Sandra Rush, and Pam Liflander, who have helped edit numerous drafts; each has added so much insight and clarity to this work and exercised emotional availability skills in bringing it to completion. I extend special appreciation to Wendy Keller, my literary agent, as she has skillfully shepherded me through the process of writing and publishing this book. Her immediate recognition of this scientific work as important for the public is the major reason for my writing this book—she also has utilized advanced emotional availability skills in getting me through this process. I am grateful to my editor at Perigee, Sheila Curry Oakes, for support, patience, and understanding throughout the year of writing this book.

I also thank my husband for being emotionally available in relationship with me and our ten-year-old daughter and always being "there" no matter what. Special thanks go to my daughter for taking a personal interest in the contents of this book and, yes, helping me with the title! I have learned much about emotional availability and secure connections from both of them.

This book is dedicated to all the children and families who have participated in our research over the years and who have trusted us with significant personal aspects of their lives. It is their generosity that has made the scientific research and this book possible!

Contents

Introduction

My goal in this book is to draw on the scientific research from child-development laboratories (both nationally and internationally) to help parents understand the connections between parenting and the emotional futures of their children. With information from hundreds of hours of parent interviews about their own childhoods and their perceptions of their children, as well as firsthand observations of parent-child interactions, I can offer information on "real" families. Most of my research involves "normal" families who have volunteered their participation. Therefore, the findings from these studies offer universal relevance. As a child psychologist who conducts developmental assessments and treats children with numerous problems, I also have culled dozens of personal stories of families as parents make the journey to correcting their children's problems with the goal of creating better futures for them—in many cases, better childhoods and futures than they themselves had.

As part of my research studies and practice, I constantly see children who are desperately seeking sources of connection. If they are not connected to their parents, they might spend hours at the computer, e-mailing strangers and in chat rooms, looking for someone, somewhere, to connect with them on any level. Unfortunately, many children's unhappiness goes unrecognized because all too often their parents are clueless as well as helpless in the face of their kids' disaffection. As a parent, I have another, even wider perspective. Because I am concerned about friendships, playdates, sleepovers, and the like, I am continually interacting with other parents and children. Many of my old friends have now become parents; most of my new friends are parents.

In this book, I describe a well-established theory of child development—attachment theory. The research offers clear evidence of why a secure attachment is the cornerstone of healthy development and how it contributes to raising secure children. Attachment theory began in the 1950s with the work of John Bowlby, a British psychiatrist and psychoanalyst, who observed young children's reactions to separation from their parents and their reactions to loss. He also studied children in unusual circumstances, such as those raised in institutions. On the basis of his observations of infants and young children as well as his extensive knowledge of the field of ethology, he concluded that the young of all species come into this world biologically prepared to love and to attach to a loving caregiver. He believed, and it has been documented, that all children are attached to the individuals who take care of them. So unless a child is raised in an institution or there are many changes in the caregiving environment (such as foster care), children attach and love their parents. It is a biological imperative because it guarantees the survival of a species. All children are better off being connected with a wiser adult than they are taking care of themselves.

A child shows attachment through a cluster of instinctive behaviors that serve to create physical closeness to the adult caregiver, such as reaching, clinging, sucking, and locomotion. From an emotional perspective, attachment is the creation of a bond between the caregiver (mother, father, grandparent, day-care provider) that helps the infant or child understand the world and form a view of the world—what we call "internal working model," that is, scripts or templates that enable individuals to understand themselves and others.

Attachment theory gives us the answers we need to raise emotionally healthy and secure children and tells us that all children in relatively normal circumstances will be ready and willing to create that special bond. However, attachment theory and research also gives us some information that might be difficult for us to hear—namely, that all children do not become securely attached just because they are born into a so-called normal home. That is, "being attached" does not necessarily mean "securely attached."

Although Bowlby believed that attachment is the key to survival and protection of the species and, therefore, a biological necessity, when our babies and children show attachment, they are not necessarily showing one pattern of attachment. Four distinct attachment patterns have been identified—one secure and three forms of insecure connection. Each will be reviewed. This book will help you identify your child's attachment pattern and make adjustments when necessary to achieve a healthy connection with your child.

Parenting experts have advocated what is called "attachment parenting." The term *attachment parenting* might sound familiar because it has been popularized in many parenting books. However, only the label has been borrowed, not the scientific research on which this topic is based. There is no scientific evidence to indicate that the practices such as "cosleeping" or "birth bonding"—the delaying of any separation or routine procedures during the newborn period until after the family has had time to bond—have much of an effect on long-term parent-child relationships. In fact, such statements have created much unnecessary guilt and worry among parents of premies and parents of adoptive children who for health or logistical reasons are unable to take part in this form of connecting with a child. There is also no good scientific evidence that "babywearing" or "breast-feeding on cue" have an effect on a child's long-term social/emotional development. Some (but not necessarily all) of these recommendations are sound advice, but they are *not* based on mainstream attachment theory or on scientific research.

Similarly, the attachment research tradition has inspired a stream of unsubstantiated and harmful parenting therapies such as "holding therapies" to induce attachment. These therapies have absolutely nothing to do with this line of scientific research and are actually harmful to children. Children who have been abused or neglected or those who have faced disruptions of affectional bonds (such as those in foster care or those who were adopted) are sometimes seen as candidates for these treatments. Such therapies involve prolonged restraint of the child, ridiculing the child, or interference with bodily functions (such as breathing). These therapies are coercive and traumatizing, and although they purport to break down the wall of resistance many children have to caregivers, they in fact instill fear, terror, and rage and reinforce the feeling that adults cannot and should not be trusted. More gentle means of working with "attachment disorders" are described later in this book.

Child-parent attachment has important consequences for children, some of it social/emotional and some biological/physiological. This book focuses on the social/emotional, but I would note here that there is evidence to suggest that positive and warm parent-child exchanges are shaping a child's brain and body as he or she grows. Certainly, a parent's caress can lower the amount of stress hormones circulating in the blood and can help a child's body regulate its own response to upsetting or traumatizing events.

My own studies as well as those of others reveal that 25 to 30 percent of families have children who do not feel secure in the parent-child connection, although many, in my view, are fully normal and do not deserve any type of diagnosis. (The percentage is higher for "at-risk" children, such as those from low-income, abusive, or otherwise stressful households.) Furthermore, studies reveal that those children who do not feel secure in the parent-child connection and do not feel that their parents have met their emotional needs go on to develop less competently than children who feel secure and who experience happy childhoods. What is striking to me is that in a substantial portion of the families in which a child feels insecure, parents do not seem to know that there is a problem! In fact, most parents seem unaware of any problem until their child's adolescence, when these problems become very obvious.

In this book, I will present an understanding of "emotional availability" in the parent-child relationship as a means toward achieving secure attachment with one's child. "Emotional availability" is a research-based, scientifically validated assessment of the quality of communication and connection between a caregiver and child. I will describe how a parent can raise a secure child through interactions that are emotionally available. *Many parents do not seem to be aware of anything being remiss in their relationships with their child. I would like to teach you the skills to become aware of security and/or insecurity and to improve the quality of your parent-child relationship.*

Many parents believe their child's emotional development is important when in fact parents also need to develop emotionally—not just monitor and encourage the emotional development of their children. The principles described in this book are not simply about teaching parents to encourage *their child's* emotional development, but about getting both parent and child to participate with each other in an emotionally available way. Because the adult has the power to start things on the right foot (or to help start over!), I invite you to read on about how *you* can shape your child's emotional development.

Although I might be using the term *parent, mother,* or *father,* I am talking about any caregiver who has a strong tie to a child. In other words, such a caregiver might be a grandparent (and many grandparents today are not only very involved with their grandchildren, some are also raising them). I also mean any important person in a child's life, including long-term nanny, aunt, uncle, day-care provider, or teacher, provided the ties are strong emotional ones. The ideas in this book are designed for a network of social relationships in a child's life—not just technically a parent. Each caregiver in a child's social network is important, and the more secure and connected relationships a child has, the better for him or her. Therefore, a biological mother, an adoptive father, a teacher, a married father, a divorced mother, a day-care provider, a grandparent, and anyone who works, plays, and/or cares for children can benefit from *Raising a Secure Child*—the more secure relationships a child has in his life, the better for his emotional future.

Although real stories of patients and research participants are presented in this book, critical information about families has been changed and/or masked to maintain confidentiality. Although the content of the stories is real, gender, names, occupations, and any other potentially identifying information are fictional.

one

Parents and Kids—
Connected for Life

Romance fails us and so do friendships, but the relationship of parent and child, less noisy than others, remains indelible and indestructible, the strongest relationship on earth.

—Theodor Reik,
Of Love and Lust (1957)

It is our first relationship, one that starts long before we are born. Genetically, it begins the moment egg and sperm come together. As the cells that ultimately form "us" divide, separate, and create proto-organs and limbs, we are constantly linked with one parent—our mother—through the physical channel of the umbilical cord. Her blood feeds us; what she eats is what we eat; the chemicals created by her emotions affect us. We are built from our parents' tissue for nine full months until we come sliding (or yelling) into the world, fully formed, hopefully healthy—and completely helpless.

Then the *real* work of parenting begins.

Parenting is a lifelong commitment. It is rarely a glamorous job, and certainly an uncompensated one in terms of monetary return. But in terms of shaping the future, parenting is probably the most important job we will ever have. As author Joyce Maynard wrote, "For a parent, it's hard to recognize the significance of your work when you're immersed in the mundane details. Few of us, as we run the bath water or spread the peanut butter on the bread, proclaim proudly, 'I'm making my contribution to the future of the planet.' But . . . few jobs in the world of paychecks and promotions compare in significance to the job of parent."

In my profession as a child psychologist and researcher in the field of child development and emotional availability, I have spent thousands of hours observing interactions between parents and children. And yet, like most first-time parents, I vacillated between feelings of confidence and terror when I was expecting my own child. Part of me felt that parenting is intuitive, that I would know just how to soothe, comfort, love, and interact with this baby. After all, she and I had experienced an extremely intimate relationship for nine months. Why shouldn't I be able to figure her out when she was in my arms instead of in my womb? But the other part of me was terrified. Would I be able to take care of her? Could I meet her needs without smothering her or spoiling her? Could I raise her to be healthy, happy, emotionally fulfilled, and eager to make her contribution to the world? In my research and my clinical practice, I had seen so many "good" parents make horrendous mistakes. Why did I think I would be any different?

As Alvin Toffler stated in his book, *Future Shock,* "Parenthood remains the greatest single preserve of the amateur." Most of us become parents with absolutely no preparation other than our own vague memories of how our parents raised us (and in many cases, we *don't* want to duplicate their efforts). Unfortunately, child-development research for the last fifty years or more indicates that most of us have a great deal to learn about being good parents. Additionally, as much as we would like it to be otherwise, parenting is *not* intuitive.

Nowhere is this more obvious, and critical, than in the area of connecting emotionally with your child. If you have ever been mystified by your child's emotional response to you, you know what I mean. You pick up your baby to play with him, and he starts to cry. Or you dangle a toy in front of your nine-month-old, and she turns away as if bored. Or one day, out of the blue, your toddler absolutely refuses to have anything to do with you. Or your school-age child screams, "I hate you!" in response to what you considered an innocuous remark. And your teenager . . . well, the parent who understands a teenager's emotions is a candidate either for sainthood or a post-doctorate degree.

Have you ever said about a baby or a toddler, "Well, they just don't know any better" when you catch them unrolling the toilet paper or pulling the dog's tail or any other small childhood naughtiness? The same might be said of us—often we don't know any better when it comes to parenting our children. Most of us come into the job with little or no prior experience and few references. Even more critical, as any parent of one or more children will tell you, every child comes with a different set of emotional desires and needs. What worked with Suzie won't work with her younger brother Sam or with her baby sister Daisy. And what Suzie needs emotionally will be very different at two years old, five years old, fifteen years old, and every age in between. In fact, your child's emotional needs will often seem to be changing day to day, if not moment to moment. Whatever is a poor, busy, beleaguered, well-intentioned parent to do?

I agree with Alvin Toffler that every parent is an amateur, but I believe you can apply two different meanings of the word *amateur* to most of us. Certainly, like all amateurs, we enter the journey of parenting with little or no experience, and we learn by doing. But second, and far more important, most of us are parenting because of love. We love our children; we want what is best for them. The problem is that we often don't know how to express that love sincerely and genuinely in ways that children will understand and that are appropriate to their ages and development levels. We are not *emotionally available* to our children. Unfortunately, the consequences of our emotional disconnection can be heartbreaking.

THE PARENTAL SIDE OF THE EQUATION

If parents *really* knew what their kids needed, I firmly believe most would respond to their children. But as amateurs, we don't know how to provide the kind of deep emotional connection our children need at every stage of development. Most parents take their kids to the doctor for "well-baby" checkups to confirm their physical health. When something's not normal, the doctor gives us instructions on what to do. Unfortunately, there are no well-baby checkups for our children's emotional health. So we compare notes with other parents: "My baby does this; does your baby do that, too?" Or we anxiously page through child-development books hoping for some sort of indication about whether or not our baby is "normal." I am convinced that we are often not given the critical pieces of information needed to observe and understand if our children are having the kinds of childhoods that will prepare them for happy futures.

I remember one playdate my daughter had with other children in my backyard. One of her friends, Nancy, began to act out the role of a mean ballet teacher, treating her students in a hostile way and using many forbidden words. Upon hearing this, Nancy's mother, Andrea, stopped in her tracks, and yelled, "Nancy, I cannot tolerate this type of talk—I don't care if it's play or not. This is my limit." Another mother turned to Andrea and assured her that "all children act mean and say such things during play." What was actually going on involved very bizarre types of meanness—not only the use of forbidden words, but also much belittling and shaming behavior toward the other children. However, the other kids didn't seem to mind because they realized this was just play, and, as in most child play, this scenario did not last long before they moved on to something else.

I think Andrea was aware that something was remiss in Nancy's behavior (in fact, many parents "know" in some sense, partly through intuition, that something is wrong with their child), but she was prevented from pursuing her gut feeling because we are all socialized to make all child behavior seem normal. Unfortunately, Andrea's gut feeling was accurate—Nancy went on to exhibit extreme acting-out and bullying with her friends. Eventually, though, with professional help, she was able to normalize her behavior.

Unfortunately, parents have acquired many flawed ideas on how to be good parents. Parents often think they are doing a good enough job because, after all, they are trying very hard to make enough money to send their children to good schools, to spend time with them, and to help them with their homework. They believe they are also taking care of their children's emotional needs—being sensitive, responsive, and connected. Most parents don't begin to question their parenting until serious problems occur, often during their children's adolescence. Earlier than that, parents might say things such as, "My child is just not a cuddler," or, "I give my child a lot of space." Although these statements might be true, they can also indicate a lack of awareness of what a truly emotionally available parent-child relationship looks and feels like.

It appears that psychologists have never really made public what emotionally connected relationships should look and feel like for both parents and children, so children suffer in silence, feeling cut off from the very people who should be giving them the emotional sustenance they need so much. Families often do not get feedback—until the cries of help cannot be ignored, until children are so severely depressed that they think of suicide or become so aggressive that they bully others at school, or until children spend years in silent fear and anxiety about life.

We might think adult-adult relationships are tough enough, but they're nothing compared with the task of relating to children. At least with adults, we can rely on verbal cues; but how can a preverbal baby express that he or she doesn't feel enough emotional connection? In fact, many parents think we cannot be concerned about babies' emotions, that because babies are nonverbal, they must not yet have emotions. Babies are just babies—cute and sweet and loving. For example, I have never heard anyone say that babies are ugly. Grown-ups really like babies, which says a great deal about how much babies fulfill grown-ups' emotional needs.

The big concern should be, however, whether adults are meeting the emotional needs of babies. For example, do our babies like us and do they feel understood by us? At least a quarter of families don't ask that question of their relationships with their babies.

It doesn't get any easier, either, as children grow. Children's emotional needs develop and change almost every day, but all too often the physical and financial stresses and strains of taking care of our children cause the goal of satisfying their emotional needs to move further and further down our list of priorities. When you add to the equation (1) our lack of expertise in parenting, and (2) the fact that often our *own* emotional needs are unmet due to the pressures of contemporary family life, it can seem that parents are set up to fail.

I'm not blaming parents for all the challenges our children face in today's world. As a parent myself, I understand the pressing and often conflicting demands of work and family. I also know how many people bring their own unresolved issues (often due to the way they were raised themselves) into the parent-child relationship. In my practice, I see many parents who want strong, happy, satisfying relationships with their children but simply have no clue how to create them.

So what do most parents do? They worry. They worry about leaving their kids to go back to work; they wonder if they are spoiling their kids or being too strict; they try their best to connect with their infants, toddlers, school-age kids, and teenagers, only to feel they've failed again and again. How can we measure our emotional effectiveness as parents? And how can we create the kind of relationships that will help our children develop into the happy, healthy, unique individuals we would like them to be?

RESEARCHING THE PARENT-CHILD CONNECTION

Several years ago, Daniel Goleman wrote a book called *Emotional Intelligence,* which became a national best-seller. In it, he described the importance of emotional intelligence (defined as a combination of emotional and interpersonal skills) when it came to predicting success and happiness in life. More important, he advocated that emotional intelligence could and should be taught to our children. But teaching children is one thing; *relating* to them is another.

Luckily, science and research are finally beginning to lend a hand to parents by studying both the emotional needs of children and the dynamics of parent-child relationships. I have been fortunate to be a part of this wave of scientific interest. For more than sixteen years, I have been deeply involved in exploring how parents and children connect emotionally. As a doctoral candidate in child psychology at the University of California at Berkeley in 1987, I developed an assessment tool called the *Emotional Availability Scales,* to be described later in the book. This simple measurement, now used in clinics and research studies around the world, is an extremely accurate calibration of the quality and quantity of emotional connection between parents and children. In my own research, as well as that of my colleagues, the emotional quality of parental relationships with children is of paramount importance. How parents talk to or hold an infant, the tone of their voices, the way they feed the child—all teach our children more about emotional connection than anything else we could do, say, or teach directly.

Happily, most parents already provide a great deal of emotional connection to their children. Somehow, some way, either through intuition or learning or just dumb luck, we manage to muddle through and help our kids feel loved. But no matter how well or poorly we've done our job so far, there is always another level of emotional connection and support that will help us deepen our relationships with our children. It's not so much what we do but how we do it that communicates our love and support to our children. We need to master the "language of love" that speaks directly to our children's emotional needs and understands what they are saying to us in return. You can learn to master the skills of emotional availability (as will be covered in detail later, including a *caregiver's emotional recruitability, child's emotional recruitability,* and *caregiver sensitivity, structuring, nonintrusiveness, and nonhostility,* as well as the *child's responsiveness to the caregiver and involvement of the caregiver*) and become fluent in the language of love that can make any child feel cherished, respected, and whole.

Research has repeatedly demonstrated that *emotional connection is the most important element in a parent-child relationship.* Parents' words and emotions create the fertile ground that allows children to develop into emotionally healthy and happy human beings. The benefits (verified by research) of parents connecting emotionally with their children are far-reaching. When parents express genuine interest, involvement, and a positive attitude, their children develop more secure relationships within the family group. Children with emotionally connected parents are more attentive and concentrate better. When parents are emotionally reachable and are able to "read" the emotional signals of their kids, the children will perform better in a wide variety of situations. Indeed, the level of emotional connection between parents and children seems to have a far greater impact than any specific coaching techniques on "how to succeed at school," "how to do your homework," "how to be a good friend," and so on. Interestingly, many parents tell their kids to concentrate on schoolwork—they give rewards for doing well and repeatedly check that they are doing their homework—but what really seems to help children with schoolwork is the *emotional* climate of the home. Children will know intuitively how to succeed in life if they have parents who are *emotionally involved* in their lives.

Receiving parental love and support can also have a dramatic effect on the child's later life. The study presented by psychologists Linda Russek and Gary Schwartz to the March 1996 meeting of the American Psychosomatic Society shows just how important building a positive relationship with your children can be to their futures. In 1960, eighty-seven male students at Harvard University had been asked to assess in writing how caring and supportive they felt their parents were. In 1995, these men (now in their fifties) were contacted again. It was found that those who had described their parents as loving and supportive had far fewer serious illnesses, such as hypertension and heart disease, when they reached middle age. These findings held up even when key risk factors such as family history, age, and smoking were taken into account. In contrast, the men who had perceived their parents as nonsupportive experienced a greater incidence of physical illness as they aged.

To paraphrase author C. Lenox Remond, parents should keep in mind that they are the first books read and the last put aside in every child's library. The effects of our parenting will last throughout our children's lifetimes. If we create the rich, supportive, emotionally connected environment that our children need, they stand a much better chance of becoming the healthy, happy human beings we would like them to be.

Based on my years of research, I can say with confidence that connecting emotionally with your child is a simple process, one that becomes easy with practice. When you know the fundamentals of being emotionally available to your child, any moment can be an opportunity for establishing and strengthening that precious connection. And if the connection weakens—through a simple error, misjudgment, change in circumstances, and so on—you as a parent can reestablish it quickly and easily.

I have seen the benefits of emotional availability again and again, in research settings and in my clinical practice. But most important, I have seen it in my own life.

Raising a child should be a profound and enjoyable experience, one that creates fond memories for both you and your child. Using the principles of emotional availability will help you create the kind of fulfilling relationship with your child that will light up both of your lives. Emotional connection isn't difficult to achieve—it just takes a little knowledge, a little practice, a little humor, and—most important—a lot of love and a strong desire to make a difference in the life of your child. Essayist John Whitehead once wrote, "Children are the living messages we send to a time we will not see." A rich emotional connection with our children is the best legacy we can leave them—and the finest inheritance they can have.

two

Is Your Child Secure with You?

It is my belief that all parents want to do well by their children. Even babies can let you know if their emotional needs are being met, but can you pick up on these cues? Psychologists and researchers such as myself have the responsibility to give parents the tools to understand their children's communication. We also must provide parents with a way to assess the quality of their relationships with their children at every stage of development. As most parents know, parenting is part science, part emotion, and part intuition. The checklists of qualities or developmental milestones we get from books and doctors can appear to be so much fiction when we're faced with a screaming baby, recalcitrant toddler, or glum adolescent. What's most important in relationships, however, is the way each person feels. I believe parents can use a working knowledge of emotional availability to enhance and deepen their connection with their children.

WHAT IS SECURITY FOR A CHILD?

As will be described later, a child's feelings of security in the parent-child relationship predicts positive outcomes for the child's future. Parents therefore may want to know how to read whether or not their child is secure.

How Can You Measure Whether Your Child Is Secure in Your Relationship?

Let me give you an example of a classic way researchers would measure the quality of security in a child-parent relationship with the youngest subjects. *Please bear in mind that although I say "baby" at many points in descriptions of security and insecurity, the same principles hold for older children.* For decades, developmental psychology laboratories around the world have been using this procedure to evaluate infants' emotional status. The results from this procedure place the infant into one of four categories:

- Secure

- Insecure/avoidant

- Insecure/dependent (also known as insecure/resistant)

- Insecure/disorganized

This experiment is the basis for a great deal of research and is used as a predictor of numerous aspects of child development. The assessment generally takes about twenty minutes and is done in an unfamiliar setting (for example, a room in a child psychologist's office or a laboratory room in the child-development department of a university). Often the interactions of the parent and child are filmed from several angles to allow assessment of the relationship more thoroughly at a later time.

This kind of assessment generally involves babies between twelve and eighteen months of age because at this stage, the child's special connection with the parent (termed infant-parent attachment) becomes clearly evident. The child can be brought in by the mother, father, or other caregiver—whoever would be considered a source of nurturing. The process itself is simple:

1. Caregiver and child are brought into the unfamiliar room.

2. Caregiver and child stay in the room together for a few minutes.

3. An unfamiliar adult (in my lab, usually a female university student) enters the room.

4. Caregiver leaves the infant and unfamiliar adult together.

5. Caregiver returns ("reunion"). Unfamiliar adult leaves the room.

6. Caregiver leaves infant alone in the room.

7. Unfamiliar adult goes back into the room to be with the infant.

8. Caregiver returns ("reunion").

Each of these events last approximately three minutes. We try to make the assessment as easy as possible for both parent and child and always halt the evaluation if the child becomes too distressed. We never let the separation between parent and child go for as long as three minutes if the baby is crying and clearly cannot self-soothe. At times, we have sent the parent back into the room after as little time as thirty seconds.

The actual assessment looks at the "reunion" episodes of the interaction. What does the child do when the parent returns into the room after a brief separation? It is believed that during stressful separation situations, a baby's "attachment system" becomes activated and heightened (in the same way that separation causes adults to miss adult loved ones). What is most interesting, however, is that *this moment of heightened attachment is a clear indication of how the baby views his or her relationship with the parent.* It is as if, at the moment of reunion, the child's relationship with the parent comes alive for the child.

THE SOCIAL/EMOTIONAL MILESTONE OF
THE EARLY YEARS

There's so much happening as your baby develops during the first year of life. Many parents read and know about different developmental milestones such as crawling, walking, and talking. Pediatricians check on these and many other factors as part of a child's well-baby checkups. But what is never checked, at least to my knowledge, is an *emotional* milestone usually clearly seen in infants nine to twelve months old. Babies develop *attachments*. Your baby will develop an emotional connection with you. Only in cases of infants raised in orphanages or institutions where there is no continuity or stability of caregiving do infants develop without attachment.

That there will be an attachment between infants and their parents is a given. What is not a given is the *quality* of that connection. More than forty years of research in developmental psychology laboratories around the world has shown that *20 to 30 percent of babies develop some form of insecure connection with their parents*. These are children mostly from two-parent, middle-income families! So being raised in a so-called "normal" context does not necessarily seem to lead to healthy emotional connections for our babies.

READING YOUR CHILD'S CUES

Most new parents (or even experienced parents with a new baby) have their hands full simply coping with the physical needs of the child. Although it might be easy to figure out when a child is hungry or wet, parents rarely recognize the emotional signs that indicate a baby is in need of emotional connection. From the moment of birth, however, babies are giving us signs about their emotional states. Parents who can read their children's emotional communications can forge healthier and stronger bonds more quickly.

In child-development studies, babies are usually categorized as either secure or insecure based on observations of their behavior. Insecure babies are further categorized as either avoidant, dependent, or disorganized. Each of these categories connotes specific kinds of behavior, and each is a result of different qualities of emotional connection of the child with the parent. By using the following information, you can learn to "read" your baby, discover the quality of your emotional connection with him or her, and determine how to create a stronger, healthier, more loving bond between you.

The Secure Baby and Child

Watching eleven-month-old Eddie with his grandmother, Lynn, was a joy. Lynn's daughter had been unable to care for her son, so Lynn had been Eddie's primary caregiver since his birth. It was obvious that the little boy loved his grandmother and felt absolutely comfortable with her. Eddie was an active baby just on the verge of being able to walk. He crawled all over the playroom in our clinic, pulling himself up on chairs, tables, and bookcases. He was happy exploring the area and happy to return to his grandmother as well.

Lynn was easy with Eddie, yet she kept an eye on him the entire time we were talking. "He's at the age where he gets into quite a bit of mischief," she explained. At one point, Eddie almost pulled an entire stack of books over on himself, but Lynn jumped up and rescued him just in time. The little boy protested, but Lynn began to tickle him and his protests turned to giggles. He snuggled comfortably in his grandmother's arms as she brought him back to her chair. Lynn then pulled a wooden truck out of her bag, gave the truck to Eddie, and put the little boy on the floor by her feet. Eddie immediately started playing with the truck, content to stay close to his grandmother and play on his own.

Lynn and Eddie obviously had an emotional connection that benefited both of them. As a result, Eddie's emotional signals were those of a *secure* baby. He was happy in his grandmother's love and secure enough to be comfortable exploring his environment on his own or in proximity to her. The relationship between grandmother and grandson was easy for both of them. This child had been given an excellent emotional foundation that would serve him throughout his life—the kind of foundation most parents would like to ensure for their own children.

In the twenty-minute situation in the laboratory, involving eight episodes described earlier (referred to as "the strange situation procedure"), the secure child will demonstrate longing for the parent and eagerness for the parent's return.

Because attachment begins during the first year of life, many of these examples are of babies, but the pattern is similar for preschool or older children. Look for the bal-

Approximately 70 percent of the normal (that is, unselected or nonclinical) population in this country are secure, like Eddie. Although each child develops at his or her own pace, you can expect to see these signals at some point during your baby's first year of life:

- *Your baby responds to you. For example, when you come into the room, your baby lights up. When you talk, your baby looks at you and smiles. When you come back into the room after being absent, your baby greets you, happy that you're back.*

- *In general, your baby seems to want to be near you, but he or she also is secure enough to be alone for short periods of time.*

- *Your baby shows age-appropriate independence, meaning that your baby can play by himself or herself for a while and you don't constantly have to be "doing" something with your baby. Certainly, all babies go through periods of being clingy and feeling that they don't want to separate (for example, when they are facing a transition such as a new daycare situation, a new nanny, or when they are ill), but such periods are fairly short-lived, and the child typically goes back to normal.*

- *Your baby demonstrates a balance between autonomy and the need for connection. This is often signaled by something called "secure base behavior," in which the child leaves the parent to explore his or her environment but then returns to the parent frequently for emotional connection. The parent is a secure base that allows the child to feel free ance between connection and moving away and for delight in interactions with you and with others. With increasing age, children become (or should become) increasingly independent, but with "refueling", never totally disconnected.*

The Insecure/Avoidant Child

Lorraine tried very hard to connect with her youngest child, Kelly, but with two other children under the age of five, she felt overwhelmed. She saw to Kelly's physical needs as well as she could; Lorraine just

---

continued...

to explore on his or her own. This kind of behavior should be clear by about nine months of age, when your baby is crawling and perhaps even walking. At this point, the child will often bring things to the parent and show off the results of his or her explorations. If your baby moves toward you, involves you in interactions, and then moves away, your baby is indicating secure base behavior.

• By twelve months of age, 50 percent of babies are walking, and their field of exploration expands significantly. However, secure babies will still return to their parents to show them what they have found in their explorations, thereby involving the parent in their expanded world. This is one of the joys of parenting: to have your baby come to you, show you things, involve you, make you an audience to his or her play, and when he or she is emotionally fed, to move away to explore the world again.

• There should be a balance between your child moving away and coming toward you over the course of time and over the course of interaction. Some researchers have called this "refueling." Your baby goes off to explore, maybe in other rooms and areas, but at times he or she looks back to reconnect, to see if everything's okay and if you are paying attention. These subtle moments of connection are extremely powerful indicators of the health and strength of the emotional bond between you and your baby. I look for this "attachment-exploration" balance in the babies and young children I see.

couldn't pay much attention to Kelly when the other two kids were around. She would put Kelly in her crib with a couple toys or turn on a video so there would be music in the room. Luckily, Kelly was a pretty placid baby and didn't make much fuss.

However, Kelly didn't seem to be that emotionally connected with her mom, either. When Lorraine came into the room, Kelly wouldn't smile or laugh. She didn't show much notice when Lorraine would try to show her a new toy or a video. By the time she started to crawl, Kelly seemed perfectly happy exploring the room on her own and rarely looked at her mom. Lorraine was relieved that Kelly was so self-sufficient, but she admitted to me that she wished her daughter were warmer. "I don't feel like I know this child the way I did my first two," she told me.

Certainly during the baby years, it is crucial for children to learn the skills of independence. But in the first year of life, babies are not supposed to be totally independent. Even when babies appear to be content with their autonomy, it is important to realize there is always a yearning inside

---

Your interactions with your child build security:

- *During the first year, you should be very attentive to your child's responsiveness and involvement. When your baby brings things to you, either in the form of objects or in the form of smiles and giggles, that is a demonstration of the child's desire to involve you in his or her life. When you initiate interactions and your baby smiles, "talks," or otherwise reacts with pleasure, that indicates the child's willingness to respond to you.*

- *Your responsiveness to your child and "joining" in his or her pleasure as he or she interacts with you and with his or her environment keeps your child coming back for more fun with you. Studies indicate that a parent's sensitivity and responsiveness toward an infant is what helps create a sense of security for the child, and that a parent's positive affect is what maintains such security over the course of time.*

them for more emotional connection with their parents. However, the insecure/avoidant child has learned to suppress the outward expression of the need for emotional connection because the parent hasn't responded to any previous attempts the child has made to reach out. Because these children don't feel secure in their parents' connection, they demonstrate very different behaviors from the secure babies described previously.

This insecurity can be born of many different factors, such as parental unavailability (physically, emotionally, or both), health challenges (for example, extended separations from parents early on) that cause the child to feel a lack of support or connection, "mismatch" between the temperaments of child and parent, and so on. Insecurity also can be caused by a lack of parental expertise when it comes to creating emotional connections with a child. For many people, after spending a decade or two at work focused on the self-sufficient, nonemotional aspects of life, it is quite a transition to become the parent of a new baby, with all the new roles that entails. Some parents spend so much of their energy providing basic care that they don't have much left for the emotional work of connecting with their children.

I believe these are some of the reasons that 20 to 30 percent of normally developing children demonstrate insufficient emotional connection. This is not abnormal or a sign that something horrible will happen. This just means, based on the type of interactions you've been having, that your baby *appears* more independent and self-sufficient but in truth, he or she still wants a strong connection with you.

In the 20-minute laboratory procedure, about 20 percent of children will seem cool and rejecting when the parent returns. The child might avert his or her gaze or make more clear and obvious signs such as physically turning around or moving away. Some children might even try to leave the room with the unfamiliar adult when the parent returns to the room. These children are considered insecure/avoidant.

As I described with respect to security, insecure/avoidance is not only a baby characteristic. Many adults mistake total independence or self-reliance for a positive attribute, but in fact interdependence or interconnectedness (balance between autonomy and connection) is the goal at all stages of life.

Many parents of insecure/avoidant children are also very independent; sometimes they think a young child can be on his or her own and not need more connection. They might view this quality as the temperament or a personality characteristic of the child. Many such parents have asked me, "Could it be his nature?" What is interesting is that some parents think that disconnection is best because this is what they themselves were used to.

A striking example of this type of perception came from my own child-development clinic. When I hire research assistants, I typically show candidates videotapes of parent-child interactions and ask them to verbally narrate what they see in terms of the emotional availability in the parent-child relationship and the quality of connection/attachment they perceive. (If a candidate's perceptions of parent-child relationships are distorted, it is very difficult to change them even with extensive training and mentoring, so I choose students who already have clarity of perception.)

One student came highly recommended with a 4.0 average in a master's program and great references on her work ethic and character. When she arrived for the interview, I showed her a videotape of a parent-child interaction. She described the interaction as wonderful, saying that the baby was very strong and independent and the mother did not stifle the baby's needs for exploration and growth. She said, "I admire

About 20 percent of the normal population in this country are classified as insecure/avoidant. The following are some signs and signals of an insecure/avoidant baby:

- Your child looks away from you and moves away from you often.

- You don't have sustained playtime together, perhaps because of your child's unresponsiveness.

- When you leave your child in an unfamiliar situation, even briefly, he or she doesn't light up and show the joy and glee you had hoped for when you return.

- When you try to initiate interactions with your baby, he or she moves away.

the fact that this baby is moving down and not just sitting on her mother's lap but going off and exploring everything in the house. This baby's going to learn a lot."

I was taken aback because my observation of the relationship was so different. The baby was squirming down because the mother was holding her in a very uncomfortable position and in a harsh and abrasive manner. The baby could easily have settled into the mother's lap had her mother been offering confident, comfortable holding. But the child had no choice but to squirm down and go it alone. When she got off the mother's lap, the child hardly turned back and immediately moved to a distant part of the house, happy to be released from her mother's uncomfortable hold. I imagined this was a child who would later move away from the family and not write home. Needless to say, this research assistant wasn't right for our clinic.

If you observe insecure/avoidant behavior in your child, it is important not to mistake such behavior as your child's nature. One woman said that she thought some babies liked to play with their mothers, but hers did not. But this kind of behavior is nurture, not nature! Babies of all different temperament types show insecure patterns. It is the history of interactions between parent and child that makes some babies seek out their mothers

continued...

- *Your child has had to be separated from you frequently or for lengthy periods, perhaps due to medical issues for either of you. Prolonged separations during the first year of life could affect the connection between you. (Here, I am not referring to daily routines such as going to day care—I mean extended separations that include overnights.)*

- *You feel disconnected from your child. Things are happening at a functional level for you, but not an emotional one.*

- *Because your baby seems disconnected, it does not mean he or she is weakly attached to you or not attached to you. It merely means there is some insecurity in this relationship that needs some work and correction to get it back on a secure path.*

for play while others don't. If we put off our babies' attempts to get close to us, they will stop seeking us out.

However, it is almost always possible to develop a better connection with your child. Especially during the first year or two, both babies *and* parents are getting used to and learning a great deal about each other.

A skeptic might wonder whether these insecure/avoidant children are merely more independent than the average child—whether they are simply more interested in other objects and toys and do not have as much need to interact with the parent. In fact, this was the view of a group of social scientists. Heart-rate studies indicated that while they were playing with toys (in a seemingly engrossed fashion) and looking away from the parent who had just returned after the separation (remember the sequence of events in which this assessment typically takes place), their heart rate was accelerated rather than decelerated. Acceleration in heart

Be sure your child doesn't become insecure and avoidant with you:

- *Read your child's emotional communications toward you. If your child is seemingly avoidant for long periods, try inserting some fun time into your day. Let the clothes sit in the washer for a while and play with your baby. As you play together, be sure you are not only physically there, but also emotionally there. Children want and need your emotional availability even more than your physical availability.*

- *When your child brings toys to you, be responsive, and make your child feel special about your relationship.*

- *Be "real" in your responsiveness—again, by being emotionally there.*

- *Give this some time. Babies don't respond to parents all the time! They need to have some autonomy, exploration, and independence, too. The balance between independence and connection is at the heart of this matter, so be available for connection when your child approaches you and then follow his or her emotional lead.*

rate indicates arousal rather than attention. If these children were truly independent and more interested in the toys in the laboratory, they would show heart-rate deceleration (indicative of attention to a stimulus). These findings have been replicated and suggest that infant insecurity/avoidance is a quality of the relationship rather than the nature of the child.

The Insecure/Dependent Baby and Child

Some insecure babies demonstrate their feelings in ways completely opposite to those just described—they become overly dependent and clingy rather than avoidant. I observed one example of such overdependence when I was working on my doctoral dissertation at the University of California, Berkeley. With a video recorder in hand, I had gone into a home with the intention of filming an hour of interaction between mother and child. I had also planned to go on a separate day to be able to capture a different mood on film. When I went into this particular home, the mother said, "My baby's not really having a good day. She's been crying quite a bit and isn't leaving my side. It's really hard to even go to the bathroom sometimes. But it's okay—I learned in psychology class that the more strongly attached my baby is to me, the better it is for her development. It gets tough at times, but it's okay because I know that being so strongly attached to me will be good for her in the long run."

I videotaped mother and baby for an hour and then left, promising to come back in a week. When I returned, the mother told me that the baby was in a different mood so I was somewhat surprised to see the same behavior occurring. The child was still crying and clingy, with the mother constantly trying to soothe her without much lasting success. As soon as the child was soothed and the mother put her down, the child would again show distress.

In the 20-minute laboratory procedure, approximately 10 percent of children show both happiness and distress in the reunion moment. They will gravitate toward the parent, seeming to be happy at the return but then become distressed. The parent's attempt to comfort such a child often doesn't produce any sustained soothing, and the child remains clingy and distressed even after the session. Such children are categorized as insecure/dependent.

Which came first in this story, the chicken or the egg? The child's overdependency could easily have been explained by the mother's oversolicitous behavior toward her. Equally, the mother's behavior could have been explained by the child's clingy dependence.

It is possible for parents to mistake dependency for a "strong" attachment. Because your child shows the characteristic of wanting to be close with you always, it does not mean that he or she is strongly attached to you. There is no such thing as a strong attachment at any age, merely security or insecurity of attachment.

When parents do not give children the space to explore their own strengths, children start to view themselves as weak. Babies with colic or another ailment can trigger this dependency dynamic. Illness can either be

About 10 percent of the normal population show an overly dependent pattern in relationship with a parent. The following signs and communications are typical of an insecure/dependent baby:

- *Often distressed and may at times even seem traumatized by small events. You might have a difficult time understanding the reason for your child's traumatization.[1]*

- *Clingy and does not easily explore away from you. He or she stays near you.*

- *Seems sensitive and is easily upset by events.*

- *Seems younger than his or her age and may seem immature.*

- *Is very emotional and may show ups and downs quite a bit.*

[1] If your child shows signs of traumatization (for example, nightmares, sudden fears, or fears of specific things or people such as men with beards) and such behavior occurs suddenly when you did not see it before, it is worth getting some professional consultation to make sure that a specific traumatizing event has not taken place. A more general and consistent pattern of overly distressed behavior is what is described here, not the type of traumatization that would be related to abuse and/or violence.

a cue to teach resilience or a cue for overprotectiveness, based on the parent's response to the child's needs.

In truth, the quality of connection is really what is important, as well as whether that connection is secure or insecure. Being strongly attached is not a positive quality for the child. In fact, it usually indicates an overconnection stemming from insecurity. In other words, the child uses overconnection as compensation for the lack of security he or she feels inside. On the parent's side, overcompensation comes from not trusting the child with independence. The results of such overly connected relationships include parental overprotectiveness and treatment of the child as younger than he or she really is.

An example of overprotectiveness is treating a one-year-old baby as an

Factors that contribute to the development of an insecure/ dependent child and how to counter insecure/dependent behavior:

- *Some children, perhaps due to persistent crying, may have come to expect a great deal of caregiving. It is worth getting some professional opinion about the possible organic (or nonorganic) reasons for the crying so the parent-child relationship can move on a healthy track.*

- *The assumption that your child is sensitive and dependent because it is his or her temperament or "nature" can actually prolong such behavior. You can work with any of your children (likely of different temperaments at birth) to help them become more self-reliant and not so easily distressed.*

- *Reward your child for expressing emotional needs in a "grown-up" way, and do make maturity demands rather than engaging in great catering services. You don't need to give up your own needs to be a good parent. In your heart, you might be feeling "fed up" that you are doing so much for your child that other kids this age are doing for themselves, but you continue anyway. It might be time for you to make maturity demands, giving a "gentle push" to your child to go beyond his or her familiar limits.*

eight-month-old, with continued spoon-feeding and without regard for the baby's budding sense of autonomy and need to do things on his or her own. Another sign is a prolonged period of breast-feeding, such as a child still at the breast at two or three years of age. During feeding, the parent might hold the baby in a supine position rather than granting some upright autonomy. The parent might also stress negative emotions, showing great concern over small cuts and bruises and supervising a baby's play time to the point of hovering.

As the child grows older, the parent might continue to be overprotective. I have seen a father who brushed his fourteen-year-old son's teeth for him so the "child wouldn't get cavities." (Note the good and noble reason for overprotection on the part of the parent.) I also have seen the mother of a normally developing fifteen-year-old adolescent still helping him put

continued...

- *Do respond to your child's positive emotions consistently, and try to respond in a less elevated or exaggerated way to distress emotions. Of course, you need to respond to cries for help, but insecure/dependent children have learned early on to heighten their emotional repertoire to get a reaction from their parents, and they continue "what has worked." Try responding to your child in positive ways, not in exaggerated ways, to distress situations only.*

- *Help your child feel strong and robust by the type of physical play you engage in and by the "discussions" you have together. I once heard a mother talking for her baby, saying, "I can do it myself Mommy, I'm a strong girl." Build confidence through such presumptuous talk, even if your child is preverbal.*

- *Be sure your child has space to explore, including floor freedom, and that you don't hover. Let your child explore (hopefully, childproofing the house will allow for greater safety and floor freedom) and support your child in his or her explorations away from you. Be ready to respond consistently when your child comes back to "visit"—such is the "attachment-exploration balance."*

on his jacket. Similarly, I have even seen college students driven to their classes by their mothers, who felt that the kids hadn't yet honed their driving skills. (Again, such parents usually have noble reasons, citing accident statistics for college students.)

Many children become so accustomed to being catered to in this way that they "require" this type of treatment. They become passive and dependent as a result of caregiving that really offers few opportunities for growth and independence and, thus, they continue to evoke such behavior on the part of their parents. Once this dependency cycle begins, it is difficult to know how to alter it because both parent and child have bought into the dynamic. The parents of such children tell me that their children are so passive that they still have to wash their hair for them— even when the child was fourteen years old! Such parents say they have to do a great deal for their children because the children just do not have it in them to do for themselves. Again, we return to the issue of nature versus nurture. Nurture can so insidiously prepare children for dependency that what actually has been created by the environment can easily be mistaken for the child's nature.

It is important to emphasize here that dependence is not the same as separation anxiety. All children will experience separation anxiety during toddlerhood, and most will revisit separation issues at different points in their development. What characterizes the insecure/dependent child is an overall quality of problems with separation that the child has internalized, rather than part of a developmental progression.

A healthy parent-child relationship shows a balance between connection and independence. The need for such a balance continues throughout childhood and into the teenage years. Child-development circles used to believe the notion that during adolescence children move away; however, that's not truly the case. A healthy adolescent moves away to gain greater independence but continues to desire connection and "refueling." The refueling might be done through other methods (such as talking on the phone), but nonetheless it involves reconnection. Asking for a parent's thoughts or advice, introducing friends, or staying near the kitchen in hopes of having that late-night talk are all ways adolescents continue to connect with their parents.

Although they appear in different forms at different stages of life, the need for a balance between closeness and connection and the desire to explore new territory are the threads that run through childhood, adolescence, and into adulthood. Indeed, a wealth of evidence indicates that romantic and marital relationships are also characterized by the balance between autonomy and connection. For example, healthy relationships usually demonstrate times of talking and sharing information and then moving away physically or psychologically "to do one's own thing." The skills of reading emotional signals and balancing the competing needs for connection and autonomy are vital for any relationship. Learning to read your baby and young child now prepares you to read your child at a later stage and, in addition, helps you read your own relationship with your partner.

The Insecure/Disorganized Baby and Child

In the twenty-minute laboratory situation, a small percentage of children show combinations of behaviors indicative of fear, such as freezing upon the parent's return, moving toward the parent and then moving behind, and so on. This pattern is referred to as insecure/disor-

---

A small percentage of babies and young children in the "normal" population show an insecure/disorganized pattern, but approximately 80 percent of abused children exhibit the following behaviors:

- *A child shows avoidant qualities at times and dependent qualities at other times.*

- *A child might show frightened behavior, perhaps being afraid of the caregiver.*

You can ensure that a child does not become confused or disorganized by doing the following:

ganized. Such a pattern is often seen in children who either have been traumatized, such as through abuse or neglect, or have become confused, perhaps by experiences that seem unstable and severely inconsistent. For example, I have seen such behavior in children who experience many changes in their caregiving, as, for example, those children who experienced divorce during their infancy and have been spending overnights with both parents after divorce. Likely, it is the lack of stability in the caregiving environment that can create some confusion for young children. I have also seen babies and young children show this pattern if their parents have not resolved issues about a prior loss (and there is no other issue such as abuse or neglect). Such loss events could include miscarriage, stillbirth, loss of a previous child, loss through giving birth to a child with a disability, loss of a parent, loss through their own experiences of abuse, or neglect or other unfortunate circumstances during their childhoods. It is "not coming to terms with" the loss that leads to problems, not merely the fact of experiencing a loss. Many insecure/disorganized children have an avoidant or dependent core that is palpable within a disorganized demeanor.

continued...

- *Maintain stable caregiving arrangements during infancy.*

- *Don't ignore your own issues related to grief and loss, lest it be transmitted to your child through your own feelings of trauma. Such unresolved feelings of loss or trauma related to loss can make your own behavior disorganized and, hence, affect your child. On your own, it might be difficult to work through all the issues related to such loss; to accomplish this, professional help may be warranted.*

- *Work on issues related to loss to avoid your own emotional expressions seeming disconnected from your child. Even though you don't feel disconnected, your emotions might not communicate the caring you really feel.*

SECURITY FOR OUR CHILDREN'S FUTURES

The four patterns just described have been shown to predict how children will develop as toddlers, school-age children, and adolescents and how emotionally successful they will be as they grow and develop. On the parental side, these patterns are a clear indication of how a preverbal baby experiences its relationship with the parent.

Just as walking and crawling are developmental milestones that children reach at particular stages of life, the infant-parent attachment relationship is an "emotional milestone" that is reached by most infants at the end of the first year. With the exception of children raised in institutions such as orphanages, by the end of the first year of life, as long as they have lived with a parent and/or spent some time with a parent, almost all children show one of the above patterns.

Obviously, we all would like our children to be secure. Secure children are easier for us to deal with, but beyond that, secure children reap many benefits from life:

- **Children who are secure (that is, have internalized an emotionally available home environment so they feel confident and secure about the parent or caregiver) are happier.** Abundant research of the past forty years has shown that children who are secure show more positive affect toward other children and seem happier. Such a positive mood is evident in both preschool and elementary school-age children.

- **Children who are secure have better relationships with peers and with teachers.** Such children seem to be more popular and/or have positive friendships. Insecure children are more likely to be bullies and/or victims in their relationships. Because they are not able to hold their own in the peer group, many insecure children seek out the teacher. Such teacher-child attachment seems to offset the neglect these children feel in their peer relationships. What should be encouraged at school with the teacher is a secure attachment (just as there can be secure attachment to a parent, there can be secure attachment with a teacher), rather than dependency on the teacher (which is an insecure attachment to the teacher).

· **Children who are secure are seen as more attractive by other children and are looked at more than insecure children.** Research indicates that secure children are more likely to be picked as attractive, despite the similarity in objective indices of physical attractiveness. It is as if such children seem more attractive because of their personalities. Secure children also receive more "visual regard" or, simply put, they're looked at by other children. In the animal kingdom, the leaders in the group are looked at more than those lower in the hierarchy. By analogy, it is as if secure children, being looked at more, are perceived as being the leaders.

· **Secure children are more likely to have a host of other positive qualities as compared to insecure children, suggesting that they are enjoying happier and more competent childhoods.** Studies that have followed secure children into their adolescent years, at least, show that the greater competence still holds.

· **Secure children are more likely to create close relationships as adolescents and adults, as well as with their own children.** There's every indication that security is stable, as long as life circumstances do not change dramatically.

· **Although security is better than insecurity in terms of the child's happiness and social competence, psychologists in this country generally view the insecure/disorganized child as problematic and view the other two insecure patterns as "normal variations."** In other words, children who feel insecure are not necessarily going to end up having problematic lives; it is merely that, compared to other children who are secure, they show less-positive qualities. These less-positive qualities do not necessarily place them in a problematic range, although the insecurity might contribute to their feelings of unhappiness and stress in relationships during childhood and beyond.

three

The Impact of Your Childhood on Your Child

Your own sense of security as a child and how you think can have enormous effects on your child's sense of security with you. One interesting exercise is to ask, "What type of baby were you?" As documented in numerous research studies, we know there is a great similarity between the type of baby we raise and the type of baby we were (unless some major changes occurred within us during our adulthood to change our view of relationships). Parents who were raised in an openly communicative and sensitive manner in their own families are more likely to have secure babies. Parents who were raised to dismiss their feelings and not to value attachments tend to have babies who are avoidant. Parents who were raised in an environment where there was a lot of negative emotion, particularly anger, are more likely to have babies who are clingy and dependent, and many of these parents continue to feel anger toward their own parents.

The following questions will help you see whether you fit into any of these three categories. A majority of "yes" answers in any group identifies your category.

Secure Child Memory

1. Were you the type of baby and young child who sought out a parent immediately when you needed some comfort?

2. Do you remember being happy?

3. Do you remember getting a lot of positive attention and caring?

4. Do you remember finding it easy to connect with others, including parents and friends?

Insecure/Avoidant Child Memory

1. Were you the type of baby and young child who did not go to a parent when you felt sad, angry, or hurt?

2. Were you the type of baby and young child who grew up feeling like a loner?

3. Did you not have very many people you could turn to, or did you just not turn to others? Were you basically self-reliant or too reliant on yourself, sometimes despite your best efforts to be more connected with others?

4. Do you remember making efforts at closeness with a parent and feeling rebuffed or just not getting the type of response you had hoped for?

5. Do you not remember much about your childhood, as hard as you might try?

6. Do you remember not being liked very much by your peers, either because you were aggressive at times or because you were a loner?

7. Do you feel that much of this discussion about feelings is "mumbo-jumbo" or "psychobabble"? Is this what your parents might say or have said about such self-assessment?

Insecure/Dependent Child Memory

1. Do you recall being very close to one parent (or more) to the point of what we call "symbiosis" or oneness with that parent?

2. Do you remember being an easily distressed sort of baby or young child?

3. Do you remember being overprotected or catered to a lot?

4. Do you recall that you were a bit younger than your age (you might still feel that way)—not necessarily in terms of appearance, but more that people treated you as younger and didn't give you enough of a chance at responsibility?

5. Did you constantly need people around you, maybe for approval?

6. Did you constantly try to please others to the exclusion of even being aware of what your own emotional needs were?

7. Did you "take care" of younger siblings or a parent so that it seemed as if you were the parent or the roles were reversed?

Whether we were secure, avoidant, or dependent as children (recall that insecure/disorganized children typically show one of the other insecure patterns as a "core"), as adults we are free to adopt new ways of creating relationships with our own children.

YOUR OWN FAMILY HISTORY

People bring all kinds of personal history into parenting—that's not a problem. The problem arises when we don't resolve those issues ourselves. Our own parents are often our only models of how to relate to children, so they usually have a powerful influence on us, no matter whether we want to emulate them or be completely different. As adults, we need to recognize the heritage we have brought with us from the family in which we ourselves were raised and to replicate what was good and eliminate what was not.

Social scientists Carol George, Nancy Kaplan, and Mary Main at the University of California, Berkeley, developed a state-of-the-art interview to assess parents' family-of-origin experiences (called the Adult Attachment Interview). The interview is very detailed and enables the interviewer to obtain information about the parent's experiences during childhood. It also does something quite tricky—it can help us understand beyond the childhood experiences of parents by going beyond the surface of what they report. In other words, we gain information on both what they say happened as well as some things they might not consciously remember.

SECURITY DURING YOUR ADULTHOOD

> Parenting has a great deal to do with one's family history—not just what we consciously remember, but, more likely, all of the largely unconscious learning that we bring to our current parent-child relationship.

Not only can we assess security in an infant or child but we can also access whether or not an adult is secure about his or her own childhood relationships.

The "Raised" Secure

Many (lucky) adults recall having positive experiences as they were growing up, and these individuals are likely to continue that positive heritage in their own families. Research (both by interview and observation of parent-child relationships) has shown conclusively that intergenerational transmission of parenting styles is a fact. In other words, if you remember that you were accepted and your parents were warm and kind to you, then you are likely to do the same for your own kids. Individuals who were raised secure usually provide a coherent account of what happened in their childhood, with minimal real inconsistencies in their story lines. For example, if a mother describes her childhood as beautiful and her parents as loving and caring, we would also expect to hear clear examples of many loving connections during childhood, such as a mother planning for a Valentine's Day party at school and utterly delighting in her child's (as well as other children's) pleasure at the party.

Many clear and detailed examples of loving childcare are typically provided, with the parent having access to a relatively full range of emotions. I have now used the Adult Attachment Interview with hundreds of mothers and fathers; I feel a genuine give-and-take, and I have a sense that I really got to know these people through this process. We call these individuals "secure." What is crucial to this book is that these secure parents seem to raise secure children.

The "Earned Secure"

Many parents in the "earned secure" classification relate well to their children, although they might be more guarded with their emotions than the "raised secure" parents because they have had obstacles to cross on the path to their security. They have passed insecure terrain and are now in secure territory, at least within themselves.

Many of these parents, however, describe horrific experiences. Does this mean that they are not secure now because they were avoidant or dependent as babies or children? What we find is that some parents, either through their own psychotherapy, help from a supportive person such as a spouse, or through other life experiences, have come to reflect on their early experiences—sometimes experiences as severe as abuse—and have come to rework those experiences. Reworking is a difficult process and

Most parents who *recall* positive and happy relationships during their childhoods *really* had such relationships, and their children benefit from such a past.

- Such parents are not recalling idealized versions of their childhood; they were truly happy during their childhoods.

- Many such parents have very easy access to their emotions. They smile easily and joke easily, and they are not overly guarded with their emotions. They can relate.

does not happen overnight. I suggest that each parent who perceives his or her child to be currently insecure should take a look at his or her own past. Were you insecure as a child? Has that insecurity within a parent–child relationship been dealt with at a conscious, adult level?

We find that when parents have become reflective about their family-of-origin experiences, their new way of thinking can transform their relationship with their own children. These parents are the "earned secure"—they have created their own sense of understanding of what happened, and in many cases they have forgiven their parents for the stresses of their childhood. These individuals are resilient, but not through "steeling" of emotions; they have coped with the emotions available to them. Because they have not tucked in their emotions to a compartment as they coped with the stress of not having emotional needs met, they can now have access to those feelings as they relate to their children.

This process entails open, coherent, and reflective thinking. The permission to reflect on the past without immediate threat of trauma or terror (although the actual events might have been painful) allows these individuals to live on a plane where emotions are permissible in relationships. These parents also raise secure children. Because they are aware of the neg-

---

A hopeful and optimistic view is that parents can create their own security in adulthood—they are not constrained by their pasts, if they don't want to be. To earn security during adulthood, you need to:

- *Have access to childhood experiences and then you can work on such memories. Professional help might be needed if you have had traumatic early experiences.*

- *Be aware that such realization and work takes time and reflectiveness. Be willing to make such reflectiveness a part of you. Take the risk!*

- *Know that not everyone chooses to do this work—in fact, it is not clear what makes people want to change. But you are clearly in emotionally healthy company if you choose to earn your security.*

atives in the past and have "unshackled" themselves from those negative effects, they have gained a freedom that they share with their children.

This holds much optimism for the future of our children. As parents
give themselves permission to examine their past, preferably in connection
with others in the family, they become freed from repeating it. Their interactions with their children are generally sensitive and caring and rarely
intrusive and hostile. In return, their children are responsive to them and
involve them in their lives.

DISMISSING PARENTS

A subset of adults (about 20 percent of the population) who recall positive experiences with their own parents actually "idealize" their family-of-
origin situation. They project a positive image of themselves and of the
adults who were a part of their childhood. Because memories of their
childhood are too painful, they distort what transpired in their family of
origin into a more consciously acceptable form. The process is unconscious; such adults rarely realize that what they remember isn't accurate. Indeed, many of these individuals have difficulty remembering their
childhood at all. It is as if certain aspects of their childhood are blocked.
When these adults are interviewed about their childhood, they provide less
"meat" and far fewer details. Often they are not very expressive and generally dismiss the importance or expression of emotions.

When asked the importance of early childhood experiences for later
personality development, these adults are puzzled by the question and say
they don't see a link.

For example, one such father, Kevin, told me, "My mother didn't
have much of an effect on me. I don't see any link. I'm my own person;
I really don't have much to do with her." Kevin was almost compulsively
self-reliant as an adult, yet he could make no connection between his almost compulsive self-reliance and his rejecting mother.

Another woman, Pauline, said that her mother was the best mother possible and everyone on the block loved her. Her mother kept a great house

and always had wonderful presents under the Christmas tree. As an unimportant afterthought, Pauline added, "She gave great parties, especially birthday parties for the three boys in the family, but she never had one planned for me. . . . She was a wonderful hostess at the parties. She was a lovely woman, and I miss her." Pauline couldn't appreciate the lack of coherence in her own description of such positive, even idyllic family-of-origin descriptions and the fact that she herself never was the recipient of one of these wonderful parties. She had idealized her description of her own mother and completely ignored any specific details that could not be incorporated into the larger picture of her mother as "wonderful." Pauline was unaware that she had had a negative early experience with her own mother. Her idealized description of her childhood was actually the evidence of a negative past.

Sadly, individuals who have little access to their emotional lives most likely will raise insecure/avoidant children. They are so dismissive of the value of relationships and of emotions as part of important relationships that it's easy for them to be good providers or good at keeping the house clean or good at some other aspect of parenting that is praised in our society. But what they lack is the ability to be part of the give-and-take of emotions. They interact in a cool and distant way toward their children. Such behavior does not mean that they love their children any less; it merely is difficult for them to interact in a loving way or to demonstrate their love. Instead, many such parents do nice things for their children and take care of other (nonemotional) more functional aspects of life. Their children are rarely happy and responsive. Many of these parent-child interactions are like "ships passing in the night" as each goes about his or her own routines. They are not emotionally sensitive to their children, and their children grow with emotional disconnects from the parents.

PARENTS WHO ARE PREOCCUPIED OR OVERCONNECTED TO THE PAST

A small group of parents are the opposite of the dismissing parents—they are actually very emotional. I don't mean this as a "healthy" option, however. Just because individuals are emotional does not mean that they can nurture healthy emotional connections.

In fact, overemotionality is what is seen here. Many of these parents are very angry about the past and what they did not receive during their childhoods. They have access to their emotions (unlike the dismissing parents), but they are "stuck" in the past and have not been able to resolve the problems so they can now have a coherent view of the present and of the family of origin as fitting into their sense of self.

Very often, the children of these parents show the insecure/dependent pattern of relatedness with them, likely because they create overconnections in their relationships. Such parents interact often in a warm way with their children. Sometimes it is difficult to see that there is anything remiss in these relationships at first glance because the parents are pleasing—but they often are either intrusive, not observing boundaries between themselves and their children, or they are inconsistently sensitive. At times, they are quite warm and nice; other times, they "fly off the handle," and are unable to regulate their emotions. It is difficult for their children to feel genuine security with them due to their inconsistent behavior. Further, many of these parents have issues with separation and see that as a threat to connectedness. They therefore respond to separations (for example, leaving a child in day care) with intense anxiety and transmit such uneasiness to their child. Not having experienced clear boundaries between family members, in behaviors and/or feelings, such parents have trouble separating themselves and their needs from those of their children.

DISORGANIZED PARENTS OR UNRESOLVED ABOUT LOSS(ES)

A last pattern seen involves parents who experienced an unresolved loss or a traumatizing event at some point during their childhood (perhaps by death, divorce, sexual abuse, or other) or during their adulthood (again perhaps by death, divorce, sexual assault or rape; giving birth to a child with disabilities; experiencing prenatal, perinatal, or infant losses, such as miscarriage, stillbirth, or Sudden Infant Death Syndrome; or the death of an older or adult child). What is important here is not so much that there was a loss as that the individual has not "worked on" and resolved issues related to this loss.

A parent with a child who has a severe illness or disability might need to go through a period of mourning the "loss of the perfect child." Only after some time and processing of what this loss means can the individual (and the couple) open new avenues of understanding and expression. Studies indicate that when parents have worked on and resolved such loss issues with respect to their children with disabilities, they are likely to have secure babies and children.

The loss of a child by death is considered one of the most difficult grief and loss issues for an individual and for a family. One of our research participants had lost two children to stillbirth after going through full labor with each of them. A heavy smoker (smoking has been linked with stillbirth), she blamed herself for these deaths and experienced much anguish during this time. When we saw her later with her five-year-old son, she seemed very emotionally disconnected both from her son and from others. In the interview, she talked about her other children as if they were still alive. Another mother, who had experienced a stillbirth one year before, gave birth to a beautiful, healthy daughter. Yet because she had not "worked on" her previous loss (and losses are not only death-related, but also include all the omissions of understanding and compassion from our own parents), when her daughter was born, she became disorganized in her thinking and psychologically and emotionally abandoned her and the family, re-creating the trauma of the prior loss in the new situation.

AVOIDING TRANSMITTING OF A NEGATIVE HISTORY

Approximately 20 to 30 percent of parents consciously report that they have had negative early experiences with their family of origin. When I speak of "negative" early experiences, I don't mean that you didn't appreciate how your mother kept house or that she was not that great a cook. I'm referring to more serious deficiencies in child rearing. Some adults report they were physically or emotionally abused, and others describe milder issues of rejection or lack of understanding by parents. Certainly actual cases of physical, emotional, mental, or sexual abuse are readily identified as negative experiences, but sometimes even cool rejection or omissions in empathy are enough to create negative early experiences for a child. For example, I have interviewed many parents who state that they were never held or hugged in times of distress. Such omissions of empathic understanding can be as serious (if not more serious) for a child's emotional development as obvious physical punishment.

If you feel (or know) you had negative experiences in your own childhood, take heart. Many individuals need to and can rework such early experiences. If childhood experiences have been negative (for example, abuse), individuals need to work at many different levels. For example, if parents were abused as children, they might vow not to abuse in their own family. But they might still engage in subtle put-downs and less-obvious signs of bullying with their children. It is as if the parent was able to eliminate obvious methods of abuse but couldn't avoid the more subtle kinds of abusive interactions they probably learned in the family of origin.

For those of you with negative childhood experiences, working on your psychological and relationship issues provides a positive "break" or discontinuity between childhood and the present. Such work must inevitably include accessing and reworking your emotions. Some of the biggest problems in parent-child relationships arise when parents refuse to access their own emotions because they wish to avoid the pain of doing so. Such individuals—who have had abusive relationships in their families of origin, for instance—might think, *You grow stronger with experiences like that, but you shouldn't dwell on the bad things in your life. You're weak if you stay at that level. You have to be strong and not let yourself get weak and full of feelings.* One parent, who had lost her father when she was five, said in a defiant tone, "Sad— no I was not sad. I was happy about it, because after he died, we had a much better life and better material possessions because all the uncles chipped in."

For people with early negative experiences, feelings are something to be avoided, dismissed, and even disposed of. They then enter their own parent-child relationships with a "stiff upper lip" and dismiss the importance of emotions in their children's lives. One such parent said, "No need to go to the hospital, right, Olivia? You're not brain damaged, are you?" when her daughter bumped her head on a nearby coffee table as she was crawling about. Such parents deny to themselves and their children the importance of emotional connection or emotional availability. Instead, they rely on what I call "functional availability." They take care of the things that are needed to keep the family running, but they rarely share their feelings with their children or ask to share their children's feelings in return.

One such mother, Sarah, devoted many hours at her son's school helping the children learn to weave. The many artistic creations in her son's school were truly beautiful. Yet along with that great "function," this mother rarely offered any emotional response to her son, Paul. During one of our sessions, Paul hurt himself with a toy sword as he played with toy knights and princesses. As Paul began to cry uncontrollably, Sarah watched coolly, as if responsiveness was not part of her repertoire. In fact, she continued to read the book she had brought into the session; she barely blinked. Finally, the observer went into the room and offered some words of reassurance to Paul, and he was then able to calm down and continue with the rest of the session.

"Functional availability" is characterized by parents doing everything for their children's basic care and survival and very little for meeting their emotional needs. The meeting of functional needs is good *providing,* but meeting a child's emotional needs as well is good *parenting.* Children deserve parents who will give them both head and heart, who will take care of all their needs. If you feel you are not connecting emotionally with your child, it's your responsibility to pursue counseling or some other means of getting in touch with your feelings.

MAKING CONNECTIONS BETWEEN THE PAST AND PRESENT

Professional help is likely to be beneficial in freeing you from your negative past so your children are freed from its intergenerational effects.

Many individuals have difficulty accessing the past, and some dialogue on how the connections can be made is likely to be in order.

One mother, Jayne, whom we had classified as preoccupied or over-connected, described a story that showed she could not make important connections about her past. She first started describing an incredibly fun childhood with great vacations in the outdoors. Jayne described great parents who took pride in each of their children. She also described incredible closeness among all family members. She said the parents gave each of the children many reasons to feel special and were wonderful with each of them. But as Jayne continued to recount her past, she began to cry more and more uncontrollably, with the recognition (on her own) that there was no reason to cry about some of what she was describing (for example, how great the vacations were). Jayne, in fact, used up half a box of tissues, continuing to wonder why she was so emotional. She then went on to describe a volcano of angry emotions about her mother, who did not live up to her promise of being caring in some ways and that Jayne felt alone as she made many life choices. She wondered why her parents never gave her their approval with respect to her career as a dancer, her boyfriends, her choice of life partner, and her husband's career. She then described her physician brother, Keith, who was in jail for committing a murder as a result of road rage, again without a pause in the recounting of the perfect family. Jayne continued to other topics about her family, not stopping to provide any detail or to make any connections between Keith and any aspect of their family life. Jayne did not recognize that her overconnected demeanor with her own child was born of her feelings about her own upbringing by parents she viewed as emotionally detached and judgmental.

I encourage you to make connections. Not making the conscious, deliberate, and reflective connections between what we have experienced and how we are parenting means we will parent in a way that is similar to the way we were parented. Although it is not possible (or necessary) to address every aspect of how we were parented and change everything in our own behaviors, it is important to pay attention to the patterns.

If you see yourself in the dismissing pattern, try to have more access to your childhood by talking to old friends, siblings, and family members. What relational patterns in your family do you all recall that led to your feeling that you need to have barricades in relationships, even in the parent–child relationship? Why are feelings and emotions in their full range not allowed in your relationships? What is the basis of your fear of being close to someone? Try to think about these issues, and seek counseling if necessary.

If you see yourself as preoccupied/overconnected with your family of origin and maybe see dependent qualities in your own child, try to come to terms with the anger you feel about your past. It is a positive attribute that you have access to feelings, but they are mostly negative feelings. Try to see some of the positive and/or *decide* to create a positive life lesson. By appropriate distancing of yourself from your family of origin, you are in fact learning to be your own person, with autonomy and separateness from your family. Look at your interactions with your child, and you might notice instances of intrusive and/or overprotective behaviors that keep him or her unhealthily connected to you. You might show signs of distress and negative affect and might pay more attention to him or her in such distress situations. Try instead to accentuate the positive rather than the distress. Knowing that you have a tendency toward hyperemotionality, decide to work on creating a more positive emotional climate, one born of appropriate boundaries between people in the family. Such observing of boundaries will help your child in his or her search for autonomy because you will have given your child permission to be his or her own person.

PERCEPTIONS OF OUR CHILDREN

Just as our thinking, reflectiveness, and decision to make connections about our families of origin can and does affect our own parenting, so do other aspects of our thinking. Inge Bretherton, Doreen Ridgeway, and I developed an interview script to help to understand the parental view of the parent–child relationship and found that a parent's insight and sensitivity in speaking about his or her child and the parent's empathy about the child's behaviors can have powerful effects on parenting as well. We found that those parents who described their children as "not close and cuddly" or "like my ex" or "not someone I feel particularly close to" but did not describe or qualify such comments with insight and empathy about the children often had children who were either insecure with them or who were emotionally unresponsive to them. In contrast, parents who described their children in ways that indicated the children were "happy and loving" or by saying, "she's my world" or "he's active and quite difficult, but it's been a really positive challenge to be a part of his life and help him to channel all that wonderful energy into his life; I feel I have been given the privilege of helping him be the best he can be" usually had children who were secure and emotionally responsive.

Interestingly, some parents who are highly reflective about their families of origin and have "earned security" still raise insecure children. In such cases, I encourage parents to make connections also with their perceptions of their children. Creating more positive perceptions and, particularly, perceptions not only tinged but also soaked in empathy for the child (seeing things from your child's point of view, finding the heart to help your child, finding and in fact changing your heart to be one that feels what your child feels) can make a huge difference. I have seen from working with families that to have this "change of heart," they not only have to see the world from a child's perspective, but they also have to garner a greater capacity to be emotionally "real" with their children, whom they previously found "hard to get to know" or whom they "didn't feel close to."

It is difficult to get to know and become intimate with your child when you keep him or her at arm's length or when you cater endlessly but without a true heartfelt connection. Be "real" and make those "real connections" with your child. Also, make sure your connection is a healthy one—don't just cater, thinking that such attention creates the context for a healthier relationship that will prepare your child for life. Instead, change your child's pattern of responding to you and others. If your child is avoidant of you, you might want to be warmer and more emotionally demonstrative toward him or her. If your child is dependent toward you and others, then treat him or her in an age-appropriate way that gives your child a sense of his or her own agency and strength. You might want to be less intrusive to give your child more chances for decision-making and problem-solving—empower your child rather than treat him or her with kid gloves.

Children have a good way of sensing how strong you think they are. If you act as if they are fragile, that sends a message to them about how much trust you have in them. Decide what the stumbling block might be to making that healthy connection and work on it. Instead of quick fixes, go for the "emotionally real."

The power of adults' perceptions was clear in a situation that involved friends of mine. In this case, it was the nanny's perceptions that almost led to a self-fulfilling prophecy, suggesting that caregiver emotional availability (as well as lack of availability) is also important.

> This family had a South American nanny, Rosa, who seemed at first to be generally good with the children. But Rosa was still hurting from her divorce and really disliked men. She likened my friends' bright little daughter, Amber, to her ex-husband and her son, all of whom were born in the same month. Rosa began treating Amber in subtly negative ways, in my opinion, unconsciously projecting her ex and son onto her. As a result, this bright, outgoing, and enthusiastic little girl was slowly becoming shy and withdrawn. Fortunately, the parents realized what was happening at an unconscious level and fired Rosa. Needless to say, it was heartwarming to see Amber return to her old self in a short time.

Traumatic relationships of the past can have a particularly powerful hold on you—be it an ex, a brother, a sister—you need to consciously draw the line between others and your child. Be particularly careful to draw that line if you think your child is similar to your ex-spouse, and you do not think well of your ex any longer, even if the similarity you perceive is a physical similarity. If anything, seeing your child as an extension of yourself (if you think well of yourself) might be a helpful strategy.

IS SECURITY AN ESSENTIAL "INGREDIENT" OF THE PARENT-CHILD RELATIONSHIP?

Most child–development professionals consider different types of insecurity "normal variations" in society, and research has confirmed that insecurity is *not* predictive of mental disorder in children or adults. In fact, some of my colleagues would argue that the independence demonstrated by avoidant children might be essential in some occupations, even superseding the need for emotional connection. Some researchers say that perhaps security should not be the goal for all children. In fact, in some cultures where autonomy is highly valued, as for example, Germany, they see a higher percentage of insecure/avoidant babies than we see in this country. In other cultures where connection is highly valued, as for exam-

---

It is less important that you know which particular pattern you are than to know that some emotional work needs to be done.

- Often, the catalyst for change is the birth of a baby. Some individuals realize that they are projecting onto the baby their own past (often referred to as "ghosts in the nursery") or that their perception of their child is crowded (they are projecting a disliked aunt or a despised ex onto this child). The nursery is crowded because the excess baggage from another relationship is there along with the parent-child relationship. Divest yourself of this baggage with the help of a professional, if necessary, or someone you trust.

- It is particularly important that an individual take the time, energy, and confidence to resolve losses. If traumatizing events have occurred, it might be important not to go it alone on this journey. A supportive presence might be of great help in the healing process. The key to resolution is to make connections, and keep making them, until the pieces fit!

- It is also important to have access to memories of your childhood. If you cannot remember much about your childhood, it might be important to try to access the memories and the emotions associated with those memories by talking to a trusted friend or professional.

ple Israel or Japan, they report a higher percentage of insecure/dependent babies than we see in the United States.

Despite some differences in the percentages of different categories in different countries, however, generally it is agreed that security predicts better outcomes than insecurity, regardless of the culture, although more research is needed in this area. My own goal for my child has always been to ensure her sense of security because I know that provides the emotional robustness for all future relationships and areas of competence. When I discussed many U.S. psychologists' views on security with a colleague from another country, she said, "In the United States, maybe you don't view unhappiness and stress for a child as a life risk, and that is what is at stake here."

---

continued...

- *If you are still angry with your parents, know that you might be over-connected through your anger. Some work to create boundaries between you and your family of origin might be helpful.*

- *If your perceptions of your child include some negatives, dwell on what might be causing that. Are you projecting others onto this child or are you sidestepping the fact that security, dependence, and avoidance are created—they are not there at birth. And just as they are created, they can be re-created—with some effort.*

- *Engage in some storytelling about your past and about your child(ren). Through such storytelling, you might have a chance to understand what went on for you and what your vulnerabilities are. Telling your story to someone you trust is an important beginning.*

- *Unleash and use your intuition, your gut feelings, and your emotions through this process.*

- *Recognize that this will be a struggle, but one that will yield many rewards for your relationships.*

four

The Importance of Emotional Availability

This chapter will describe how "emotional availability" in your relationship with your child will help your child feel more secure. Emotional availability measures and predicts the quality of the relationship between parent and child. More emotionally available environments promote secure attachments, and less emotionally available environments create insecure attachments. The richer the emotional relationship between parent and child, the more likely it is that the child experiences the parent as emotionally available.

Numerous studies have shown that a history of emotionally available caregiving creates security within the child. For most children, the relationship starts at birth; for others, it starts at the point of adoption or foster care. If the parent-child relationship has been an emotionally available one, the infant is likely to feel security. If the history of interaction has been less than emotionally available or inconsistent because a caretaker has been only moderately available at times and unavailable at other times, the likelihood of child insecurity begins to increase.

HOW WE OBSERVE EMOTIONAL AVAILABILITY

Typically, we assess emotional availability in a clinical or research laboratory setting. If it is a baby and parent, we provide some age-appropriate toys and leave the baby to play on the floor, saying, "Play as you normally do." We film about a half-hour in the laboratory. Particularly with babies, we often go into the home with video camera, and say, "Go about your normal daily routine." We have filmed parents and children in various scenarios: as the parent is vacuuming, during a feeding, during bath time, as well as during play. We like to get a variety of contexts so we have a sense of what the normal day is like for them. Because the contexts in the home can be so varied, our observations last an hour or two. For older children, we usually see families in the laboratory. Typically, we have the child and parent play together for about five minutes with Etch-A-Sketch, with the parent operating the vertical dial and the child operating the horizontal dial. The task is to cooperatively draw a boat or a house. A model sketch is usually presented to them. They then are asked to engage in fantasy play with some toys that include knights and princesses and other parts to evoke imaginative play (usually twenty minutes). Similar contexts are used with older children. The idea is always to provide some age-appropriate toys and to videotape them as they play for at least twenty minutes to a half-hour.

At all ages, including babies, we film parent and child in a stressful context, after a "reunion," in which the parent has been out of the room for a few minutes, leaving the child with an adult stranger, and then comes back into the room. Such a reunion can give us much interesting information about how the baby or young child reacts under stress to the parent. This is sometimes very telling about whether the baby or child feels comfortable going to the parent for support during a time of stress.

THE EFFECTS OF GOOD EMOTIONAL AVAILABILITY ON A CHILD'S FUTURE

After many years of clinical research and observation of interactions between parents and children, the importance of emotional availability in the healthy development of children has become very clear. A few examples of the effects of good emotional availability are the following:

· **Infants and children who have emotionally available relationships with their parents are more likely to also show the secure pattern.** Thus, emotionally available interactions during the first year of life and beyond create trust and security in children, with all the positives that such a secure pathway affords.

· **Children who have emotionally available relationships with their parents are less aggressive and less likely to be the targets of aggression from other children.** I recently conducted a study funded by the National Science Foundation on how emotional availability affects children in terms of peer interactions, the child-teacher relationship, and the learning experience. We found that the emotional connection a parent is able to establish with a child (not just from the parent to the child from the child back to the parent) before the child is in school is highly predictive of that child's aggression as well as victimization.

In this study, we observed children in classrooms throughout the kindergarten year. We also asked their teachers to report on child-peer relationships as well as child-teacher relationships. We found that healthy emotional availability between parent and child usually led to less aggression by the child in kindergarten and less victimization of the child by others' aggression. This doesn't mean that the child was never aggressive, nor that other children were never aggressive toward the child; but in general, the greater the emotional availability in the parent-child relationship, the less likely the child was to be involved in any aggressive episode or dispute with other children. Children from emotionally available relationships used a variety of skills in navigating sources of aggression, including ignoring the children who were aggressive, having clever "comebacks," and the like. It might also be that children in emotionally available relationships with their parents are more emotionally available themselves and, therefore, have social allies in the classroom who support them during peer interactions.

· **Children from emotionally available homes have better peer relationships.** They are more positive and proactively social in interactions with their peers; they are more gracious to others and have a certain air of confidence. These children are more likely to be helpful to other children and seem to sense the feelings of other children and respond in a sensitive manner to them. They are more willing to have positive interactions with their peers, more likely to help out their peers, and more likely to respond in a positive or helpful way to any interaction they begin or respond to with their peers. For their futures, children who are emotionally available or whose emotional availability has improved over time will have more skills to understand others and to work with them in collaborative ways. These are important skills for children to learn—as important as their academic learning—because these skills of emotional availability create healthy connections with others in relationships. For children to have these skills of emotional availability, they have to be in a network of emotionally available relationships—with their parents, with their teachers, and with others. In such a network, they "feel" what it's like to be in a healthy relationship. They will also likely then contribute to other children's senses of security and emotional availability, thereby enhancing what happens in the community and in society in general.

· **Children who have emotionally available relationships with their parents are more attentive in school and suffer less from the effects of learning problems.** Attentiveness is a very good sign of early learning. If a child is attentive and focused on the task at hand, the child is more likely to absorb what is going on in the classroom. However, if a child isn't attentive to the teacher and is easily distracted, he or she will not be able to pick up information from the environment.

In the same National Science Foundation study cited earlier, we observed and scored eye movements of children for a whole year to measure children's attentiveness and lack of distractibility in school. We discovered that children from emotionally available parent-child relationships were more attentive while the teacher was teaching. Emotional availability also appears to be related to teacher-rated academic competence.

In addition, emotional availability appears to mitigate the effects of some learning problems. Although learning disabilities are inborn in many ways, learning problems also can be related to the level of emotional connection. Children are less able to concentrate on what is going on in school if they are busy thinking about the problems at home. If they are emotionally satisfied and fulfilled at home, however, they come to school ready to learn and are able to concentrate on school instead of being preoccupied with other issues. Interestingly, we find this relation between emotional availability and observed attentiveness in school even when we take into account the effects of a child's age-related language ability. A healthy, emotionally available home life prepares our children to pay attention and concentrate in school.

We also have evidence that emotional availability is related to knowledge of vocabulary words and of humanities, even after we take into account the child's language level. We theorize that this is because emotionally available parents are more likely to talk to and be involved with their children at many different levels, both emotionally and intellectually.

· **Children from emotionally available homes seem to relate better with their teachers.** If emotional availability in the parent-child relationship is high, the teacher-child relationship in the school has fewer "bumps," so to speak. That is, the children experience less conflict and show less dependence, and the teacher is less likely to see such children as "problems" in the classroom. Basically, teachers are more likely to see those children as allies or kids who are "on the right track." Such children are less likely to be the ones getting the negative attention in the classroom. These findings have major import for our understanding of school readiness. We should be thinking about preparing our children for school many years before they actually set foot into the doors of any formal institution. Our children's preparation begins at the time of birth, and the parents' emotional availability is one of the most important ingredients in that preparation.

What I think about as a researcher, clinician, and parent is that 20 to 30 percent of parent-child relationships are in the gray to dark zone of emotional availability. This suggests to me that 20 to 30 percent of parents might not know that there is room for significant improvement in their relationships with their children. This is not about abuse, neglect, or even obvious rejection; it is about parents not being emotionally connected to their children in a healthy way. Most parents are generally involved and caring; the problem arises when the parents' version of "good enough" parenting and the children's point of view of the same thing are different. If children aren't feeling emotionally connected to their parents, the consequences can be subtle yet pervasive. Emotionally unavailable parenting predisposes children to unhappiness or being emotionally shut down and might create either emotional disconnection or unhealthy emotional overconnection with the very people who care most about them—their parents.

PARENTS' EMOTIONAL AVAILABILITY—IS IT "INTUITIVE PARENTING" OR A "WORK IN PROGRESS"?

The ability to be available emotionally to our children is not something that is "inborn" or "instinctual." Parenting is sometimes described as "intuitive." However, what is "intuitive" is not always better than what is learned. In fact, viewing parenting as a learned quality—like learning on the job—rather than an intuitive exercise can help every single one of us do better at this important job. Being intuitive is not necessarily better!

Many aspects of your thinking (feelings of rejection or trauma from the family in which you were raised; not seeing your child as the extension of yourself; projecting onto your child someone from your past or someone you dislike from your present), however, can alter your ability to view your child as he or she really is. Such distortions might impair your ability to be an intuitive parent. It is not that you aren't or couldn't be intuitive in your immediate emotional response, but simply that there is an "obstacle" that keeps emotional communication from being open and expressive.

Many aspects of emotionally available parenting involve a set of skills each parent can develop with some information and guidance. Indeed, as parents, we must learn our emotional availability skills anew with each child because each child's needs are different, and those needs will change as our child grows. We are indeed "works in progress" when it comes to being emotionally there for our children.

EMOTIONAL AVAILABILITY—NOT A "TRAIT"

Luckily for parents, emotional availability is a quality of *relationships* rather than of individuals. It's not as if some individuals are emotionally available and others are not; everyone has the potential to create emotionally available relationships. It is mostly a question of degree. Many parents have had the experience of feeling that it is easier to connect emotionally with one child than with another. Some individuals are more emotionally available in one relationship and less emotionally available in another. Indeed, our research has shown that emotional availability is unique to a particular relationship rather than a "trait" of the individual. Therefore, this connection has to be nurtured in each relationship. Such findings provide hope for the improvement of emotional availability in all the important relationships of our lives.

Emotional availability in the parent-child relationship also produces some additional benefits for parents. For example, emotionally available parents are less likely to be depressed and stressed. Perhaps a better way to put it might be that the less depressed and stressed parents are, the more likely they are to be emotionally available to their children. As many parents know, being stretched thin and feeling that nothing is going right affects your ability to relate to your children. We also have observed, however, that the greater the emotional availability in the parent-child relationship, the more likely parents are to report that they are happy with their children and that they view their children as high functioning. The quality of the emotional relationship you establish with your child is related to how you view yourself and your child, suggesting that the overall emotional connection you have with your child predicts how you rate other qualities about yourself and your family.

THE EMOTIONAL AVAILABILITY ASSESSMENT

In research laboratories both nationally and internationally, we observe parent-child interaction and then rate the quality of interaction on several different scales. Because this observational instrument requires long and intense training, I will not provide it here. I do believe, however, that if parents are given the "tools" to observe their own interactions with their children, they can do an effective self-assessment.

If you aren't able (or don't wish) to visit child psychologists or developmental psychology labs for a formal scoring of emotional availability, the following simple self-diagnostic quiz I created for this book should help with your self-assessment. The following questions are divided into two sections. The first section is for parents whose children are under two years of age. The second section is for parents of older children (ages two through early adolescence). It's best to answer only the questions appropriate for the age of your child. The self-assessment, or quiz, could give you some idea of what qualities to look for in your relationship.

To evaluate your own emotional availability, you must use a continuum-based measurement. Read the following questions and mark the response you believe best represents your behaviors and feelings and those of your child. Use a rating scale from 1 (almost never) to 3 (sometimes) to 5 (almost always).

Section 1

Emotional Availability Self-Assessment

for Parents with Children Under Two Years Old

	ALMOST NEVER		SOMETIMES		ALMOST ALWAYS
	1	2	3	4	5
1. My baby is upset whenever I leave the room and seems to play mostly near me.	□	□	□	□	□
2. My baby doesn't seem to notice when I come back into the room.	□	□	□	□	□
3. My baby doesn't crawl/walk to me much.	□	□	□	□	□
4. I wish my baby were happier when he/she is with me.	□	□	□	□	□
5. My baby looks at me and listens to me when I try to talk to him/her.	□	□	□	□	□
6. My baby likes to be with me the most.	□	□	□	□	□
7. My baby is lots of fun to be around.	□	□	□	□	□
8. My baby is very independent and mostly likes to play on his/her own.	□	□	□	□	□
9. My baby seems to "light up" when he/she sees me.	□	□	□	□	□
10. After I leave the room, my baby seems really happy when I come back.	□	□	□	□	□
11. My baby barely notices me.	□	□	□	□	□
12. My baby is "cranky" most of the time.	□	□	□	□	□
13. My baby seems to understand what I mean most of the time.	□	□	□	□	□
14. I feel my baby tries to communicate with me.	□	□	□	□	□
15. When I try to play with my baby, he/she seems to be busy and mostly moves away.	□	□	□	□	□
16. It's hard to get my baby to play with me for very long.	□	□	□	□	□

	ALMOST NEVER		SOMETIMES		ALMOST ALWAYS
	1	2	3	4	5
17. I wish my baby could play a little more on his/her own.	☐	☐	☐	☐	☐
18. My baby and I have lots of fun together.	☐	☐	☐	☐	☐
19. When my baby seems to not want to play with me, I feel hurt.	☐	☐	☐	☐	☐
20. I don't feel close to this baby.	☐	☐	☐	☐	☐
21. I try to see things from my baby's per-spective.	☐	☐	☐	☐	☐
22. When things go wrong, I get bent out of shape easily.	☐	☐	☐	☐	☐
23. I am usually in a good mood around my baby.	☐	☐	☐	☐	☐
24. When things go wrong, I tend to be flexible.	☐	☐	☐	☐	☐
25. Even if my baby doesn't get it right, I let him/her have the experience.	☐	☐	☐	☐	☐
26. It's difficult for me to say "good-bye" or separate from my child when I leave the house or leave him/her with a sitter.	☐	☐	☐	☐	☐
27. I shadow my child's every step as if it could be his/her last and worry much too much.	☐	☐	☐	☐	☐
28. It is hard to soothe my baby and he/she seems to be distressed a lot.	☐	☐	☐	☐	☐

Section 2

Emotional Availability Self-Assessment

for Parents with Children Older Than Two Years

	ALMOST NEVER	SOMETIMES			ALMOST ALWAYS
	1	2	3	4	5
1. My child is upset a lot.	☐	☐	☐	☐	☐
2. My child doesn't talk to me much about what goes on at preschool/school.	☐	☐	☐	☐	☐
3. I wish my child smiled more and seemed happier.	☐	☐	☐	☐	☐
4. My child listens to me when I talk to him/her.	☐	☐	☐	☐	☐
5. My child seems happy when with other children.	☐	☐	☐	☐	☐
6. My child has lots of fun with me.	☐	☐	☐	☐	☐
7. My child has few friends.	☐	☐	☐	☐	☐
8. My child seems sad to me.	☐	☐	☐	☐	☐
9. Others (for example, teachers, my friends) have commented on my child not seeming happy.	☐	☐	☐	☐	☐
10. My child and I do a lot together.	☐	☐	☐	☐	☐
11. My child listens to me when I discipline him/her.	☐	☐	☐	☐	☐
12. My child tries to talk to me when he/she has something on his/her mind.	☐	☐	☐	☐	☐
13. When I try to talk to my child, he/she seems disinterested in my joining in.	☐	☐	☐	☐	☐
14. My child likes to be on his/her own and is a bit of a loner.	☐	☐	☐	☐	☐
15. I feel I don't have a lot of control, and my child is the one with control around here.	☐	☐	☐	☐	☐
16. I don't feel like I know this child.	☐	☐	☐	☐	☐

	ALMOST NEVER		SOMETIMES		ALMOST ALWAYS
	1	2	3	4	5
17. When my child seems not to want to play with me, I feel hurt.	☐	☐	☐	☐	☐
18. My child cries a lot and seems to get bent out of shape easily.	☐	☐	☐	☐	☐
19. I listen to my child when he/she tries to explain things to me.	☐	☐	☐	☐	☐
20. I try to see things from my child's perspective.	☐	☐	☐	☐	☐
21. When things go wrong, I get bent out of shape easily.	☐	☐	☐	☐	☐
22. I am usually in a good mood around my child.	☐	☐	☐	☐	☐
23. When things go wrong, I tend to be flexible.	☐	☐	☐	☐	☐
24. When I see that my child isn't getting it right, I jump in to correct him/her.	☐	☐	☐	☐	☐
25. It's difficult for me to separate from my child for school, sleepovers, or playdates.	☐	☐	☐	☐	☐
26. I shadow my child's every step as if it could be his/her last and worry.	☐	☐	☐	☐	☐
27. My child seems to need a lot of assurances and reassurances of my caring and attention and seems to use distress to get attention.	☐	☐	☐	☐	☐

Scoring Your Test

Section 1:

Questions 5, 6, 7, 9, 10, 13, 14, 18, 21, 23, 24, and 25: If you answered 3, 4, or 5 on these questions, your emotional availability is relatively high. Responses 1 or 2 suggest you need to do some work on emotional availability in these areas.

Questions 1, 2, 3, 4, 8, 11, 12, 15, 16, 17, 19, 20, 22, 26, 27, and 28: If you answered 3, 4, or 5, you might want to do some work on your emotional availability with this child. If you answered 1 or 2 for these questions, your emotional availability with your child is pretty good.

Section 2:

Questions 4, 5, 6, 10, 11, 12, 19, 20, 22, and 23: If you answered 3, 4, or 5 on these questions, your emotional availability is relatively high. If your responses were 1 or 2, you might need to do some work on your emotional availability with this child.

Questions 1, 2, 3, 7, 8, 9, 13, 14, 15, 16, 17, 18, 21, 24, 25, 26, and 27: If you answered 3, 4, or 5, you might want to do some work on your emotional availability with this child. If you answered 1 or 2 for these questions, your emotional availability with your child is probably pretty good.

Remember that emotional availability isn't something you have or you don't have—it's a continuum of connection that will change, grow, and evolve throughout your child's life. If your scores indicate you are less emotionally available to your child than you would like to be, take heart. Many parents don't realize that they have to improve their emotional connection with their children until it's too late. But if you've realized this early on, it is correctable and can be improved with some simple techniques.

Be aware, however, that as with any relationship, making changes can take time. Parent-child relationships have a great deal to do with history, and if you have a history of being less than emotionally available, it will take your child a while to adjust. The more emotional availability you show as a parent, the more responsive to you and trusting your child will be. The earlier you start, the better foundation you and your child will have for your future together.

There is a link between emotional availability and security in the parent-child relationship:

- *By the end of the first year of life, children can be characterized usually into one of four attachment patterns: secure, insecure/avoidant, insecure/dependent, and disorganized. Although it might seem simplistic to narrow down the uniqueness of a parent-child relationship into one of these four categories, research has indicated that a secure attachment is an important predictor of children's future, as will be described in later chapters. We worry most about the disorganized pattern, as it has been linked with the least positive adjustment for children.*

- *How do children come to show these patterns of behavior, particularly security versus insecurity? If you and your child interact with one another in more emotionally available ways, your child is more likely to be secure. If you and your child interact with each other in less emotionally available ways, however, your child is less likely to be secure in his or her relationship with you.*

- *Security of the child and the emotional availability of the relationship are not traits of individuals but qualities of specific relationships. In fact, children can have very different relationships with each member of the family (for example, securely attached to Dad, insecurely attached to Mother, and secure with teacher). The important thing about this message is that you are not born with a certain fixed amount of emotional availability. Further, your child's security or emotional availability toward you is not inborn, either. With the emotional work described here—some of it simple and some of it involving profound changes in your thinking and way of approaching relationships—you can create the type of relationship you hope for.*

- *The Emotional Availability Self-Assessment provides some indication of whether there is work to be done. Because the assessment shows you what types of behaviors to look for in your child's relationship with you, it provides a window on improvements over time as well. As your child improves the quality of his or her connection with you, you are likely to have a different "feel" in the relationship, and this "feel" will be reflected in your changed responses to the self-assessment.*

The Eight Principles of Emotional Availability

I have heard parenting described as "a dance on a tightrope over an alligator pit"—it's much too easy to make a mistake and fall, and the consequences can be serious when you do. However, when you know the eight principles of emotional availability, it's like having a balance pole or, even better, a guide rope that you can hang on to as you negotiate your ever-changing relationship with your child.

In our research, we evaluate parent-child relationships by separating its qualities into eight areas. We then score each quality on a numbered scale (1 to 9 in some cases; 1 to 5 in others). These principles are what clinicians, researchers, and other child psychologists look for when they are evaluating a parent-child relationship. To conduct this assessment, we observe the parent-child relationship. To conduct your own assessment, you can observe your own relationship with your child, or that of someone close to you, such as your partner.

Many of these eight principles are things parents do naturally—some of the time. However, most of us could use these principles more frequently and deliberately and, thus, create deeper bonds with our children at every age, at every stage of development, in tough times or great times, and every time in between.

If it feels strange to you to "deliberately" build an emotional connection with your child, you're not alone. I find that the general perception of most parents is expressed as, "But I love my child, and he [or she] knows it. Why would I have to keep eight different principles in mind just to do something that comes naturally?" Loving our children is one thing; communicating that love in ways that are appropriate to their age and development is another. Emotional availability is a research-based, scientifically validated measurement of the quality of communication and connection between parent and child.

Some of these principles measure the presence of a particular trait or attitude (sensitivity, recruitability, structure, and so on), a couple measure the absence of such traits as hostility and intrusiveness, and still others evaluate the child's response to the parent rather than the parent's connection with the child.

All relationships are two-way streets, and often the most telling evaluation of the quality of the connection lies not with the parent's actions but with the *child's response*. Sometimes—and certainly, most often—the parent has shaped the child's emotional availability as the child grows up. However, we must recognize that all children come into the world with their own temperaments. One child might be quiet and less demonstrative, another hyperactive and overly affectionate. It's how a parent responds to a particular child's temperament and needs and how the child, in turn, reacts to the parent, that makes the difference between a high- and low-quality emotional connection between the two. One of the reasons the Emotional Availability Scales have become so valuable in research settings is because of their ability to evaluate such relationships objectively, measuring action and reaction, communication and response, regardless of the child's or the parent's particular emotional predilections.

I describe these principles in terms of what we look for in a clinical setting, where parents bring their children into a clinic or research lab and are observed for anywhere from ten minutes to an hour. The following interactions I describe are cases with children in an age range from nine months to ten years. I hope to give you concrete examples of the ways each of these principles might show up in your own life. I have tried to avoid a lot of psychological jargon, but you might find some of the descriptions a little clinical. Don't worry—the rest of this book will give you examples of how these eight components work in the context of real life. I guarantee that once you understand these components, you will find them easy to apply to your own relationship with your child and you'll be far more likely to respond to your child in a manner that will connect and support both of you.

I have put the eight principles of emotional availability in the form of questions. I have deliberately used the same questions that form the basis of emotional availability research simply because the terms are recognized and accepted throughout the field of psychology. By asking yourself these questions, corresponding to the eight principles of emotional availability, you can assess the quality of your own emotional connection with your child. I hope they will make it easier for you to determine what you are already doing well, and where you can put a greater focus on deepening your relationship as a parent.

These eight questions are: (1) Are you "emotionally recruitable" by your child? (2) Is your child "emotionally recruitable" by you? (3) How sensitive are you to your child? (4) Do you structure interactions with your child appropriately? (5) Are you available to your child without being intrusive? (6) Is there any overt or covert hostility present? (7) Is your child responsive to you? (8) Does your child allow you to be involved in his or her life?

1. ARE YOU "EMOTIONALLY RECRUITABLE" BY YOUR CHILD?

Sandy, a young mother, took her three-year-old adopted son, Jeffy, to a community pool. The little boy was very active and prone to inattentiveness—he was what many people would describe as a "handful." However, Sandy was very good at playing with Jeffy and keeping him on task. She also gave him a lot of space, but when she called him to come and play with her, he would run back to her with gusto. Although Jeffy demanded a lot of his mother's attention, she was responsive to his needs. Sandy was engaging and lively, and there was a lot of laughter between mother and son. They obviously enjoyed being together. It was clear that the time at the pool was their "special time," an opportunity for mother and son to connect with each other.

Another mom, Jennifer, was at the same pool with her child, Sherrie, a little girl of about five years old. Jennifer had encouraged Sherrie to take her boogie board and swim around, but very quickly Jennifer settled back in a lounge chair and started working on her needlepoint. Sherrie would occasionally yell, "Mommy, watch me!" and Jennifer would respond, "That's great, dear," looking up momentarily and then returning to her needlepoint. After a while, the little girl stopped asking for her mother's attention. Even when Sherrie hit her foot on the edge of the pool and started crying, Jennifer's demeanor barely changed. After a few moments, she coolly put down her needlepoint and went over to her daughter. "You should know better than to swim that close to the side of the pool," she said as she reached to touch the child's hair. But Sherrie brushed away her mother's hand, very clearly not wanting the consolation. Jennifer shrugged and went back to her needlepoint.

Both mothers spent about the same amount of time at the pool with their children, but the quality of each mother's emotional interaction with her child was markedly different. What children truly want is not just their parents' time or attention, but their connection as well. Children need to be able to recruit parents emotionally; they should find their parents open and willing to connect with them emotionally. Children should not have to spend much effort recruiting parents, who should make sure they are available to be recruited.

Of course, at times you might be preoccupied with other tasks—such as earning a living, attending to other children, taking care of chores around the house, or even taking care of yourself. But there are many simple ways to be emotionally recruitable by your child and still tend to the day-to-day requirements of life.

Let's look more closely at Jennifer's interaction. When her little girl shouted, "Mommy, watch me!" she did not need to drop her needlepoint, rush to the edge of the pool, and cheer, "Sherrie, that's amazing! Show everyone what an incredible swimmer you are—everyone, watch my little girl!" because it wouldn't be true emotional recruitability. Instead, the behavior would demonstrate the kind of overcompensation and false emotion that, according to research, actually indicate a very poor parent-child relationship. If Jennifer had put half of her attention on Sherrie while she kept doing her needlepoint, so when her child shouted, "Mommy, watch me!" she looked up and said with genuine warmth and encouragement, "Great, Sherrie—you made it all the way across the pool!" she would have helped Sherrie feel her mom was emotionally available. This kind of specific response—one that makes it clear to the child that her mother has indeed been observing her—delivered with an obviously real emotional connection, will indicate that the mom is involved in the child's activities while allowing her daughter to learn, grow, and explore for herself.

The key to emotional recruitability is not simply paying attention to your child, it's the genuine caring and warmth you bring to the interaction. One of the most wonderful things about children is the fact that their emotions are so close to the surface. When children are happy, sad, upset, or joyful, or if they find something funny or scary, they communicate it—immediately! Adults lose much of this awareness of their own feelings so it is vitally important when you are with your children that you allow your best emotions—love, reassurance, caring, and warmth—to come to the surface easily and often.

Emotional recruitability also has to do with picking up on children's signals and responding appropriately to them. When children want your attention, do they want you to kiss them? Cuddle them? Teach them? Help them? Cheer them on? Advise them? Laugh with them? Cry with them? You can demonstrate your emotional recruitability by responding appropriately to the stated and unstated needs of your child. No, you don't have to be able to read their mind! Luckily, reading a child's needs is usually pretty simple.

2. IS YOUR CHILD "EMOTIONALLY RECRUITABLE" BY YOU?

What makes a good mother or father? How do you know when you encounter one on the playground, walking down the street, in day care, or perhaps in your own home? Good parents aren't determined by what they do but by how they are around their children. When you think of good parents, don't qualities such as warmth, emotional connection, and strength without rigidity all come to mind? But how can you really tell whether people are good parents? You watch their children. Specifically, in a clinical setting, we watch the child's emotional response to the parent—his or her openness, comfort, security level, and general emotional recruitability by this particular adult.

A parent's emotional availability is not enough to create a strong connection with a child; the child also must be emotionally available to the parent. As I said earlier, certainly some children are less disposed temperamentally to be recruitable, but ultimately the emotional recruitability of children has to do with the way they are raised. The most important factor is the quality of emotion you offer your child. If you are consistently warm, loving, caring, and supportive, your child will most likely mirror what he or she receives.

In the example of the mothers and children at the pool, three-year-old Jeffy might appear to be the more difficult child to recruit emotionally— he was certainly more hyperactive and scattered than five-year-old Sherrie. Yet due to the connection that his mother, Sandy, had obviously created over time, when she called him to come and play with her, he returned willingly. Jeffy felt safe enough to leave Sandy and explore his environment, yet he clearly enjoyed their interactions just as much. He was eager for and open to the emotional connection offered through his relationship with his mother.

Sherrie was obviously seeking emotional connection with her mother, Jennifer, when she called out, "Mommy, watch me!" yet it was also clear that she felt she had to demand her mother's attention rather than assuming it would be there. Once Sherrie had asked for the attention and was refused, her level of emotional recruitability dropped dramatically. When

Jennifer tried to reestablish a connection when the little girl injured herself, Sherrie turned away. She was no longer emotionally recruitable by her mother in that circumstance. In truth, Sherrie was simply mirroring the lack of emotional connection she had received from her mother.

When a child is emotionally recruitable by a parent, there's a palpable sense of strong connection between the two. Junior can be off exploring or playing and Mom can simply be watching, yet her quiet supportiveness tells her son that it's okay for him to be on his own. In this emotionally connected atmosphere, Junior feels safe and happy—but he will return to Mom for emotional "refueling" every so often. The mother's emotional availability fosters the child's willingness to be available in return.

In school-age children, emotional recruitability manifests in the child's willingness to verbally connect with the parent. For example, most parents will ask their kids, "How was school today?" Children who feel connected with their parents will usually be willing to talk about their activities and share some of the incidents of the school day. Emotionally recruitable children will also wish to include their parents in special activities such as sports, recitals, ceremonies, and so on. When there is a healthy emotional connection between the parent and child, the child also will feel free to invite over friends to play or for dinner, thereby including the parent in some aspects of peer relationships.

Parents of emotionally recruitable older children will usually experience both a sense of connection and a feeling of growing independence on the child's part. Like toddlers who can explore their environment because they are confident their parents are in the room, older children who maintain a secure relationship with their parents feel free to explore an ever-widening universe of friendships, situations, and challenges. Because these children feel certain of the love and support of their parents, they can be far more open to discovering and developing their own abilities and emotions.

In clinical or research settings, because parents know they are being observed, we often see them being attentive, nice, and positive with their children. However, if this is not the parent's typical behavior, the child usually makes it clear by his or her response. Specifically, there is a visible lack of emotional recruitability in the child. It is as if the child were saying,

"Mom, I'm dumbfounded that you are so nice to me because you're not like that at home," or "Mom, get off it, you're putting on an act," or perhaps, "Mom you're not giving me any responsibility for growing up. You do everything for me, and some of this I'd like to try all by myself." Signs of a lack of emotional recruitability in a child range from ignoring the parent's requests, to turning away from the parent, to consistent demands for attention (and a show of surprise when it is offered), to refusing to play with the parent or taking over the game or activity completely once the parent tries to get involved. In older children, lack of emotional recruitability manifests as unwarranted secrecy; a lack of enthusiasm when it comes to sharing news, events, or activities; an unwillingness to include parents in any part of their lives; refusing to invite over friends; spending as much time as possible outside of the home; and so on.

If children are unresponsive to overtures by their parents, chances are, the parents were unresponsive to begin with—like the little girl in the swimming pool who rejected her mother's caress. If you had seen only that one moment of the mother-daughter interaction, you might believe the child was simply not warm toward her mother: *Perhaps she just isn't a demonstrative child,* you might think. Certainly there are children whose temperaments are more phlegmatic, or who prefer a greater degree of independence. But time and time again, research has shown that the quality of the parent's ability to connect emotionally with the child contributes greatly to the child's willingness to connect with the parent.

How do you get your child to be emotionally recruitable? It starts with your being emotionally recruitable by your child. Children learn from parents what being emotionally connected feels like and then they respond in kind. You have to create an environment for your child that is rich in love, security, and emotional sharing. In your child's life, the most important gift you can give is connecting with him or her emotionally.

Remember, this kind of relationship should not feel like pulling teeth! In an emotionally connected relationship, the parts fit together. Parents offer warmth and caring to their children, and the children respond in kind because they feel loved, cared for, and supported. Children want their parents to be part of their emotional lives, and vice versa.

3. HOW SENSITIVE ARE YOU TO YOUR CHILD?

How many times have you heard parents say (or even said yourself), "I just can't figure out my child," or "I didn't know that was coming"? These statements are common when parents refer to adolescents (who constantly amaze and surprise us), but they are equally true with infants and young children. Often, parents tend to think they can read and know what is going on with their children, but in truth, they are either guessing or theorizing based on what they remember from their own early days (or perhaps learned from their other children).

"Recruitment" is a way to express your (and your child's) willingness to create and maintain an emotional connection. The word suggests that you can be counted on and that you are a participant:

- *I am not suggesting that you be hyperemotional or fake emotionality. Being overly demonstrative and exaggerated in expressions is not at all the aim in becoming "emotionally available." Maintain your unique and personal style—just allow for the space between you and your child to be filled by being "real."*

- *Take the lead in becoming emotionally available, whether it is for the first time if you just had a baby, or belatedly if your child is older. Show the way!*

- *I guarantee that your child will become as available to you as you are to your child. Relationships are dynamic—we often get back what we invest. Many dads have expressed the difficulty they find in showing their feelings to their children—likely, because men are generally not socialized to be emotionally expressive in their other relationships. Yet most dads are emotionally connected (in a healthy way) with their children. If it is difficult for you to show your feelings, start with small steps in emotional communication. Dads don't have to look like moms as they interact—far from it. Dads need the space to find their style of emotional connection with their children, and each style will be unique.*

Sensitivity is your ability to read your child and be emotionally and openly communicative with him or her. Sensitivity is the tool that allows you to create a strong emotional connection with your child. It refers to a variety of qualities in a parent, such as responsiveness, accurate reading of your child's communications, ability to resolve conflicts smoothly, and so on. When you are sensitive to your child's needs, you can offer him or her the response that is appropriate to the moment. This usually makes the child feel loved, supported, and connected, because you have read his or her needs and filled them in an appropriate way.

Sarah's one-year-old daughter, Meg, is just beginning to walk. In our clinic, we observed their interactions for about an hour. It was obvious that Sarah was sensitive to her daughter's emotional and physical needs. When Meg would bring Sarah a block or play toy, Sarah would respond warmly, admiring the toy and asking Meg questions about it. Both the tone of Sarah's voice and her clear interest in Meg's activities were sincere and appropriate (that is, not overenthusiastic or false). When Meg toddled away to investigate something on her own, Sarah chatted casually with the researcher while still keeping an eye on her daughter. After a while, Meg started getting frustrated with the wooden train she was playing with because she couldn't get it to move. Noticing Meg's frustration, Sarah went over and checked in with her daughter, asking, "What is it, honey?" She then offered her another toy. After playing with Sarah for a few minutes, the child went off exploring again and Sarah returned to her seat.

Sarah's responses showed she knew her daughter well and was attuned to her physical and emotional needs. She was comfortable letting Meg explore on her own, but she also was interested and connected with whatever her daughter was doing. She didn't overwhelm Meg with false attention or emotion; she also was able to diffuse the potential frustration about the toy quickly and move the child on to other activities. Sarah is an excellent example of an emotionally sensitive parent.

Infants and young children often cannot tell us what they want and need in words, but they do communicate nonverbally. This includes communication about their emotional needs as well as their physical ones. When Meg came to Sarah to show her the toy, it was obvious that she wanted her mother's attention. However, Sarah also picked up the subtler signal of Meg's frustration with the train and the need for some help and/or redirection. Many mothers are very good at deciphering their children's nonverbal clues, whether it be facial expression, body language, behavioral cues, or others. "When my son comes home from school, I can tell in a minute whether it's been a good or bad day," one mother reported. "When he's had a bad day, he gets this furrow between his eyebrows. Even when he tries to tell me everything's okay, I know something's up if that furrow is there. I don't push him about it, but after we chat for a while, he'll usually clue me in to what's going on."

Some of the most important nonverbal clues are signals of avoidance because they are signs that the child is becoming emotionally unrecruitable. Moms report, "My baby doesn't come to me enough," "I wish my baby were more affectionate to me," or "My baby would rather play by himself than with me." But they don't interpret these behaviors as signs that their children are feeling a lack of connection with them. Many parents take the view, "Well, my baby's just like that; it's his [or her] temperament [or genetics]." But in our research, we see children of all temperaments being responsive or unresponsive, within the range of what's "normal" for them. Often, when there's a problem with a parent's level of emotional recruitability, we see the child being more responsive with one parent than the other. No matter what your child's temperamental tendencies, it's up to you to read the positive and negative signals your child is giving you and shape your own emotional connection to suit his or her needs.

Of course, no parent can be attuned to a child at all times; everyone misses signals every now and then. It's the overall level of sensitivity to your child that is important. When we measure sensitivity in a clinical setting, we look at a variety and number of parent-child interactions over a period of time, rather than examining one particular instance. You should do the same when assessing your own sensitivity. Here are some of the key traits of a parent who is sensitive to his or her child:

- **Is predominantly positive in both facial and vocal expressiveness.** Especially when dealing with infants and preverbal children, your facial expression and voice are what communicate your level of emotional connection and caring for your child. A sensitive parent is predominantly positive rather than bored, discontented, or harsh.

Paul works at home, and it is his job to pick up his son, Ethan, from preschool each day at noon, get him lunch then put him down for his nap. Although Paul's work as a graphic designer can be very demanding, he makes this time with Ethan their special time. He is attuned to his son's moods and needs, and is good at responding to both verbal and nonverbal cues. In contrast, Paul's wife, Deborah, who is an attorney, is not particularly sensitive to Ethan. She admits that too often she "brings her day home" with her, and her fatigue causes her to respond harshly to Ethan's demands for her attention. Even when she means to be warm and caring, her face doesn't communicate her emotions well. Sensing this, Ethan turns more to his father than his mother for emotional support and connection.

- **Is appropriately responsive to circumstances and the child's emotions.** If you laugh and smile at everything your child does, you will come across as unauthentic and not spontaneous. Indeed, it is often inappropriate to be positive to everything your child does, as this would seem more like a performance than real emotion. A general positive attitude is more important to a child, as long as it is genuine and emotionally based.

Carl, a divorced father with two children from a previous marriage, vowed that he would be a better father when he and his second wife had their daughter, Lisa. But if you ask most observers, they'll tell you that Carl tries too hard. Lisa, who's seven, is involved in gymnastics, and whenever Carl sees her do anything—a somersault, a back bend, a cartwheel—he praises her enthusiastically and extravagantly. But his response is inappropriate for the level of achievement, and Lisa knows it. It feels false to everyone but Carl, who thinks he's being a "good parent."

If Carl were more sensitive to Lisa's needs, he could offer support and encouragement in a more genuine way, at a level of positive emotion appropriate to what Lisa is experiencing. This would create a stronger sense of connection between father and daughter.

· **Displays congruence between verbal and nonverbal expression.** If your words are caring but there is no warmth in your face or voice, what message do you think your child receives more clearly?

Joanna has three children under the age of five. She tries to be warm and caring with her children, but she is frequently preoccupied with household tasks. When her five-year-old son, Brandon, proudly shows her his latest drawing, she responds, "That's beautiful, dear! Why don't you put it on the refrigerator?" However, she barely looks at the paper, and her voice sounds distracted.

Brandon is confused: He's getting one message from his mother's words and another from her tone and actions. Joanna is trying to be sensitive to her child but can't. This kind of pseudosensitivity creates confusion for the child.

Jim is a big, bluff, hearty kind of guy who came from a family that always teased each other unmercifully. When he had a son, Jim's idea of affection was to croon to his son, "Jimmy, you're a little stinker, you know that? How'd you get to be soooo ugly?" Jim's adult friends found this to be funny, but as his son Jimmy grew older and started to understand the words his dad was using to express his affection, he grew confused and started to turn away from Jim. Jim, on his part, didn't understand what was going on. "I'm just teasing the kid!" he'd protest. "Can't he take a joke?"

Yes, he could—if Jimmy were old enough to understand that his father's tone and emotion were genuine and the words were meant to be funny. The sensitive parent expresses the emotion he or she wants to communicate through words, facial expressions, and vocal tones. The child should get one message, rather than being confused by conflicts between verbal and nonverbal communication.

· **Shows clarity of perception and appropriate response.** Being sensitive to your child means you can read your child's signals and communication accurately and then respond in a manner appropriate to the child and the situation.

Emily's two-year-old daughter, Sydney, is deaf. When they came to our research laboratory, I was interested to see how the two would interact. It was delightful to watch them together: Emily was clearly attuned to Sydney's needs, discerning when her daughter became bored with the puzzle she was working with and moving her smoothly to another activity. Emily could "read" her daughter's emotional cues with ease and accuracy and respond appropriately to the child's needs.

If your child begins to show boredom during play, it is important for you to recognize such signals and adjust your behavior accordingly. If your perceptions are distorted (for any of a number of reasons), you might not be able to soothe your child if he or she becomes upset. In some cases, you might even label your child's expressions and emotional states inaccurately ("You're not upset—you're just faking!"), mimic sarcastically ("Oh, gee, Johnny took your favorite toy. Boo-hoo!") or behave in other mismatched ways to your child.

Karen became a mother when she was sixteen years old, and her own immaturity seems to prevent her from interacting appropriately with her son, Matthew, age four. When another little boy started a fight with Matthew on the playground, Karen came up to Matthew and jerked him away. "You're always getting into trouble!" she scolded him. She didn't notice that Matthew wasn't responsible for starting the fight.

Matthew protested and then started to cry, which caused Karen to snap, "Stop that. You're a big boy now, and big boys don't cry."

Because Karen lacked the emotional maturity to deal with her son's distress, she reacted with anger instead of a more supportive response.

· **Is aware of timing.** During the course of a day, or simply an afternoon, parents and children interact in many ways—playing, feeding, bathing, joint "chores," and so on. When it comes to assessing a parent's sensitivity to the child, the timing of many of these activities can be more important than the content. Children rely on a sense of rhythm and progression in their days—they need some kind of order to provide a sense of security and safety. Sensitive parents are careful not to introduce abrupt transitions between activities. They soothe the baby before they put it down for a nap. They don't initiate play or other interactions out of the blue or interact with their children to the point of overstimulation.

Awareness of timing becomes even more critical with older children and teenagers. Knowing when to broach difficult subjects or ask questions is a vital parenting skill.

Chuck knew his teenage daughter, Mary, had an important math test coming up. Math wasn't Mary's strong suit, and Chuck wanted to help her, but he also knew that Mary hated to admit she needed help in any subject. The week before the test, Mary brought an English paper home and proudly showed it to her father: She had received an A+. Chuck praised her highly, read a little of the paper, and commented on how well she had expressed herself. Then he said, "I always did really well in math and science when I was in high school, but I could never write compositions. I was really grateful that my mom was so good at writing. She checked stuff for me and helped me with my English papers. And I always looked over the checkbook for her to make sure her math was right!" After they both laughed, Mary admitted she wasn't as good at math as she was at English and mentioned the upcoming math test. "Maybe I could help you study," Chuck said. "I think I can remember my algebra. I'd sure like to give you a hand if I can."

Because Chuck was sensitive to Mary's emotions, he was able to offer help in a way she could receive it. He also acknowledged her excellence in one area before bringing up discreetly the place where she needed assistance. The timing and manner of his offer showed his emotional sensitivity to his daughter.

· **Is flexible in terms of attention and behavior.** A parent whose attention is flexible can do other things and still be able to respond to his or her child. If a parent's attention is less flexible (like Sherrie's mother, Jennifer, at the pool), the parent "tunes out" when absorbed in a task and "tunes in" only when he or she is ready.

Flexibility in behavior should be an obvious requirement when it comes to being a caretaker for your child, but it is even more important when it comes to being emotionally sensitive to your child's needs. Two areas in which flexibility in behavior is critical are getting a child to accomplish a difficult goal (eating vegetables, for example) and parent/child play (a child will change the game and the rules in a heartbeat, and the sensitive parent will adjust accordingly).

Getting her older son toilet-trained had been a real battle, so with Alison's younger son, Charlie, she decided to adopt a more flexible approach. Instead of requiring Charlie to tell her whenever he needed to urinate or defecate and then standing over him until he did, Alison told Charlie, "I think you're a big enough boy now that you can start to use the toilet instead of going in a diaper. Let's try this. Whenever you need to go, you tell me, then you decide whether you want to use the toilet or your diaper. If you want to use the diaper, fine, but if you're ready to go like a big boy, I'll take you to the toilet." Alison also set up a chart on the wall, and every time Charlie used the toilet he got to put a sticker on the chart. Alison had to be very flexible. For the first few weeks, Charlie elected to use the diaper a lot more than the toilet. Even when he said he wanted to use the toilet, he sometimes wouldn't make it in time. Alison continued to make toilet training a game, rewarding Charlie when he acted like a "big boy" but encouraging him in whatever choice he made. Even though Charlie took longer to train than his older brother, the process was far more enjoyable for both mother and son.

Pat and Arthur have very different styles when it comes to playing games with their kids. In some ways, Pat is just another "big kid." When she plays with her five-year-old son, she becomes a firefighter, a horse, an astronaut, or whatever the game requires. She's very creative, too, suggesting ideas for new story lines and ways to play, but never insisting that her ideas are better than her son's. In contrast, Arthur is far more structured in his interactions with both his nine-year-old daughter and his young son. He insists they follow the rules exactly when playing board games, and he is clearly uncomfortable when it comes to "pretending." He loves his kids, but he relates to them as he thinks an adult should, rather than being flexible enough to enter into their play in ways that connect on the level of just having fun. Because of this, he seems less emotionally available than Pat.

Linked to flexibility in play is another trait of the sensitive parent: variety and creativity in modes of play. How creative are you as a parent? How good are you at eliciting a positive response from your child? How willing are you to join in your child's activities in a playful rather than didactic (teaching) way?

· **Shows acceptance of the child.** One of the simplest ways for us to assess parental acceptance is to notice how parents address the child as well as whether they talk to the child at all. A more sensitive parent typically speaks to the child as if he or she were a separate, respectable person with clear needs, wishes, and goals. Even with very young children, a sensitive parent will offer choices, ask the child's opinion, and be willing to accommodate the child's requests within reason. A sensitive parent also holds conversations with the child, even a baby. A baby understands a great deal of nonverbal communication and grows with verbal conversations. A sensitive parent will generally describe actions to the baby, helping the infant be a part of the parent's world. Conversely, a more insensitive parent might make disparaging comments either to or about the child, sometimes in the form of jokes or offhand remarks. This type of parent might treat the child as a possession or a doll, make condescending observations within the child's hearing, or act as if the child is far younger than he or she is ("infantilizing" the child).

Every since Katherine's daughter, Anne, turned twelve, there has been a lot of friction between them. Anne wants to dress like Britney Spears, while her mother wants to keep her in little-girl jumpers and ankle socks. Katherine insists that Anne is still a child, makes fun of Anne's attempts to mimic the artists on MTV, refuses to allow her to try on lipstick at home, and refers to the afternoons Anne spends with her best friend, Cynthia, as "playdates."

Katherine is having a difficult time accepting that her daughter is growing up, and she refuses to offer the emotional support Anne could use. If Katherine simply recognized that Anne is changing from a child to a young woman and acknowledged her awareness of the differences, Anne would be less likely to want to "grow up" even faster than she is. With a little awareness and emotional support on Katherine's part, this could be a time when mother and daughter become closer, a closeness that would serve both of them well as Anne enters her teen years.

· **Shows empathy.** Empathy is the ability to take the perspective of the other and to feel what he or she feels. Much of sensitivity is about empathic understanding of the child. With a toddler, the sensitive parent is empathic of the child's issues with autonomy and/or with tantrums. With an older child, the sensitive parent is empathic about problems with peers. The sensitive parent is able to feel empathy for the plight of the child and about the trials and tribulations of growing up. Thus, the empathic parent refrains from shaming or belittling and instead helps the child understand his or her feelings.

· **Shows the ability to handle conflict.** How conflict situations are handled is a very clear indicator of the degree of parental sensitivity.

No parent is perfect, and a certain amount of conflict or mismatched interactions between parent and child is normal. It is common to see parental insistence on a goal (helping clear the table, for example) meet child resistance (Melissa wants to watch TV instead). How parents and children move from conflict to more harmonious states is as important as the quality of the harmonious state itself. With a sensitive parent, conflicts are usually resolved with negotiation and co-determination of outcomes (Melissa will help clear the table for five minutes before her show comes on). If the parent is less sensitive, insistence and resistance provoke rising levels of anger and frustration. The parent finds it difficult to relinquish control and/or give credence to the goals and desires of the child. The result is something

The ability to hear the voices of your children and give them the feeling that you understand them is what it's all about:

- *Many parents know that it can be difficult to "read" an adolescent but that they need to try anyway. Babies have voices that need to be heard also. Listen to and understand the emotional signals and communications of a relationship with a baby as well as a young child. Long before there is clear verbal give and take, your child is telling you what he or she needs—if only you listen and understand.*

- *A parent cannot be sensitive without the child. Sensitivity is looking to your child's experience of you and adjusting your behavior accordingly. When you are able to hear your child, not just "hear" yourself in the interaction, then you are truly sensitive to your child.*

- *One mother was heard to say, "I don't really know this child." Work on the stumbling blocks to your sensitivity. Try to explore what it might be that is keeping you from feeling empathy toward your child.*

- *Are you and your child enjoying each other? Nothing is a better indicator of the health of a parent-child relationship! Let your own intuition be at work here as well.*

like, "Clear the table right now, young lady, or you won't see any TV tonight!" from the parent, and then the child feels frustrated and powerless and might break a few dishes "by accident."

Sensitive parents don't have to demonstrate their emotions in a certain way. They might be soft-spoken or animated, gentle or strong, low-key or vivacious. Often men and women have completely different styles when it comes to being sensitive to their children. The real test is not so much the style of the parent, but their willingness to be attuned to the needs, desires, and goals of their children and to express themselves in an emotionally connected manner.

4. DO YOU STRUCTURE INTERACTIONS WITH YOUR CHILD APPROPRIATELY?

In our research studies, parents who structure well (for example, breaking play tasks into smaller pieces, limit-setting) might actually seem to be providing few clues and suggestions to the child, but the child almost automatically picks up such suggestions. This indicates the parent-child interaction is a highly familiar routine, one that is comfortable for both parties. It also indicates that this parent has an intimate knowledge of what works for his or her child.

Structuring by Limit-Setting

Research has shown that children who are raised in an emotionally connected yet consistently structured environment have less drug use, show less promiscuity, and get better grades.

Even though we want our kids to keep growing and learning and trying new things, as parents, we realize that our kids sometimes don't know how to set limits appropriate for their age and abilities. Who has to do it for them? We as parents do! Limit-setting and discipline are other forms of structuring behavior. It is important for you to provide appropriate rules and regulations for your child (depending on age and stage of development) and then stick by them—and for you to be comfortable in doing so. You must be firm but not harsh.

Limit-setting and discipline are an important part of the parent–child relationship. Limit-setting also should include preventive measures whenever possible. Remember that toddlers like to explore, so rather than having to tell your child, "Don't touch" all the pretty knickknacks in Grandma's house, you might very quietly remove everything breakable that might be within your child's reach during a visit.

Too much or too little structuring and limit-setting behaviors are equally bad. Even inconsistent structuring can be difficult for a child. Parents who create a certain framework of structure but then back off at the first challenge or difficulty leave the child feeling as though they can't trust the structure—the scaffold isn't steady beneath their feet. Some parents are overstructured in some circumstances (around school or drugs or sex, for example) and completely unstructured in others (not asking the child to do homework or unconcerned about when the child gets home for dinner). In these cases, discipline and limit-setting are inconsistent, with predictable results. Children who are faced with inconsistent structure are getting mixed messages, and often they respond with confusion, frustration, and eventually defiance.

> Not too long ago, a teenage girl, Brittany, was referred to me as a real discipline problem. She had a history of problems in school, was abusing alcohol, and had become pregnant. The mother, Beth, accompanied her daughter to the session and complained, "I don't know why she's so wild. I never asked anything of any of my kids. The only thing I ever demanded of them was that they go to church on Sunday and not take the Lord's name in vain." She also described a household in which there were no rules or expectations for positive behavior.

Beth had a lot of rules and structure around religion but provided almost no structure in any other part of her children's lives. Brittany interpreted this as meaning that her mother didn't care about her and only cared about shoving her version of God down her throat. It's no wonder Brittany acted out and ran wild.

We often see low structuring behavior when parents play with children in our clinics. In one such case, a father played with his son for a half-hour without making one suggestion or contribution to the game. He did everything the child wanted, certainly, but added nothing himself in the way of new activities or independent ideas. There was some structure simply because parent and child were playing together, but it was definitely not an optimum, vital experience for either father or son. In some cases, parents provide no structure at all. In the lab, we see parents who play alongside their children but not *with* them. It is as if they were playing separate games, with no interaction at all. Limit-setting and discipline also tend to be nonexistent in these cases, with predictable consequences.

Kids need structure and limits. They need boundaries, if only to have something to push against so they know they're growing. But structure can be perceived as either jail bars or scaffolding, depending on how it's done by parents. Structuring might not be the most pleasant part of emotional availability, but when parents can set frameworks for their children in a supportive and caring way, children will feel secure, focused, and happy.

> Eight-year-old Todd was a child who always pushed the boundaries set for him. He rode his bike farther and faster than anyone; he climbed higher trees than any of his friends. But his parents were always firm when it came to the rules around Todd's behavior. He wasn't to endanger himself or others; he wasn't to stay out late without calling first; and he was to act in a responsible manner when it came to his five-year-old brother, Mike.
>
> One day Todd got caught up in a game he was playing with his friends, and he left the playground, not telling Mike where he was going. Mike, who was busy on the monkey bars, didn't notice Todd was gone until twenty minutes later. He looked around for his older brother for about ten minutes and then started to cry. A neighbor noticed Mike's distress and drove the boy home.
>
> When Todd came home later, his dad asked him what had happened. Todd admitted he had forgotten about Mike. "My friends and I wanted to ride bikes and so we left," he said.
>
> "Todd, I know you want to be with your friends, and most of the

time that's just fine. But Mike's not old enough to ride bikes, and you were supposed to be keeping an eye on him," his dad replied. "Mike was really scared when he realized you weren't there. You know that leaving Mike alone broke a rule. So no bike riding for a week, and when you're done at school this week, you're to come straight home every day."

"No fair!" Todd protested.

"Sorry, Todd, but it is fair. In the future, if you aren't able to keep an eye on Mike, you can bring him home before you go off with your friends."

Todd's dad did a great job of providing structure. The rules for Todd were clear, simple, and easy to follow. They allowed Todd room to be active and explore while still demanding that he be responsible. When the rules were broken, the consequences were also clear, immediate, and appropriate to the violation. The punishment was meted out without a lot of emotion or hostility on the father's part. This kind of structuring allowed both Todd and his father to feel comfortable and confident in their relationship with each other.

Structuring During Play

"Structuring" doesn't simply refer to setting limits for appropriate behavior for your child. Optimal structuring provides consistent (but not overdone) clues and suggestions as well as a framework, rules, and regulations for your parent-child relationship. It's not about guiding every moment of your child's life, but providing a supportive frame in a relaxed, unforced way.

Optimal structuring usually has both verbal and nonverbal components. Using more than one form of communication helps give the child a greater range of clues to the desired response to the parent.

Conversely parents who are following the lead of their children and letting the children structure a particular game or other play must attune themselves to the verbal and nonverbal clues their children are providing. Sometimes your child will tell you, "Mommy, you're not playing the game right!" but more often there will be nonverbal hints of the child's wanting to take the game in a different direction.

During playtime with the child, the parent who understands how to structure offers guidance but not direction. The parent is an active participant in the play, providing information, breaking down steps to help the child complete a puzzle or game or task, and physically helping the child when the child wants it (but not until then). Such parents might allow the child to win the game or diminish the importance of parental victory.

Connie was delighted when Alexander, her six-year-old son, declared, "I want to learn how to play chess!" Connie had played the game all her life and had entered a few tournaments in high school. She wanted to make sure, however, that Alexander regarded chess as a game, not as a competition between them. Connie explained to Alexander what the different chess pieces were and then showed him how to set up the board. Then she took him through a few basic moves, explaining how each piece moves in a different way. She made the game into a story about gallant knights, valiant pawns, sneaky bishops, gracious queens, and powerful kings. She let Alexander make his own moves, seldom offering advice but making sure he remembered the basics of the game. At age six, Alexander's attention span was limited, so they played together only as long as he remained interested in the game. The more he understood, the more interested he became. Connie deliberately let Alexander win the first few games they completed. After that, she would occasionally win a game and explain how she did so.

Connie's goal was to foster her son's interest in chess and share her love of the game with him. Because she was able to structure his experience of chess in ways appropriate to his age, attention span, and abilities, Alexander grew to love and appreciate the game. The relationship between mother and son was also deepened by their common interest, but more important, by their emotional connection during the process of learning.

From the time she could walk, Sonny always loved messing around the kitchen while her mother, Louise, cooked. As the child grew older she demanded that her mother let her "help" with the cooking. Louise was very careful to give her daughter specific tasks appropriate to her age. She had her put rice into a cup and then use a spatula to level off the top. She asked Sonny to mash up a cooked egg yolk with a fork and then put the paste into the potato salad Louise was making. As Sonny grew older, she learned how to beat eggs, measure flour, roll out cookie dough, and so on. Louise always gave Sonny specific instructions, showed her how to carry them out when necessary, then thanked her for her help. Eventually, Louise could tell her daughter, "I need three eggs beaten and then mixed into the ground beef for the meat loaf" and be confident her daughter could handle it. By the time Sonny was seven, she was making simple cakes and side dishes on her own, with her mother offering the occasional suggestion. Louise created a favorable structure in which Sonny could learn more and more about an activity she enjoyed—cooking—at levels appropriate for her age and abilities. The structure also helped Louise enjoy the experience of teaching her daughter, thus strengthening the connection between the two.

One of the most important components of structuring is providing a supportive frame in which the child has a chance to explore and try new things. Parents have to allow children room to grow, and any structure they establish must be flexible enough to give children increasing amounts of autonomy. Good structuring is like a scaffold: within it, children can climb higher and higher, learning more and more, confident that there is a solid framework to support them every step along the way.

Parents who feel they always need to be liked might have a difficult time setting limits. They don't want to risk alienating a child by setting limits. A great way to set limits is to first have an emotional connection with your child, and that emotional connection can really be forged through play. The more you play and interact with your child, the more you can expect that he or she will listen to your limits. Because you have joined his or her world, your child will return the favor.

Structuring and limit-setting are crucial aspects of parent-child emotional availability:

- Many parents realize that to be sensitive, you need to read your child's signals and communications, but they are surprised that to structure during play, you again need the same skill and inclination. As you play, make sure you are following your child's lead rather than the other way around, but also provide well-appointed suggestions and be a participant. Being emotionally available in such a play situation also means that you attend to, acknowledge, and take notice of your child's emotional reactions and preferences. Play is your child's time with you.

- Play with your child so that you get to know him or her. Without one-on-one play, it is tough to get to know your child enough to know how to structure. That half-hour a day would be the most desired slot of time for your child, so set up the emotional connection by arranging regular playtimes that enable you to hone your structuring skills.

- During play and other times, be a participant rather than a removed and distant presence. How do you become a participant without becoming intrusive? One of the nicest techniques you can use is to "describe" rather than prohibit. If you see your child do something he or she should not be doing, rather than saying, "Don't" or "I told you not to do that," or other such intrusions, merely describe. For example, if your child is about to put a wet glass near the television, say, "Sweetie, you are about to put a wet glass near the television." If your child is killing one dinosaur with another during play, say, "The dinosaurs are fighting." These comments are descriptive and make your child feel that you are a participant without being judgmental or prohibitive. They make you emotionally present, yet nonintrusive.

- Structure play that is appropriate to your child's age and development. Good structuring usually involves making suggestions that might help your child get where he or she needs to go while letting your child think he or she is doing it on his or her own. Teaching over your child's head or setting overly strict or overly lax and permissive limits is less likely to help your child than setting clear, understandable, and consistent limits. Structure play by giving a "gentle push" rather than "taking over."

5. ARE YOU AVAILABLE TO YOUR CHILD WITHOUT BEING INTRUSIVE?

Intrusive parental behavior can take many forms. If parents set the pace and tone of interactions too often, this can be intrusive. Asking too many

continued...

- *Our studies have indicated that structuring becomes particularly important as children approach school age. Parents who structure well during play have children who do better in school in a variety of ways. So along with your sensitivity, your structuring provides your child with a sense of trust and support.*

- *Just like with sensitivity, nonhostility, and the other components of emotional availability, it is important to be consistent. It builds trust!*

- *Limit-setting is often difficult for a parent, particularly one who has a deep need to be liked as a peer. What parents don't realize sometimes is that children can find other peers and they need parents to set limits. If you play with your child, you can then set limits that are effective. Children like limits because they instinctively know that parents struggle with setting limits. Such struggle is appreciated and is a sign of parental caring because it takes work!*

- *Our studies also show interesting links between the different components of emotional availability. For example, parents who structure their children's interactions and set appropriate limits also seem to manage their own aggressive impulses well (that is, they are nonhostile and peaceful). It is likely that such parents instinctively know or have learned that they need to contain child misbehaviors, and if the children are the ones who have the control, parents respond by being hostile. It is easier to be peaceful with a child who listens to you than a child who is defiant. A subtle nod is often acknowledged by some children, whereas yelling is the only thing that more defiant children acknowledge. To get the effect and expectations you want, play with your child. The more you join your child's world, the more you can expect from your child in terms of attentiveness to your requests.*

questions, directing the course of play rather than letting the child take the lead, making suggestions, and creating frequent theme changes are all indicative of intrusion into the child's autonomy.

One of the ways in which we see parental intrusiveness is with overstimulation. For example, during physical play with a child, the parent might get rougher and rougher until the child reacts adversely. Overstimulation is a frequent risk with babies, especially for first-time parents. It's all too easy for well-meaning parents to play with the baby too much, make too many cute faces when the baby is looking away (a signal the child has had enough), pick up the baby and jiggle him or her when the baby is tired, change the baby's position for no particular reason, and so on. It takes practice to learn to read your child's cues and to recognize when the baby or child wants to interact with you and when it's time to leave him or her alone.

As the child goes from infant to toddler stage, intrusiveness can take the opposite direction. Instead of overstimulating, the parent becomes overprotective. For example, a parent who doesn't allow a normal, well-developing preschooler the chance to walk up and down stairs might be considered intrusive. However, the determination of intrusiveness depends on the child's level of development. Your one-year-old child might not be ready for the stairs, but your two-year-old might be. Cutting your five-year-old's food is definitely intrusive, but at three or even four, you'd better take charge of the knife if you want to avert the possibility of disaster.

Intrusiveness can also manifest in overdirectiveness. Children have to be given room in which to experiment for themselves, but an overly directive parent does not allow the child to develop his or her potential. Some parents spend a lot of time directing their children to accomplish certain activities, "helping" them succeed at games, and "showing" them the best ways to do things. In extreme cases, overdirectiveness can take the form of physically moving, pushing, or manhandling the child.

Sally wanted to teach her daughter, Kim, to knit. She had tried several times, but the little girl couldn't seem to get the hang of it. Sally talked her through each step, her voice getting louder and louder as her frustration increased. Finally, Sally took Kim's hands in her own and "showed" her how to make stitches correctly. Kim burst into tears and said, "I don't want to learn to knit!" Instead of a chance to develop a deeper emotional connection, Sally's intrusiveness had made the knitting lesson a source of upset for both her and her daughter.

The reasons behind parental intrusiveness can be conscious or unconscious and include traits such as the following:

· **An overdeveloped need to control the environment.** This can be a reflection of the parent's obsessive-compulsive tendencies. If the child does not do things exactly as the parent would like them done (as in the example of Sally and Kim), criticism or perpetual corrections may be the result.

· **Viewing the role of parent as that of a teacher.** This can often arise with parents, who feel the children they take care of have to catch up developmentally, emotionally, or educationally, or a combination of all three. We sometimes see such behavior in foster parents who feel that their role is to teach and help a child catch up.

Dan, an artist, uses every opportunity to teach his son, Kevin, about art, instructing him on the proper use of line, color, shape, form, and texture. Unfortunately, Kevin isn't interested in technique—he just likes using paints and crayons. Dan's efforts to teach his son continually backfire as Kevin gets bored and Dan gets frustrated. Dan's overdirectiveness creates a great deal of tension between father and son.

· **Subtle or not-so-subtle personality dysfunctions.** A parent with narcissistic tendencies (read "self-centered") might come home from work and want the child to stop whatever he or she is doing and be with the parent. Such a parent might feel rejected if the child doesn't want to stop watching television and, therefore, might turn off the set (intrusive behavior).

· **Issues about control in the family who raised us.** A parent might overcontrol because he or she was controlled in an authoritarian way in the family in which he or she was raised. Such forcing of a child, as in "you must clean your plate," can eventually lead to eating disorders in children and adolescents. This parental behavior can stem from the belief that children need to be told and controlled on many matters, rather than simply trusted to be autonomous individuals who can share in decision-making with the parent. Similar power struggles can occur around sleeping. Such power struggles often resolve when children are given some control.

· **Achievement, overachievement, or perfectionistic needs.** Sometimes parents push too hard due to their own agendas. You might be teaching your child how to play with toys, rather than allowing your child to discover. You might expect your child to do everything your way, rather than you following your child's lead. Inside, you might be feeling that you know better and will give your child a head start if you transmit this knowledge. Your need to be the perfect parent can actually make you intrusive. If you are pushing your child too far, he or she might burn out. It is important to stop running every aspect of your child's life. Many parents tell me that they feel they are not being good in their role unless they interact with and teach something to their child all the time. Do not overinvolve yourself. Just sit back and relax sometimes. Of course, some parents are rarely involved, and that is not helpful, either.

Optimal nonintrusiveness is the ability to be available to your child without being intrusive. Parents who score high in this area let their children take the lead while playing and base their own interactions on the children's direction. There is a sense of ease and spaciousness in their time with their children. Discipline is firm without being harsh, and it is context-appropriate; it does not upset the relationship when used. Parents set limits by using gentle reminders, changing moods (helping a rambunctious child calm down, for example), and preventive measures such as offering the child a new activity or removing a possible problem (an inappropriate game or book, for example) from the environment. When sifting activities, nonintrusive parents take advantage of spontaneous moments rather than abruptly making transitions.

Most important, remember that intrusiveness is determined not solely by your actions as a parent, but also by your child's response to your efforts. One child's fun roughhousing is another child's overstimulation. It all depends on the response of your child.

6. IS THERE ANY OVERT OR COVERT HOSTILITY PRESENT?

Our research indicates that 20 to 30 percent of parents show some degree of hostility (irritability, bad words, and the like) toward their babies and/or young children. Not surprisingly, these percentages get higher as children move toward adolescence.

Many well-meaning parents become intrusive at times. In other words, sometimes caring a great deal can lead to intrusive behaviors, such as wanting the child to eat enough, wanting him or her to do well in homework, or knowing that staying with the wrong crowd can only be bad for the child. What, then, does a parent do?

- *As with all aspects of emotional availability, intrusiveness is not just a quality of the parent but a quality of the relationship. What might feel intrusive in one relationship might seem like true caring in another relationship. If you are feeling or you are made to feel intrusive, ask yourself if your child has shut you out in any way. If so, you might intuitively feel that you are being intrusive because the relationship has become less of a two-way street. It is then necessary to bring things back to a nonintrusive form. Sometimes just the recognition of your intrusiveness can do the trick.*

- *Being overly forceful about eating is rarely the answer to eating difficulties and can often exacerbate the problem. The soundest advice, given by pediatricians, is to have food available but not control, let alone overcontrol, its intake. Power struggles rarely help.*

It is normal to feel some degree of irritation or anger toward a child every now and then. Being completely responsible for the well-being of a tiny, helpless human being is sometimes exhausting, frustrating, and maddening. However, emotionally available parents are able to avoid projecting those emotions on or toward their children. Such parents can regulate their emotions so their children do not feel like the targets or the sources of the parents' distress.

Remember, as a parent, you are seen by your children as their primary source for everything—food, security, love, health, and so on. When you take your feelings out on your child, you threaten the foundations of his or her very life. Develop the ability to diffuse hostility and frustration so it is not directed at your child (or indeed, expressed around your child) as a key component of creating an emotionally available relationship.

The topic of yelling or screaming is worth mentioning. Such parental outbursts can be just as scary and humiliating for a child as physical abuse. Apologizing as quickly as possible is not a complete remedy, but never-

---

continued...

- *Power struggles also rarely help in the area of peers. Having dialogues with and coaching your child is very different from intrusion. Even if your child isn't initially available for the dialogue, the ice might melt with time, and true dialogues, rather than diatribes, rarely seem intrusive to children.*

- *"Be there." At some points in development, particularly in adolescence, just being a physically available, nonintrusive presence can be what your child needs. You can respond and interact as you are "invited" to join— such "being there" or "being available" is very reassuring, not intrusive, to children and adolescents. For example, as you drive your child to soccer practice, it might seem less intrusive to talk about "that crowd" than if you sat your child down for a serious talk. The quality of being available and emotionally present, without feeling an urgency or desperation to take over, is an important aspect of "emotional availability."*

theless should be done to show respect to your child. Working on the connections between how you were treated when you were a child, your perceptions of your child's perceptions, and the reasons for your hostility can
make a clear difference. One mother who was generally very sensitive and
caring told me that although she has worked on many issues related to the
emotional unavailability of her own mother, when she is tired or stressed,
she "becomes her yelling mother." In the future, give yourself a time-out
before the "point of no return."

Research has indicated that when children hear yelling, they become
energized and frenetic in their activity. Much of the yelling or intrusiveness delivered by a parent is meant to stop unwanted child behavior, yet
such hostility fuels the very aggressive and overly active behaviors it is sup-
posedly designed to stop because when there is yelling, the child hears the
negative energy but cannot process the words. For example, if you yell,
"Don't do that!" your child likely hears the negative energy and little of
the content.

Recently, Bob has been going through a very stressful time. He was
laid off from his job and had to take a different position at a lower salary.
He now has to work much longer hours. Having grown up with an abusive father, however, he is completely committed never to let his own
negative emotions affect his relationship with his family. So Bob has developed several strategies to help him leave his troubles behind when he
comes home. Bob uses the drive between the office and home as his
chance to unwind. He plays jazz, which he loves, on the car stereo, and
he makes a conscious effort to put any bad moments of the day out of
his mind. Bob has also set up a signal system with his kids. If the day has
gone well and he is in a good place, when he walks in the door he calls,
"Where are my boys?" That means he's ready for anything—his two sons
(ages seven and nine) can tackle him, tell him about their day, ask for help
with homework, and so on. If, however, Bob walks in and says nothing,
the kids know he still needs a little space and time to unwind. Most of
the time, the kids will wait awhile until Bob has had a chance to hang up
his coat, put up his feet, and maybe spend a while talking with his wife
about what's bothering him. But Bob has an agreement with himself that

no matter what, he'll come to the dinner table in as good a mood as he can. His kids feel supported emotionally because they know how important they are to their father and that even though he is going through some rough times, his negative emotions are not directed at them.

Often parents think they are "keeping the lid on" their negative emotions when they are around their children, but unless they can process and handle such emotions, there is a tendency for them to "leak." This leakage usually creates covert rather than overt hostility. Signs that your child might read as covert hostility include a slightly raised voice, boredom, impatience, and so on. This can progress to, for example, resentment, "huffing and puffing," rolling your eyes, teasing with an edge, raising your voice, being easily irritated, or showing a long-suffering attitude. Covert hostility can produce passive-aggressive behaviors or cause you to disconnect emotionally from your child as punishment. Therefore, you must be wary and deal with your negative emotions by all means available (psychotherapy, talking to a spouse or good friend, introspection) to prevent their impact on your emotional involvement with your child.

Even "leaks" of covert hostility can be detrimental to a child. In our research, we go into people's homes and videotape parent-child interactions for an hour or more per session. For obvious reasons, we usually don't see overt signs of hostility, such as yelling or hitting, during our time in the home. But we do see low levels of covert hostility, such as rolling the eyes or making a sarcastic comment ("What a mess you made," or "What a dirty little girl you are," for instance). We see the same thing in classroom settings. A parent might go into the school classroom and compliment the child on a picture well done and then turn to the teacher (within earshot of the child) and say, "What is it?" (with a laugh). These are leaks of covert hostility, and they signal to the child that the parent has some negative feelings toward him or her. On another note, hostility that is in the environment (for example, yelling between spouses) even though it is not directed toward the child, also affects him or her.

In its most pronounced form, hostility becomes overt. Parents are overly harsh, abrasive, and demeaning, either facially, vocally, or both. They might threaten and/or frighten the child with teasing, shaming, ridiculing,

I have seen many parents who show a capacity for sensitivity but who also fly off the handle easily. Parenting is not about sainthood. All children push their parents' buttons sometimes. But as a parent, one of the most important lessons you can teach your child is how you (in regular, day-to-day life) regulate your emotions when the going gets rough.

- *When you are tired, stressed, or pushed and pulled in different directions, you are at risk of losing your cool. You later regret it. Before the point of no return, give yourself a time-out. After making sure that your child is safe (for example, he or she is not in the bath or on a changing table), just excuse yourself.*

- *If you have crossed this boundary, do apologize to your child. Adults do make mistakes, and children can see that correcting mistakes is possible. Restore justice and fairness by an apology—relationships should be just and fair, not angry and unfair. By apologizing, you at least show that you are holding yourself to the same standards that you hold your child. Many adults mistakenly feel that they have privileges that children do not have and that their own behavior is not the point.*

- *Through your own nonhostile, peaceful, just, and fair interactions with your child, you are teaching him or her to interact in this way with others. When you are covertly hostile, impatient, shaming, or putting others down, you are subtly bullying your child, and your child is learning an important negative lesson—that he or she can be bullied by others in relationships and that he or she can do the same to others. More obvious lessons about violence, the permission for violence, and the like are learned in overtly hostile relationships. Children carry these templates into their other relationships. A third-grader once told me, "My mom threw this paperback at me in the kitchen." He was also a child who showed aggressive displays with peers on the playground. Parent-child emotional availability in the home will teach your child emotional intelligence, but most lessons occur when you are least aware that you are "onstage."*

and so on. Sometimes the threats might be in the form of a joke ("I'll send you to an orphanage if you keep that up"), but the child takes such threats of separation or abandonment very seriously. In some circumstances, the hostility is not directed at the child but is a significant part of their environment. A parent who habitually loses his temper and yells at anyone and anything, for example, would be demonstrating overt hostility. Unfortunately for their health and sense of security, as a rule, children are very emotionally attuned; when they are young, they cannot differentiate between hostility at home and hostility directed toward them. Be aware of your expressions of unresourceful emotions, and do your best to handle them quickly in ways that will not affect your child.

continued...

- *Some parents see a lot of covert (or overt) hostility in their own behavior and feel bad that they have "stepped over the line." Many more parents use threats but don't ever carry out such threats—they don't even have any intention to. Nonetheless, threats of violence ("If you do that again, I will throw you against that wall"), threats of separation ("I'm going to leave you kids if you do that"), and threats of loss ("I'll kill myself") are as real to a child as the action. Such threats are frightening and lead to your child being frightened of you, even though it might seem difficult for you to believe that saying something threatening (and never intending to do it) can seriously frighten your child and make him or her feel insecure with you and his or her own world.*

- *We have them for only a short time and then they go off with their life lessons. One father said to his son, "He only remembers all the things I did wrong, but I also did so much for him." This father was right. Hostility is remembered—not necessarily at a conscious, mental level, but at the level of feelings. Memory is not objective; it is emotional. To build positive emotional memories, unload stress, think positive thoughts, relax as much as you can, take time-outs, find supportive networks of friends and family (parents need support!), but do limit even covert hostility. Children remember about us (and about others) the emotions they feel when they are with us.*

7. IS YOUR CHILD RESPONSIVE TO YOU?

Once again, we're back to the child's side of the parent-child equation. I hope you're beginning to see that the components of emotional availability are part of a whole relationship construct, with many different factors interrelating and interacting to form a healthy (or unhealthy) whole. Ultimately, any relationship is about just that: the act of relating to each other. In the parent-child relationship, ideally the parent has the most responsibility and flexibility in creating something that both parties will enjoy. However, the only way to tell whether the relationship is working is to see how the child responds to the parent's attempts to connect emotionally.

In our research, we see a child's responsiveness to the parent reflected in two aspects of the child's behavior. First is the child's eagerness or willingness to engage with the parent when the parent offers a suggestion or moves to interact with the child. What we are looking for is a child who looks up and talks to the parent in an enthusiastic, engaged tone—a child who appears eager to connect with the parent. What is important is not just the response itself, but the emotional quality of the response from the child. If the child ignores the parent when approached or generally appears bland or blasé to the overture, then obviously the child is not demonstrating an optimum emotional response. If the child looks up and talks to the parent but uses an unenthusiastic tone, that is not an optimum response, either. In a few cases, the child might even need to be encouraged to respond to the parent. Conversely, we have seen situations in which the parent doesn't bother to reach out to the child or bother to initiate contact, and the child continues to play on his or her own. In those cases, it is clear that emotional responsiveness is limited not by lack of response on the child's side, but by lack of initiation on the parent's. Remember the little girl, Sherrie, in the swimming pool, described earlier in this chapter? By the time her mother paid attention to her—when the child was hurt—the little girl no longer responded to her mother. Her level of emotional responsiveness had decreased because her mother had not responded to her earlier.

The second aspect of a child's behavior that indicates lack of optimal responsiveness is what we call a "negative cycle of connectedness." When a child is approached by the parent and, instead of ignoring the overture, becomes whiny, complains, insults the parent, cries, or appears anxious or fearful, something is obviously wrong. The child is responding negatively to the parent's attempt to connect, and this often indicates a dysfunctional means of maintaining contact.

> Patty was a premature baby, and her lungs were not fully developed. Throughout her infancy, she had had trouble with asthma, bronchitis, and a range of other lung-related problems. Her parents were both so concerned about her health that practically every time Patty coughed, they would rush her to the hospital. They found it difficult to relate to their daughter without an overlay of fear and worry. Whenever Patty's parents tried to play with her, Patty would become whiny and push them away. The family had created a negative cycle of connectedness.

This is not to say that smiling, laughing children are always considered emotionally responsive. Some children will smile and laugh a great deal during a play session, but if the emotion is directed only at the play activities, and it is clear that the child is avoiding the parent by focusing emotion on the imaginary world of play, it is obvious that the child is not connecting with the parent. Also, some children use nervous, overbright smiles and laughter as a way of pleasing others, rather than to indicate happiness.

Children who are emotionally responsive to their parents usually demonstrate a generally happy and content countenance. They are content pursuing autonomous activities, but they also respond in a positive way toward the parent at appropriate points. Their response generally shows pleasure and eagerness without any sense of urgency or necessity. They smile or laugh appropriately and usually attend to their parents' comments, questions, suggestions, and demonstrations with ease. Emotionally responsive children might not respond to every request, however, especially when they are engrossed in play. But there is the sense that, for the most part, the child is comfortable with and willing to respond to the parent's overtures.

If the emotional responsiveness is not optimal, the child might respond but seem unenthusiastic about doing so. The child might respond slowly and reluctantly, continuing play as if he or she didn't hear the parent. The child who always responds to the parent in an overeager, overly bright way is also not optimal; this might indicate a reversal in roles (the child feeling like he or she has to take care of the parent). In the most serious cases of emotional nonresponsiveness, the child's emotional health might be in danger. Here we see the kind of avoidance behaviors described earlier—ignoring parental requests, turning away from parents, strong protests that appear inappropriate, and so on.

Remember the description of the secure child in Chapter 2 as showing a balance between exploration and wanting to be close to you.

- You can do your own observation of your child's emotional connection with you by taking note of his or her responsiveness toward you. Remember, responsiveness is not obedience or compliance. It is emotional responsiveness toward you, with a balance between connection with you and explorations away from you. A child who shows positive responsiveness toward the parent is likely to be secure with that parent. So go on and observe whether your child is responsive to you—seeming generally happy and content in his or her life and showing a balance between "moving away" and "moving toward" you.

- Some children are emotionally responsive but show many signs of distress, whining, and the like. These children have become accustomed to drawing people in through negative cycles of relatedness. They have learned that if they are distressed, they will receive caring, and if they whine, someone will come to soothe them. Many of these children engage in dependent interactions with their teachers as well, staying near the teacher and being comforted by adults. Rather than engage in catering behavior that would encourage and prolong this type of responsiveness (an unhealthy kind), trust your child to grow emotionally, and subtly and kindly demand more mature emotional responses from your child.

When I say "responsiveness," I am not referring simply to the child's compliance with the parent's wishes, but to the emotional richness, happiness, and tenderness shared between parent and child. Therefore, the importance of a child's responsiveness cannot be overstressed. This measure is the best clinical criteria for assessing the child's emotional availability to the parent. As a parent, it is your best, clearest indication as to whether you

continued...

- Many children show pleasing behaviors toward parents and/or others, as if they are engaging in caregiving or parenting behaviors. If such a pattern of pseudoforms of mature behavior is going on, again let your child know that he or she does not need to "take care of others"—that he or she is the kid. We have seen such behavior in children when a parent is depressed or traumatized; the children take it upon themselves to "make things right." Obviously, such behavior is burdensome for the child and can be framed into a more positive and healthy direction. Play with your child and in the context of play, you can show that your child is heard and that he or she does not need to be the pleaser all the time; he or she can also be pleased.

- Some children seem avoidant and unresponsive. If during play or otherwise, your child seems not to "return the serve," then try not to keep "hitting the ball." Instead, wait for your child to come to you, then elaborate and show pleasure in positive sharing of emotions together. With consistent availability and emotional responsiveness on your part, your child will begin to relearn the language of relationships and will likely become less avoidant and unresponsive over time. Many children (especially foster and adopted children) have become so unresponsive and avoidant over time that it is a challenge to win them over. The same strategies can work with them, except the parent needs to know that he or she is in it for the long haul. Progress can be met by several steps back in such relationships. The idea is to maintain the trust and consistency and to "surprise" such a child about relationships by not giving up in the face of such challenges.

are connecting emotionally with your child in ways that touch his or her heart. If you feel your child is not being responsive, the best thing you can do is to tune up your sensitivity. Remember, children connect with us when they feel loved, safe, cared for, and their needs are being met. As the parent, you have more tools for "reading" your child's needs and emotions than your child does. If you can meet your child's needs in a responsive way, your child is more likely to respond to you in kind.

8. DOES YOUR CHILD ALLOW YOU TO BE INVOLVED IN HIS OR HER LIFE?

This is a measurement that will gain in importance as your child grows and matures. Parents usually must be totally involved with babies' lives simply because babies can do nothing for themselves. But as your baby grows, goes to day care, then preschool, then elementary school, then middle school, then high school, then beyond, your child will be the one who decides just how much he or she wants to let you in. Evaluating your level of connection when it comes to your child's allowing you access to his or her life is a key measurement of emotional availability.

When we assess involvement in a clinical setting, we look at the degree to which the child attends to and engages the parent in play. Typically, children will make parents either the audience for their activities or engage them as playmates or support people. Asking questions, narrating a story line, requesting assistance, or demonstrating materials to parents are all examples of involving behavior. Sometimes children will involve parents simply by looking toward them. A healthy parent-child relationship has a balance between autonomous play and requests for parental involvement. The child appears eager but not anxious to engage the parent. The relationship is a comfortable, positive one for both parent and child.

At lower levels of involvement, children show more interest in the task at hand than in engaging the parents' attention. It seems that these children are more oriented toward solitary play with occasional reference to parents. Parents appear more like tools the children use when needed, rather than a desired audience. As the amount of involvement decreases, these children might avoid their parents altogether, literally turning their backs on them. Or the opposite might occur: The children might overinvolve the parents, insisting they cannot play by themselves, offering toys and constantly speaking to, looking at, or seeking physical contact from the parents. These actions might be accompanied by anxiety, whining, "acting out," complaining, and other forms of negative emotional expression. Such behaviors suggest that the children are assuming the lion's share of responsibility for maintaining contact and interaction with their parents. At the most severe levels of uninvolvement, children do not seek to involve parents at all. If parents try to engage the children, there might be some response, but the children make no attempt to elaborate on the exchange and do not initiate new ones. It is as if the children are completely uninterested in the parents. Of course, many children will show a range of involvement, depending on their mood, but here we are talking about what your child is *usually* like.

One of the ways we measure a child's involvement with the parent is through "storytelling talks." We meet with the child separately and ask him or her to tell a story about his or her parents. Often, uninvolved children will tell stories about being angry with their parents or stories in which

---

If your child is responsive to you, your child is also likely to be involving you in his or her life. But take note—is your child involving you in positive or less positive ways?

- *Your child's involving behavior, such as running up to you to tell you something as you are about to leave his or her school and giving you a kiss, is a sign that your child is including you in his or her life. It's a wonderful sign.*

- *Conversely, your child is also involving you if he or she has started bullying other children at school and you are getting regular phone calls from the teacher or principal. Negative forms of involving are a child's cries for help. Children don't know how to describe that they are feeling depressed or rejected or angry and, thus, they act out. Your responsiveness to your child during such times is a gift.*

they are hurt and their parents don't comfort them. Conversely, children who enjoy involvement with their parents will relate incidents in which their parents took care of them, about going on outings or adventures with their parents, or perhaps about going on adventures by themselves and being warmly welcomed by their parents when they returned.

The highest compliment your child can pay to you is the desire to involve you in his or her play, problems, school, and life. Healthy levels of involvement mean you have earned the love and trust of your child. It is one of the last, best measures of the success of your efforts to create a strong and supportive parent-child connection.

Of course, in real life, the eight elements of emotional availability are not separate at all; they are interrelated in complex ways in your child's life. And best of all, most of the time you connect emotionally with your child without having to think about it. Research is very useful because it is able to analyze what good parents do, consciously and unconsciously, to build healthy relationships, as well as how parents with challenges are not accomplishing the same thing. However, research can sometimes make the process seem clinical and overwhelming. It is not. Parenting is a job for which you take all the information you consider useful, put it in the back of your mind, then deal with the child in front of you. It's kind of like sailing a boat. You can study nautical theory and the dynamics of wind and waves, and this knowledge can help you figure out what to do on a boat, but when you're out at sea, with waves hitting the sides of the boat and the sail flapping in the wind, you don't stop to think, *How much air pressure does that sail need to get me across the lake?* You let the knowledge you've studied and absorbed help you as you make the split-second decisions required by the circumstances of the moment.

The eight elements of emotional availability can give you a strong basis for connecting emotionally with your child if you simply remember the basics. Be available emotionally to your child. Share your emotions. Be sensitive to his or her needs. Provide structure without intrusiveness. Look for the ways your child wishes to involve you in his or her play.

The Two Sides
to Emotional Connection

This chapter will help parents (new parents, adoptive parents) or any care-giver who feels he or she needs to connect at a deeper level with his or her child.

THE PARENT'S SIDE OF EMOTIONAL CONNECTION

"She doesn't love me." You'd be surprised how many times I've heard those words—from parents, not from children. Although it might not seem like it at times, parents should be the ones in charge of the emotional relationships with their children. Parents have more of everything—more knowledge, more control, more power—and, therefore, more ability to change. Although it's easy to forget, it is a parent's responsibility to foster the qualities of emotional availability in themselves so their children can learn to replicate those same qualities.

Parents need to nurture emotional availability. It's not true that some children come into the world with emotionally available personalities and other children are emotionally *unavailable*. Yes, some babies cry more. Yes, some babies are more receptive to cuddling. However, except for severe situations (for example, autism), most children can become emotionally available to their parents, provided that *parents react and interact with them in emotionally available ways*.

How Parents Modify Nature

Every parent can tell you that children come into this world with their own unique temperaments. Mary was a wakeful baby, but Penny slept through the night right away. Tommy was placid, but his sister Karen seemed scared by the slightest noise. Josh loved hugs, but his brother John pulled away from them. Daily, I hear parents in my clinic say things such as, "That's just the way my child is—sensitive," or "She has cried like that from the day she was born."

As research and parents' own observations will tell you, right from the start, some babies will cry a lot and others won't cry as much. In the first three months of a child's life, clear differences are apparent in the amount a child will cry, and in many ways, the level of crying is completely unrelated to what the parents do. But the relation between baby crying and parental behavior is much stronger as the child grows. When a child's caregiver is quick to respond to crying during the first three months of the child's life, that child will cry less by the time he or she is nine months to a year old.

One of the core debates in child development is how much *nature* (genetics and/or inborn temperament) plays in a child's personality versus how much is contributed by *nurture* (environment, especially the emotional environment created by a child's caregivers). Certainly, quite a bit is inherited. A child can be more or less difficult, more or less sensitive, more or less shy, more or less anxious, and so on. But the level of a child's emotional connection with a parent or caregiver is *not* inherited. The relationship between parent and child develops over time. It is not determined by the child's *nature*. Rather, it is based in *nurture*. And initially at least, it is based in the nurture provided by the parents. According to a wealth of research evidence, the parent-child relationship is a more crucial determiner than inborn temperament of how children ultimately will respond to their world.

Nature Versus Nurture in Children's Conduct Problems

One area in which the importance of nurture is clear is in the area of children's temperament and conduct disorders (a mental health term for a child's illegal behavior, such as stealing, assault, truancy, and so on). Extensive studies have compared levels of conduct problems in children of different temperaments (difficult versus easygoing). Children from favorable home environments seem to have few conduct problems, regardless of whether they have difficult or easy temperaments. *It is only when the home environment is unfavorable that temperament seems to affect the level of a child's conduct problems.*

When the home environment is unfavorable, children of different temperaments respond differently. Children who have easy temperaments and come from unfavorable home environments have a low incidence of conduct problems, almost as low as easygoing children from favorable home environments. In contrast, children with difficult temperaments who come from unfavorable home environments have a high level of conduct problems. In this case, nature (temperament) is less of a predictor of conduct problems than nurture (home environment). When *both* nature and nurture are unfavorable, the child is most at risk for conduct disorders such as aggression, truancy, and so on.

As parents, the greatest lesson to be learned from these studies is that as long as the home environment is favorable (nurturing and loving), even children with difficult temperaments have a low level of conduct problems. In other words, *a favorable home environment effectively can neutralize a child's unfavorable inborn temperament.*

As researchers, we usually find that a combination of nature and nurture—what is inborn combined with what occurs in the environment—will determine the child's path in life. The amount and quality of nurturing in the home environment will shape that child's character in either a positive or a negative direction.

Nature Versus Nurture in Children's Sense of Security

Another area in which temperament is often a "candidate" is in the area of children's security. This emotional milestone of infancy and childhood is considered to be mostly related to parental nurture, not a child's nature. Although a child might have a disposition toward a particular kind of temperament—sensitive, outgoing, shy, and so on—an abundance of research indicates that a child's emotional relationships are far more important in shaping a child's sense of security than any inborn factors.

Some studies do indicate, however, that nature and nurture can interact with one another, but rarely is nature the sole explanation. One study by Jay Belsky, who is now at the University of London, indicated that infants of easy temperaments who are involved in insensitive caregiving are more likely to become insecure/avoidant, whereas infants of difficult temperaments who are involved in insensitive parenting are more likely to become insecure/dependent. As another example, Shamir-Essakow's dissertation with adviser Judy Ungerer, a leading researcher in child-parent attachment security at MacQuarie University in Sydney, Australia, showed the effects of parent-child relationships on children who were temperamentally disposed to be socially inhibited—fearful of novel situations, objects, and people. (A Harvard study led by Jerome Kagan indicated about 10 percent of children fall into this category.) The MacQuarie University study found that socially inhibited children whose relationships with their parents made them feel secure were quite open to forming relationships with others. That is, their shyness or inhibition did not prevent them from relating to others. However, socially inhibited children who did not feel secure in their relationships with their parents (and in particular, those who were insecure/avoidant) seemed closed off to relationships in general.

ALL ABOUT FUNCTION RATHER THAN EMOTION

Paula was an excellent homemaker. Her house was tidy, and she was a wonderful cook. Paula was always doing something for the benefit of her son, Henry, such as cutting up small slices of bananas and putting them in front of him. Paula was very attentive, following Henry with her eyes as he explored the kitchen. She had even set up her cupboards in a "child friendly" way, with grown-up things on higher shelves and the child's things on lower shelves. Paula clearly knew how to run a household. Everything was in order and set up for the best interests of a child, including the food served and the functional, clean, even germ-free atmosphere of the home. There was just one thing missing: emotional connection. Paula's home resembled a well-oiled machine.

Although she knew a great deal about the functional aspects of parenting, Paula didn't know what to give her baby emotionally. And after living ten or eleven months with a mother who didn't attend to his emotional needs but only to basic functional needs, Henry just shut down. Paula's baby gave off almost no emotional signals. Had Paula known that anything was remiss in the relationship, she certainly would have done something because she seemed so well intentioned and focused on her baby. But because Paula didn't know how to read the emotional signals of relationship, she thought her baby was fine.

Given all the work parents do, it is easy to overlook what children need most: *emotional* reactions. Meeting a child's emotional needs is the most important job of parenting. As was demonstrated in Paula's home, it is not enough to be physically available. In fact, emotional availability actually matters *more* to children than mere physical proximity. Robert Emde (one of the leading psychiatrists of our time and one of my collaborators and mentors in developing the system and theory on emotional availability) and James Sorce at the University of Colorado Health Sciences Center, with their colleagues, designed a study scenario in which the parent was reading a newspaper and, thus, was physically available but emotionally unavailable to the baby. In this situation, babies smiled and explored less indicating that emotional availability was needed more than physical availability. (Unlike Paula's baby, most of the babies in the study had been raised in emotionally available homes and, therefore, were able to signal their displeasure.)

Emotional disconnection is noticed and missed, even by babies. In another study, Edward Tronick and his colleagues at Harvard developed a brilliant way to understand how children respond to sudden emotional discon-nection called the "still face" procedure. Mothers were instructed to become suddenly stone-faced and unresponsive after a brief playful interaction with their babies. Again, most babies protested and showed clear displeasure at the mother's emotional unavailability, indicating that physical availability is not enough. This study was designed as a simulation of parental depression and indicated that even a temporary lapse in one's emotional presence can have a clear effect on babies. It is no surprise that studies on actual parental de-pression also indicate the negative consequences on children.

As was the case with Paula and Henry described earlier, if your child senses you are emotionally unavailable, he or she can shut down and never develop the basis for emotional connection with others. Babies raised in situations of relative emotional unavailability basically give up and turn inward. They get used to the lack of connection and won't demand it. Any emotional "signals" go underground, and the child becomes even more difficult for the parent to read. In some cases, this lack of early emotional connection can lead to serious psychological problems such as depression. Studies of babies in orphanages, where there was a great deal of physical caring and availability by caregivers but little opportunity for focused emo-tional connection, indicate that many such children became depressed dur-ing the first months of life.

Through lack of time or lack of awareness, children's emotional needs sometimes can get lost in the day-to-day effort to keep them fed, clothed, and clean. Luckily, building a better, stronger emotional connection with your child isn't difficult. It doesn't take huge amounts of time or the abil-ity to read your child's mind, but it does take focus and some specific, easy-to-learn strategies. No matter what your child's age—from the moment after birth until the child becomes an adult—you can strengthen and, if needed, heal your emotional connection with your child and create greater satisfaction and love for both of you.

Emotional Availability—Being "Good at Repairs"

In the early days of research into emotional availability, investigators described qualities such as maternal sensitivity as an almost "exquisite responsiveness." Maternal sensitivity was described in all positive terms, and only beautiful qualities such as clearly perceiving the baby's needs, promptly responding to the infant's signals and communications, and being aware of a sense of timing were included in this concept. A mother was supposed to "sense" her baby's needs the instant the child emerged from her womb.

However, as any mother or father will tell you, nothing could be farther from the truth. Parenting is a process of trial and error—with the emphasis on *error*. Children have different needs, and even if you are the most experienced parent in the world, what worked with your firstborn probably won't work with your second—especially when it comes to emotional needs. Emotional availability is not "perfect parenting." In fact, emotional availability acknowledges the importance of the parent's ability to consistently "repair" the relationship with the child after conflicts. It is much more realistic to look at emotional availability as being "good at repairs" rather than being "perfect."

This need for relationship repair is apparent even with babies as young as six months of age. One study analyzed moment-to-moment interactions between mothers and their babies during play times. It showed that 50 percent of the exchanges between mother and child were nonsynchronous—meaning there were consistent conflicts or emotional "bumps" in the parent-child relationship. This suggests that repairing our relationships with our children is a normal aspect of emotional availability. Many of us recognize the need for relationship repair with our older children, but we are less aware of doing this with our babies. Even during play, if we look at moment-to-moment exchanges, we are consistently repairing our relationships to move our children out of conflict and into a more harmonious emotional state.

Signaling Your Temporary Unavailability

At this point you might be thinking that I am describing "supermoms" or "superdads" who are so secure with their children that they never have to signal their unavailability to their babies or children. Not so! It is completely unrealistic to define emotional availability as being physically and emotionally present for your child all the time. Indeed, such attention actually would be *un*healthy from both the parent's and child's points of view. You actually are doing your child a favor when you give him or her the opportunity to connect with other aspects of the world.

Emotional availability is an *overall* quality of the relationship between a parent and child, not something that is evaluated on a moment-to-moment basis. In other words, *emotional availability is the overall experience your child receives from your relationship*. Contributing to this overall experience is the opportunity for your child to be autonomous. Your temporary unavailability will allow your child to engage the world on his or her own.

Recently, Claudia brought her one-year-old baby, Sonya, into our clinic. Whenever her mother left the room, even for ten seconds, Sonya showed extreme distress—full-blown crying and complete unsoothability by anyone else. As soon as Claudia returned, Sonya settled only reluctantly and would not let Claudia out of her sight for the rest of the session. We asked Claudia about their life together, and she said that she had never left Sonya with others, even with grandparents, and that she took the baby with her everywhere. Claudia reported that Sonya showed extreme distress whenever she left her, even for a moment to go to the bathroom. Claudia, therefore, tried to keep her unavailability to a minimum because it distressed her baby so much.

With another mother, Caroline, the scenario was very different. She was concerned about the emotional "health" of her baby, Sammy, if she were to do work around the house that did not involve him. Caroline sometimes felt guilty about needing to clean or do other tasks. She brought these concerns to my clinic, where I reassured her, "It's important for babies to be able to explore independently and experience the world autonomously," I said. "Such explorations occur best in proximity to the parent, certainly. But in a healthy emotional relationship, the presence of a parent can trigger a child's need to move out into the world. Children will explore other areas of the house in a way they would not think of unless a parent was readily—although not completely—available." I recommended that Caroline experiment with encouraging

The Two Sides to Emotional Connection 117

Sammy to explore while she did housework near but not necessarily in the same room with him.

Caroline later came back and told me her guilt had vanished. She discovered that if she established a nice emotional connection with Sammy and then set him up with some toys, she felt comfortable taking care of her work and he felt comfortable exploring his world of toys on his own. Both mother and son reconnected frequently as they both "worked," and those reconnections would reconfirm their emotional tie. The cycle of "moving out" and then "moving back together" would start again.

Caroline's experience describes perfectly the kind of relationship a secure mother and baby share.

Being constantly available is not good for creating healthy emotional availability. Of course, I don't mean that you should take off for a month's vacation and leave your new baby at home! However, babies need to explore the world on their own, with parents available for monitoring, should it be needed. In this way, your baby feels your presence, garnering a sense of safety and security, but also senses that you have other tasks, and that doing them with gusto is important to you.

How We Connect with Our Sons Versus Our Daughters

Not too long ago, I read a newspaper column in which a mother theorized there must be a male-linked gene that helps little boys make truck noises while they play. I think most parents will agree that even if we wish to raise our children in a gender-neutral environment, differences between little boys and little girls simply exist. Perhaps some of these differences might be genetically hardwired to gender, but study after study shows that differences in the way a parent connects to a male child versus a female child has an enormous impact on the child's development, especially in the way the child learns to develop emotionally with others.

For instance, I recently conducted a study of mothers and their eighteen- to twenty-four-month-old toddlers in relation to emotional availability. Happily, we found no differences between how emotionally available mothers are with their sons versus their daughters. We also observed which party took the lead in emotional interactions. At the same or similar levels of emotional availability, we found that when a mother was smiling and the toddler was not, the girl toddler was more likely to match her mother's face by smiling. (This is called "repairing" the interaction.) However, a boy toddler would more likely do nothing, or the mother would assume the facial expression of the boy. These findings suggest that emotional availability during parent–child interactions looks different for the two genders and that girls get more experience in "repairing" interactions than boys.

As a parent, it might make sense for you to be more aware of your emotional interactions with even very young children and to give your son greater ease and exposure to the entire range of emotions. It might well be that giving our sons more experience in the repair of interactions that involve emotions will help increase their trust in dealing with their own emotions and the emotions of others.

In a separate look at the same group of families, we found that mothers were more likely to follow their boy toddlers' lead than their girl toddlers' lead. (Remember, though, that there were no differences in the extent to which mothers were emotionally available toward their girls versus boys.) For example, if the boy initiated an interaction by saying "Hi," the mother was more likely to follow his lead by sitting down and starting a conversation with him. In contrast, when a girl toddler said "Hi," the mother was likely either to leave her alone or create a simpler interaction with her—simply saying "Hi" in return or smiling at her but not starting a conversation. This research indicates that emotional availability in mother-son versus mother-daughter interactions can look different when you analyze the interactions in a more detailed way. Boys seem to be given the lead in "directing" interactions with their mothers, thereby gaining greater experience in competence, leadership, and control than girls. In contrast, girls seem to be given more opportunities in noticing and adapting to their mothers' emotions, giving the girls greater experience with the world of feelings. Both findings confirm what we see in males and females in our society.

In a separate study in my own laboratory, this time with nine-month-old babies, we found that mothers (even those who were equally emotionally available to their sons and daughters) were more likely to relate to their girls with a slightly rougher edge than they did to their boys—a reflection, perhaps, of the tendency of women to "smooth over" interactions with men while feeling no need to do so in their interactions with other women. This finding indicates that mothers should pay greater attention to their interactions with their girls and try to give them a greater experience of being a part of smoother interactions.

One wonders, of course, whether fathers are "rougher" with their sons. One study found that emotional availability was clearly different in mother-child versus father-child interactions, and that father-son interactions scored lowest in emotional connection. It might be that the father-son conflict during childhood and adolescence we so often hear about actually begins much earlier than reported, perhaps during the toddler years.

These studies as well as several others indicate that we treat our boys and girls differently. We offer our boys greater opportunities for interaction and acknowledge their taking the initiative by following their lead more; we give our girls greater experience in regulating their emotional interactions. This difference, of course, has value and may indeed be guided by the tendencies of each gender—boys tend to take the initiative, girls tend to be more expressive of their feelings. As a parent, however, you can help your son or daughter strengthen his or her "weaker" sides, so to speak, by offering both sexes the same opportunities for initiative and emotion. It makes a great deal of sense to be aware of the level of emotional connection between yourself and your child and to put a gender lens on your interactions. If you encourage your son to be more expressive of his feelings (and to recognize feelings in others), or you support your daughter in taking the initiative in play by following her lead, you might raise a more competent girl or a more emotionally expressive boy. Further, these studies suggest that mothers and fathers might need to do some "reworking" in relation to their interactions with their children of the same gender.

The Power of Parental Perception Revisited

Let's look at another example of nature versus nurture in a child who is sensitive "by birth."

Maria brought her two-year-old son, Carl, to see me at our clinic. She told me Carl was born shy, sensitive, even hypersensitive. "He cries all the time," Maria said. "He won't respond to anyone he doesn't know. He's not outgoing with other children. I don't know what's wrong with him." From the way Maria talked about her child, it was clear that she saw Carl's temperament and general lack of boldness as negative or weak. (This kind of response might arise when the mother is of the same temperament and was not treated in a sensitive manner during her own childhood development, or for other reasons.)

Maria tended to respond to Carl's crying or fear by deriding him, telling him to "be a little man," or by ignoring his emotional distress. She seemed somewhat hostile and impatient; rather than empowering Carl or strengthening his sense of confidence, she talked down to him. When Carl was unwilling to explore his environment on his own, Maria became intrusive, trying to make Carl try out a new toy. When asked about her behavior, Maria said, "I have to be hard on him or he won't ever try anything new."

Maria viewed Carl as difficult to be with, both for her and for other children. As a result, she didn't pay much attention to structuring his play time, delivering well-timed or well-appointed suggestions about how to play, or setting up playdates with other children. Unfortunately, Maria's perception of Carl and her resulting behavior caused Carl to develop a kind of shell, an armor. He became less responsive to Maria and less willing to attempt to include her in his play. He also shut himself off from others.

When a parent's perceptions do not allow a child to learn new ways of relating to others and to the world, such perceptions can become a self-fulfilling prophecy. Maria's behavior was not leading to an emotionally close relationship with her son. Let's look at Maria's actions in view of the eight elements of emotional availability. Because Maria viewed Carl's sensitivity as a problem, she responded negatively to his attempts to recruit her emotionally (element #1), telling him to "be a little man" rather than picking him up and reassuring him. As a result, Carl stopped responding to his mother's emotional overtures (element #2). When Carl stopped responding to her, Maria's sensitivity to his needs decreased (element #3). She also became more hostile (element #6), demanding that Carl stop being so afraid and trying to force him to try new things (element #5) by over-structuring his play (element #4). But Carl refused to respond to Maria's demands (element #7), either ignoring her or starting to cry even harder (element #8).

Luckily, parents can change their level of emotional availability fairly easily, beginning with changing their view of their child's nature. When parents change their view of and their behavior toward their sensitive child, the child's view of the parent can change as well. I suggested to Maria that she change her view of Carl's sensitivity and regard the trait either as positive or, at the very least, neutral. "You're communicating to Carl that something's wrong with him," I said. "And no one wants to feel that there's something wrong with who we are."

If she regarded Carl's sensitivity in a positive light, I told Maria, she would find that he would respond quickly and positively to her encouragement and that he would interact more boldly with his environment. "Positive attributions about our children can have powerful effects on them and on us," I said. I then confided to Maria, "When my daughter was born, she cried nonstop for four months. While I was soothing her, I sang her songs I made up about how easy she was and how fun everything was around our house." (I sing some of those songs around our house to this day—they still make both of us laugh.) I reminded Maria that sensitive children respond very well to their caregiver's shaping, so in those terms, Carl's sensitivity would make her job as a parent easier.

For the next few weeks, Maria and Carl came to the clinic for observation and coaching. Maria learned how to encourage Carl whenever he attempted something new or exhibited a little more boldness. She also became more nonintrusive in Carl's play, allowing him to explore his environment in his own time and on his own terms and praising him when he did so. She made a point of being patient with Carl's difficulties, supporting him to learn on his own and, thus, creating greater self-confidence in him. Outside the clinic environment, Maria set up playdates for Carl with other toddlers, allowing her son to have more experience with his peers without her constant supervision. I encouraged Maria to enroll Carl in a nursery school for a few mornings a week to give him an opportunity to develop without any (potential) overprotection on her part. (There is evidence that when parents provide more social opportunities for shy or sensitive children, the children often grow out of shyness.)

Carl responded to Maria's new style of nurturing with more openness to his mother's interactions. As he was allowed to explore on his own and was genuinely praised for every small increase in confidence, he began to enjoy more creative and challenging play. He also became more open with other children. Carl was still sensitive and a little fearful when presented with new people and situations, but he quickly overcame his shyness with a little reassurance from his mother or a little time to explore new situations on his own. Because children are able to get over their inborn shyness, it is likely that shyness can be overcome with nurture.

Our positive perceptions of our children can have an immediate and long-lasting effect on our children's self-esteem, and evidence by Susan Campbell at the University of Pittsburgh shows that positive perceptions can have a life of their own. One very interesting study evaluated both a baby's temperament and the parent's perception of the baby's temperament. Researchers observed young babies and objectively evaluated their temperaments on a scale from easy to difficult. Each parent was then asked to rate his or her baby's temperament on the same scale. Many months later, the babies were reevaluated on the same temperament scale. Researchers found that a parent's positive perception of the child's temperament had a positive effect on the child over time. Children who were assessed originally as difficult (based on the researchers' objective observations) but whose parents viewed them as easygoing were measured as much easier in temperament (judged again by objective observations) when they were older.

This effect of parents on a child's emotional responsiveness demonstrates one of the fundamental rewards for a parent's positive perceptions: *Our children become more responsive to us.* Children are responsive to parents who try to establish a healthy connection with them. Certainly, a child's level of emotional responsiveness is affected by its inborn nature, but I would rate nature as only 20 percent of the equation. The other 80 percent of emotional responsiveness has to do with what the child feels is coming (or not coming) from the parent. As the adult, you are the one who is supposed to have some control over your behavior and your emo-

You, as a parent, can create an emotionally available connection with your child.

- *Be available to be emotionally "recruited" by your child.* Be present with your child. Pay attention to him or her when he or she requests it, either verbally or nonverbally. Praise your child for his or her accomplishments, and support your child in learning from his or her environment. It is so easy in today's busy world to have your mind on a million other things even as you interact with your child. Being physically close does not make up for emotional unavailability.

- *Offer your child opportunities to become emotionally "recruited" by you.* Reach out to your child during play time and other moments. Look for the ways your child responds favorably to your overtures. Realize that the way your child responds to you might not meet your pictures of an "emotional" response. Some children respond emotionally by smiling, some by hugging, some by clinging, some by asking for your company. Learn your own child's emotional vocabulary and what constitutes a favorable emotional response for him or her.

- *Be sensitive to your child's emotions and the way he or she communicates them.* Maintain a positive attitude and an atmosphere of openness to your child's emotions. It's important for your child to know that he or she can express both positive and negative feelings and still keep your love. Remember, you can acknowledge the feelings while still shaping your child's behavior. If you respond favorably to smiles and hugs and do not respond at all to whining, for example, your child will quickly learn what it takes to get the emotional connection he or she is seeking. Be sensitive to your child's unique emotional vocabulary. Also, be aware that repairing interactions is okay, and that you should try to give both your son and daughter the experience with control as well as the experience with expressing and responding to emotions. Let your daughter as well as your son take the lead in play. Do respond positively when your son as well as your daughter becomes emotionally expressive.

tions. As a parent, it is your responsibility to set up a climate of healthy, available emotional connection with your child.

The emotionally available parent enters into a child's world, creates pleasure, allows rather than pushes, and encourages rather than forces. The result is a strong, emotionally fulfilling relationship for both parent and child, one that will allow both parties to grow in happiness and love.

continued...

- *Guard against expressing overt or covert hostility toward your child.* Children are very perceptive and will pick up any hostility immediately. Even if you are feeling stressed or aggravated, do your best to put those feelings aside when you interact with your child. If the child produces feelings of hostility in you, you might want to seek outside help in dealing with your emotions.

- *Be available rather than intrusive.* Children want and need to explore the world on their own, but they also need the security of having a parent nearby. When your child is playing, be available for interaction rather than pushing yourself on the child. Don't interject yourself in the middle of play to show your child how to "do it right" or to "help" him or her. If your child invites you to play, do so. When appropriate, gently encourage your child to explore play on his or her own. Don't be afraid to signal your unavailability at appropriate times. Give your child the space he or she needs to explore the world and be sure to establish the emotional connection that will give your child a secure place to come back to. Be a positive emotional follower, and be available without feeling the need to take over or to perform for someone. Wait for that special look or smile, then reward those signs by joining in with your child and sharing in the positive emotions. Engaging in this style of interaction gives your child a feel for reciprocity in relationships, and that is a valuable gift to offer.

THE CHILD'S SIDE OF EMOTIONAL CONNECTION

A friend of mine recently returned from a family trip to Disneyland with her nine-year-old daughter, Margaret. "We went on all the rides, we saw the *Beauty and the Beast* show—it was great!" my friend enthused. "It's a trip we'll remember forever." But later, when I talked to my own daughter, Erin, she told me she had heard a very different report from Margaret. At nine (going on nineteen), Margaret felt her mother had treated her like a baby in Disneyland, forcing her to go on "boring" rides like *Pirates of the Caribbean* and see "stupid" shows like *Beauty and the Beast* instead of taking her to Space Mountain and other more adult rides. "My mother just doesn't get it," Margaret had complained to Erin. What had been a great trip for the mother had been for the daughter a painful and boring example of her mother's obtuseness.

Another parent told us that her son had a wonderful, idyllic childhood, with every summer vacation in a beautiful village in Spain where they owned a summer home. However, her son was depressed and suicidal. She

---

continued...

- *Encourage and reward your child's responsiveness to you*. When your child's overtures are accepted and rewarded with your attention and love, your child will want to involve you in his or her life. When you are invited into your child's play, join in. Be an active and eager partner in your child's life when your child requests it. Being able to express your feelings in appropriate ways is often the invitation for your child to express his or her feelings.

- *Be emotionally involved in your child's life*. Remember that emotional availability is based on your feelings rather than just your actions. Offer your child a strong, healthy, emotional connection, and he or she will respond in kind. When your child is emotionally available to you, parenting will be so much easier! Your child will listen to you more easily, will cooperate with you (will even be nicer to younger siblings!), and will have a happy childhood. The "gift" of emotional availability is truly the best gift you can give your child. In return, your child says thank you by becoming emotionally available toward you.

could not understand that her experience of these wonderful summers was not his experience—his was one of loneliness, with no friends nearby.

The most important thing about emotional availability to a child—be it a baby, preschooler, or school-age child—is the child's experience, not what the parent *believes* is the child's experience. A great deal of research indicates that the reality of childhood is less important than what the child *perceives* as his or her reality. In other words, according to a parent, the child might have had a very favorable childhood, but the parental recounting of events is less important than what the child recalls. We call such recollections "internal working models," or "representations." These representations are not meant to be an accurate rendition of early events, but rather subjective experiences related to the emotions and emotional availability the child experienced at the time—again, not necessarily the emotional availability that was *delivered,* but what was *experienced.* One cannot know everything a child experiences, of course, but reading a child's emotional cues and behaviors related to security/insecurity are all important, and through such "reading," a parent can understand whether a child is secure.

For instance, different siblings in the same family sometimes describe clearly different circumstances attached to the same event. Certainly, different children could experience even a very objective event such as the death of a parent differently, partly because that death could affect the children in different ways. Or the experiences following the death of the parent could be quite different for different children, with possibly the older one facing greater maturity demands and becoming the caregiver to the younger, and the younger having more opportunities for self-expression as a result. Abuse during childhood also can have different effects on different children in the same family, based on the experience of each child and how he or she copes with the abuse. Individuals can have very different types of experiences from the same family members or the same events, due to the unique interaction of the individual with others and the environment.

A growing interest in the field of child development involves what we call the *nonshared family environment*—that is, the unique response of each family member to the environment created in the home. A great deal of research in the field of behavioral genetics now focuses on the effects of the nonshared family environment on individuals as they are growing up. It is believed that the nonshared family environment is just as important (if not more) as the shared family environment in predicting child development. (The *shared family environment* comprises elements that are the same for all siblings in the same family, such as the effects of social class, the schools the children attend, the neighborhood the children live in, and so on.)

Research indicates that part of the reason siblings develop so differently is that they have such different interactions with family members related to what they evoke emotionally from others in the family. This is certainly something that parents with more than one child can understand, as they know that part of their behavior with each child is determined by what that child evokes in them. For example, a father might treat his athletic son with rough-and-tumble affection and camaraderie but have trouble expressing affection to his more bookish younger son. I have lost count of the parents who have come to my clinic saying, "I don't have any problems relating to my other kids, but this one pushes my buttons. I get angry at the drop of a hat, and I don't know why."

Parents who are trying to establish emotionally available environments for their children need to focus on what each child is experiencing from the child's point of view, not their own. This might seem like a daunting task, especially when your child is preverbal or when the child enters the teenage years and often seems to stop communicating altogether. I want to make very clear here that although it is a parent's responsibility to understand the child's side of the emotional availability dynamic, I am not interested in "parent blaming." As a parent, the most important thing you can do is simply to make emotional connection a priority of your parent-child relationship.

Parents can explore a child's emotional experience by three very simple methods:

- *Learn to read and understand* your child's emotional expressions.

- *If you are having difficulty interpreting your child's emotional signals, ask* what your child is feeling.

- *Listen* to the response. Really listen to your child's experience and expressions of feelings.

Reading Your Child's Emotional Cues, Starting in the Baby Years

Based on our research, it seems that during infancy, children are disposed to form an emotional connection with at least one significant person. The attachment between a child and his or her primary caregiver seems to be independent of that child's relationship with the caregiver's partner or other nonrelated caregivers. Your baby's feelings of emotional availability toward you can be independent of any other emotional situation in his or her life (for example, feelings toward your spouse, ex-spouse, nanny, etc.). If you attend to your baby's emotional experience, if you nurture your child and create a strong emotional bond from the start, then you can help your child develop high levels of emotional availability regardless of what he or she might be experiencing with other family members or caregivers.

Your responsibility as a parent, then, is to learn to read and interpret the cues your child gives *you* about his or her emotional availability to you. Each child will have his or her own emotional "vocabulary," or ways of expressing positive or negative emotions. This vocabulary is often a combination of nature and nurture. Some children are more naturally quiet or sensitive, whereas others are outgoing and boisterous. The ways parents respond to their children's emotions will quickly shape the children's levels of expression.

Connie expresses her pleasure with an activity by laughing out loud. Connie's father is very sensitive to noise. He expresses his annoyance about Connie's laughter either overtly ("Shut up!") or covertly (looking at her with exasperation or leaving Connie alone while he reads in another room). Connie quickly learns to temper her emotional expression, thus depriving her father of a valuable way to read his child's emotional responsiveness.

Let's assume that as a parent you don't want to stifle your child's emotional expression but simply want to reassure yourself of your child's emotional availability to you. Reading the cues of most children's recruitability is simple. If your child looks happy, if your child involves you in his or her day, and if your child is emotionally positive and responsive to you, then it is likely that your child is emotionally recruitable. But what if your child does not give off clear cues; for example, what if your child is a quiet child? Your job as a parent is to learn your child's particular emotional vocabulary. This task is much easier if you have a relatively solid emotional connection with your child. If you love your child, if you want to nurture and deepen your relationship with your child, then your ability to understand who he or she is and what he or she means is heightened.

However, if you feel a lack of emotional connection with your child, then you are less likely to express your emotions—and so is your child. This kind of emotional constriction often shows up in a lack of facial expressiveness on both sides. We often see parents whose faces show little change in emotion when they are with their children. These children are then left uncertain of their parents' emotional availability to them, which might cause the children to become less likely to give off emotional cues themselves.

Another way a lack of emotional connection manifests is in the parent's tendency to categorize a child as one thing or another (quiet, loner, sensitive, and so on), rather than relating to that child as an individual. When we label a child in a particular way, we often cease to look for ways in which the label does not apply to the child.

> Mort told me that his daughter Holly was a loner. "Whenever I see her at the day-care center, she never seems to want to play with other children," he said. But when I interviewed Holly's teachers, they said Holly was actually very gregarious when Mort wasn't around. When her father was in the room, however, Holly focused all her attention on him. If he told her to go play with the other children, she would tend to go off by herself and wait until Mort paid attention to her again or left, at which point she would approach the other kids. The dynamic between father and daughter was reinforcing Mort's labeling Holly as a loner, even though she demonstrated very different behavior when he wasn't around.

A lack of emotional expressiveness and a tendency to label a child are clues that some work is needed to strengthen the emotional connection between parent and child. It falls to the parent to begin the process. You must first become more emotionally recruitable by your child. You must establish the connection that allows you to understand what your child is communicating.

So what are we looking for? One of the signs of good emotional recruitability is your child's willingness to be responsive to you when you ask your child to do something or when you play with him or her. By "responsive," I do not mean that your child has to jump to please you. In fact, at all ages, your child should demonstrate a good degree of autonomy and respond in an age-appropriate way. (An adolescent "jumping" as soon as he or she is asked to do something is usually not an age-appropriate interaction!) Your child's healthy willingness to respond to you shouldn't seem to be "people pleasing," compliance, or obedience. Rather, it manifests as your child being full of life and pleasure and being emotionally responsive to you.

A baby who wants to involve a parent in his or her world might laugh in response to a parent playing peekaboo. A toddler might show the parent a new toy or ask the parent's help in putting together a puzzle. An older child might ask questions about a tough situation with a friend, talk to the parent after school, or tell the parent how he or she feels about Grandma coming to visit. This kind of involvement is how children tell their parents that it "feels right" to them to have their parents in their lives. (And, yes, even adolescents involve their parents. In fact, the myth of the detached adolescent is just that: a myth. Although there is greater autonomy during adolescence than during childhood, there is still positive involvement of the parent[s].)

Children usually try very hard to involve their parents. However, the ways they choose to involve parents can be either positive or negative. Most parents are all too familiar with the negative attention-seeking tactics of their children. However, it is vital for parents to recognize such attention seeking as a cry for help. When a child cries for prolonged periods and, thereby, solicits adult interest, that child likely needs connection but doesn't know how to go about getting it. Such behavior is often a habit born of the child's lack of skill in creating positive ways to get attention from adults. Clearly, working with our children to help them develop some positive coping skills is in order, as is working on ourselves to be more emotionally available to our children.

By living in an emotionally available environment, children learn to be emotionally available to others—not only to their parents but also to other children, their teachers, and the world in general. For example, I am currently working on a project designed to smooth children's transition from preschool to elementary school. Our studies so far indicate that *a child's level of emotional availability is highly related to his or her school competence.* Certainly school competence is affected by parents' emotional availability; but equally important for positive school outcome is the child's emotional availability to the parents. (Although the child has a contribution to this dynamic, it is based on the quality of the relationship created between parent and child, and not on the child's temperament.)

The "Value" of a Child's Emotional Responsiveness to the Parent

The child's side of emotional connection needs to be recognized and felt by parents because that is what keeps parents emotionally available. It is difficult to be an emotionally available parent without the child's active participation. When parents experience their kids as emotionally unavailable, the joy of parenting is greatly diminished. I have seen parents put herculean efforts into connecting with children who have "shut down" toward them. I often wonder how parents stick it out with such children. But why did the child shut down in the first place? If we are hardwired as babies to connect emotionally with at least one significant person, what can get in the way of the parent-child bond?

In my observations of many parents with their children, the breakdown in the relationship usually occurs due to one of three reasons. The first is a fundamental mismatch in temperament between parent and child. A gregarious parent has a baby who likes solitude, or a quiet parent has a child who cries a lot. In these cases, it is up to the parent to adapt to the child's temperament and, as described earlier in this chapter, help shape the child's behavior toward more of a middle ground. In spite of children's temperaments, parents can create emotional availability, and children can become responsive and involved.

Second, circumstances occur that cause a parent to disconnect emotionally from a child. Depression, divorce, a death in the family, or problems with other children, for example, can affect a parent's ability to express feelings or even to feel at all. The child, who often is affected by the circumstances as well, cannot understand why that parent isn't emotionally there, and the child closes off in response.

Third, the parent simply isn't reading the child's emotional cues correctly. The child might be signaling his or her emotional disconnection through behaviors such as turning away, refusing to smile, or actively seeking to leave the area where the parent is, but the parent either misinterprets the behavior or doesn't see it as a problem.

Improve emotional availability in your child.

- *You must be positive toward your child in words and deeds as well as in facial and vocal expressions.* When my daughter was in preschool, I watched one of the other mothers drop off her son at the school. Every day when she left, the mother would say to the son, "I love you," but the words sounded like a brush-off. The mother always looked distracted and was never particularly warm. I never saw her hold or caress her son. The son was well clothed and clean, but the amount of emotional connection between mother and son was nonexistent.

  Saying you love your child without showing them behaviors that display loving, or doing great things for your child (keeping a clean house, sending him or her to great schools, buying the best jackets for winter) without being emotionally available suggests to your child that you are willing to give him or her anything but yourself and your feelings. Make time to acknowledge your child's feelings, and be sure your child experiences positive feelings from you. In so doing, you also help your child use his or her emotions.

  We all have seen children who are really difficult to read—they are so inhibited in their use of facial expressions and gestures that their emotions seem not to be there. If we help our children to use and express their emotions, they will not feel that they have to maintain such a tight control over their emotional lives. Interactions—lively interactions—and dialogue can help such children feel comfortable expressing a range of feelings.

I once saw the impact of two of these forms of emotional disconnection in a mother and daughter I observed for my dissertation at
Berkeley. Aleysha was pregnant with her second child when her own
mother died suddenly. A long period of mourning ensued, and Aleysha's
feelings of depression had not lifted when her baby, Makayla, was born.
I observed Aleysha and Makayla in their home when the baby was about
nine months old. I noticed that Makayla seemed to move away from her
mother during play and did not include her in many of her everyday ac-

---

• **Let your child accomplish goals while you cheer or help him or her succeed.** *A child's first steps are almost always an event of celebration. But the
joy for both parent and child comes from the fact that these are the child's
first steps all by himself. or herself. Similarly, helping your child find solutions
or accomplish goals for himself or herself is different from "taking over" these
accomplishments or power, such as doing homework for your child or demanding that your child play piano because "it's good for you." Your child's
emotional responsiveness to you will grow when your child feels your support for his or her efforts in areas where he or she wishes to succeed.*

• **Help your child learn to manage his or her own negative emotions.** *As an
individual who (hopefully) has learned to cope with your own feelings, you
must help your child learn to manage his or her anger and other negative
emotions. One of the best ways you can do this is through example.*

   *Tom learned this lesson very painfully one day when he was driving his
son David and daughter Lisa to school. Tom was an impatient driver, who
constantly yelled at other drivers when they got in his way or failed to use
turn signals. Right after Tom had shaken his fist at the car in front of him and
called the driver a "stupid idiot!" he looked in the rearview mirror and saw
David hit Lisa and call him a "stupid idiot!" Tom realized that David believed
such behavior was acceptable because he saw his dad do the same. Tom
talked to David and explained that it was not okay to call others "stupid" and
let anger get the best of him. From that point on, Tom worked hard to control his anger when the kids were in the car so he could be a good example
for his son.*

tivities. Aleysha said, "I thought most babies like to play with you," but she said she hadn't given Makayla's behavior much thought. My research assistant ran into them at a playground nine months later and later commented to me, "I think Makayla has really shut out her mom." She described the mother and daughter as "ships passing in the night." What was a natural process in life—mourning one's own mother—gave way to Aleysha's shutting down her relationship with her daughter.

Aleysha had observed Makayla's behavior of not wanting to play with her, but she had not interpreted that behavior as a problem. Therefore, she did not intervene to break the cycle of disconnection that can happen when parents become preoccupied with their own issues. I am not suggesting that mourning is inappropriate or unhealthy—far from it. If you have experienced a loss or another life-changing event, you need to be aware of what your children are experiencing as a result and remain emotionally available to them, even during difficult times.

When you are in control of yourself, your child learns that he or she can be in control, too, and regulate his or her own anger and other negative emotions.

As my research and clinical work have shown, it is much easier to be the parent of an emotionally available child. Therefore, it makes sense for you to work with your child by using the techniques outlined in this book to deepen your child's experience of emotional availability. Then you can start with a foundation of equality in the relationship, where your emotionally available child accepts and welcomes you as an emotionally available parent, and vice versa. If low emotional availability has been part of your history as a parent, work at changing that as soon as possible, before your child concludes that emotional unavailability is all he or she can hope for in your relationship. Allow your child (and yourself) to experience the riches that an emotionally available relationship can bring.

seven

Creating Emotional Connections

Emotional availability can be of enormous help for brand-new and experienced parents alike because it provides a simple set of guidelines for creating one of the most nebulous yet important elements of a happy childhood: a strong, healthy, age-appropriate emotional connection between parent and child. In the sixteen years since I began studying emotional availability, I have seen thousands of children and parents interacting, and I have observed how parents successfully build secure, strong, happy relationships with their kids at every age. Based on these observations, I have come up with a list of ten very specific ways parents can nurture their emotional connection with their children. These "exercises" might seem simple, but when you understand how these activities and suggestions produce an atmosphere of emotional availability, you will also understand their importance.

The first three ways have to do with activities that parents can use to establish the all-important sense of security by the end of the child's first year of life. For children older than a year, these activities can still promote that secure bond, as well as help parents reconnect with children after a difficult transition (such as a divorce) or when the relationship gets off-track. The remaining seven ways are some of the best-kept secrets of creating a healthy emotional connection. Each can help create or enrich emotional availability between you and your child.

TEN WAYS TO NURTURE EMOTIONAL CONNECTION WITH YOUR CHILD

There are likely to be myriad ways one can nurture emotional connection, but here are some I have found to be powerful: (1) Play with your child, (2) use music (particularly with babies and young children), (3) videotape your interactions, (4) take time to observe your child carefully, (5) describe your interaction to a trusted other or write them down, (6) try (really try) to understand your child's experience, (7) share a range of emotions with him or her, especially positive ones, (8) be an emotional follower rather than the leader, (9) be real and genuine with him or her, and (10) work on your emotions, especially the kinds you experience when you are tired or stressed.

#1. PLAY WITH YOUR CHILD

One of the best ways in which emotional connection (or reconnection) can happen is through play. When parent-child relationships experience stress, we often observe a lack of playtime. I'm not talking about taking your child to the playground and letting your child play, or arranging playdates, or taking your child to preschool and making sure he or she has an opportunity to play. It means actually playing with your child.

So much of what a parent does is like the job of a maid: preparing meals, taking children to school, cleaning them, making sure they go to bed, and so on. Who has time for play? However, daily activities can be done in a playful way.

Researchers know that the types of play children engage in can be used as accurate measures of childhood emotional development. For example, the ability to pretend, in and of itself, is a very good sign. Pretend play that has positive themes and a good-things-come-out-of-bad-things quality indicates the child feels secure and emotionally connected to you as a parent. But if your child's play is very aggressive and destructive (featuring earthquakes, floods, or killings, for instance), don't worry. Children use play as an outlet for a wide range of emotional expressions, including aggression and anger. (This is a far more appropriate form of blowing off steam than hitting another child!) Don't be worried if your child's play allows for a wide range of emotional expression. You should allow your child to act out those themes, then you can begin to structure your child's play toward creating positive outcomes for the pretend situations.

For example, you could say, "Wow, the whole family got swept away by the flood! Where did they end up? Did they land on a beach somewhere? Did a helicopter come and save them?" Structuring toward more positive themes gives your child experience with problem-solving rather than simple "catharsis" (letting out angry feelings). Just be sure that when you suggest or structure positive alternatives in the context of play, the child doesn't feel you are taking over his or her game. One of the nicest things a parent can do for a child is to join in play rather than taking over. Remember, young children live in a different world, not just a smaller or simpler adult world. If you want to strengthen your connection with your child, enter your child's world and join into the world of nonverbal play. Through playing, parents can begin to learn about a child's internal world—the world that he or she might not be able to reveal in other ways.

When you play with your child, so much information comes out about what's worrying him or her, what's on his or her mind, and what issues he or she is working on, as well as (of course) having fun together. And no amount of verbal questioning ("How was your day at school today?" "How were you with your friends?" "Would you like to do this?" and so on) can substitute for the communication that happens and the interest that is conveyed when you play with your child. It is most important to follow your child's lead. Slow down and let your child be the leader, then comment on and try to elaborate interactions.

Mei-Lin was playing with her four-year-old son, Han, at our clinic. Han had constructed an elaborate building with blocks and had put several toy figures inside the building. Then Han violently knocked the whole construction down, shouting, "Earthquake! Earthquake!" Mei-Lin remembered that in the kitchen the previous night she and her husband had been discussing a recent earthquake that had affected the California town where Mei-Lin's parents lived. Although Mei-Lin had talked with Han about his grandparents and assured the little boy they were all right, it was clear from his play that the earthquake was on his mind. Mei-Lin said to Han, "That was a pretty bad quake to knock over such a big house. How can the people get out? Should we call the firemen to come?" (Mei-Lin knew her son loved fire engines.) Han agreed, and they both went to the toy shelf in search of a fire engine. Han picked out the one he wanted, and Mei-Lin asked, "What kind of sound does a fire engine make?" Han started rolling the engine along the floor toward the pile of blocks, making siren noises. Mei-Lin let Han direct the "rescue" operations, moving the blocks off the "people" one by one, both of them exclaiming when another figure emerged.

Mei-Lin had successfully entered her son's world of play. She had made a suggestion (the firemen) that helped him move from the disaster of the earthquake into helping the people in his play world. Then she let Han take the lead and shape the rest of the story. It was an enjoyable and bonding experience for them both.

#2. USE MUSIC

Music can help tremendously by allowing and giving permission for emotional interaction between you and your child. Getting a feel for the give-and-take of rhythm can create the context for emotional give-and-take as well. Music also can facilitate connection because it allows you to connect with your child without constantly having a formal "interaction" and interact without expectations. Indeed, the only expectation should be for both of you to have a good time, and even that shouldn't be forced.

There is no expectation for interaction and the only goal is to be together in an enjoyable atmosphere, but music also can help "turn off" your mind and allow you to experience feelings. Many parents are so used to being cerebral or intellectual (maybe because they have careers that require it) that they allow their feelings to fall by the wayside. But being with a baby or child is more about feelings than anything. Exercises such as holding, touching, humming, and other kinesthetic activities help you stay at the level of "now" with your child. Being with your child in an unpreoccupied way—rather than needing to do or say something or thinking of other things that you need to do—is important.

You can incorporate music into your child's life in thousands of ways: You can create music together by singing or dancing. At other times, you can have it in the background. Try music with words, or make up your own words to the music. Sing lullabies. Play children's music and sing along to the silly songs. Think of different kinds of music. People often think music has to be classical such as Bach or Mozart, but widen your selections. Try African music. Try drums or percussion instruments. Take a couple pots and wooden spoons and make your own percussion section with your child. Don't put on a CD or a video and leave the room; use the music to connect emotionally with your child.

From the moment his daughter Maggie was born, Nate loved singing to her. On the nights she was fussy, he would walk the floor with her on his shoulder, crooning old Beatles songs in her ear. He got every CD of kids' music he could find and learned all the words. He would sing to Maggie when he bathed her, when he changed her diaper, when he fed her. As soon as she could hold two blocks, he showed her how to bang the blocks together in time. Music was Nate's special link to his daughter. No matter how crazy his day had been or how tired he felt when he came home from work, all he had to do was see his daughter and croon the Rod Stewart song "Wake Up, Maggie," and her face would light up and he would feel himself relax completely. When Maggie sang, "Baa baa black sheep" for the first time at eighteen months of age, Nate thought he had never heard anything so beautiful. Music truly created a very special bond between father and child.

#3. VIDEOTAPE YOURSELF IN INTERACTION WITH YOUR BABY OR YOUNG CHILD

Felix, a proud but busy dad, brought his eighteen-month-old son Bobby to our clinic at his wife's urging because she didn't feel father and son were bonding well. We videotape most play sessions at the clinic, and Felix was somewhat surprised when I suggested he watch one of the tapes of him playing with Bobby. But after he saw the tape, Felix understood. During the session, Felix had interacted with his son briefly, but then turned away to make a call on his cell phone. When Bobby started to make noise playing with his toys, Felix hushed the child. When Bobby wouldn't be quiet, Felix got up and moved to the corner of the room so he could keep talking on the phone.

What Felix saw on the tape was Bobby's reactions to his father's lack of attention. Felix saw how often Bobby would glance at his father to see if he was noticing him. Felix also saw that Bobby's noisiness sometimes came from the child's absorption in play, but also was an attempt to get his dad to notice him. "I thought when kids played, that was all they focused on," Felix confessed. "I thought that it wouldn't matter that I was on the phone as long as Bobby was occupied. But Bobby was looking at me and wanting my attention a lot more than I ever suspected. I guess I'd better start paying more attention to my son."

Videotaping you and your child together is a great way of spotting your own patterns as well as giving you the chance to pick up some of the subtle cues your child is offering about his or her emotional wants and needs. I usually suggest that parents videotape a minimum of twenty minutes of interaction (several hours if possible, as defenses go down with longer time in front of the camera) and then watch the tape with someone they know and trust. (Another person might be able to pick up things you wouldn't, simply because he or she will have a more objective perspective.)

As you watch the tape, ask yourself questions such as, "Why did my child do that?" "Why did I do that?" "What was I thinking when I did that?" "Why did my child (or I) react in this way?" Take a look not only at yourself and your child but also the relationship between the two of you. What is developing? Here are some pointers on what to look for:

- **Parental sensitivity:** Do you create fun times in relaxed, confident, and emotionally positive ways? Are you genuine in your expressions of emotion? Would your child trust you to be predictable in your interactions with him or her? Rather than always being task-oriented, do you allow for fun in your relationship without forcing it?

- **Parental structuring:** Do you make suggestions during play by breaking down larger tasks into smaller, more understandable parts? Do you set appropriate limits for your baby or young child around what is and is not acceptable behavior? Do you prohibit in consistent and gentle ways?

- **Parental nonintrusiveness:** Do you create a quality of "being there" in an emotionally connected way? In other words, are you comfortable being available to your child without necessarily having to do or say something? Do you rarely take over interactions but instead allow your child to lead and assume the role of an emotional follower? Do you sit back and let your child initiate interactions with you, or are you always the one initiating?

- **Parental nonhostility:** Do you manage your anger well and try to create the type of climate in the interaction that is emotionally well regulated? When you need to express anger, do you do it in clear and crisp ways, rather than in unmodulated or uncontrolled ways that might scare your baby or young child? Do you try to find positive outlets for your energies so you are not left feeling bored or insidiously resentful of all the giving you do as a parent? Such positive outlets allow you to be with your child in a patient and measured way rather than in overtly or covertly hostile ways.

- **Child responsiveness:** Does your child respond to you when you initiate interaction? Does your child seem emotionally engaged? Does he or she seem to look forward to your initiations of interactions and invitations for play?

• **Child involvement of parent:** Does your child initiate interactions with you? And do these initiations lead to some elaborated play between the two of you? Does he or she seem to make you an audience to his or her play?

#4. TAKE THE TIME TO OBSERVE CAREFULLY

When I asked Lorraine to describe when her daughter Kelly had learned to walk, she had to think a moment. "When you've got three kids under the age of five, they start to blur together," Lorraine admitted. "Let's see . . . Kelly started walking at thirteen months, I think. Maybe she was a year old. I'm not sure I remember exactly." When pressed to describe her daughter, Lorraine used terms such as "easy," "quiet," "not a bother." But she had very little sense of her daughter's likes and dislikes. "I just can't pay that much attention to her," Lorraine said. "You know how it is—the youngest in the family always has the fewest pictures in the family album and the least fuss made over them."

As a parent, you are the expert on your child, and the way to become the best possible expert is to observe your child's behaviors and the events in the child's life. Often in the clinic, we find that parents who have insecurely connected children describe them in vague generalities and recall their time with them in less than vivid ways. The only way you can describe your child and how he or she is developing, as well as how he or she reacts to situations, is by knowing and describing to yourself (or to others) what went on at the kitchen table, the soccer game, the parent-teacher conference, or the Halloween party at school.

It is also helpful to keep a written record of what you observe in a scrapbook or journal. This record is something you can review with your child as he or she grows. Children love to hear their own histories. It makes them feel secure that someone has been looking out for them.

#5. DESCRIBE THE INTERACTIONS YOU HAVE WITH YOUR CHILD TO A TRUSTED OTHER, OR WRITE THEM DOWN, AND SEE IF THEY MATCH THE GUIDELINES FOR THE EMOTIONALLY AVAILABLE PARENT

There are many different ways to be emotionally unavailable in a relationship with your child and for your child to be emotionally unavailable to you in return. But a truly emotionally available relationship between parent and child has eight very specific characteristics. These eight elements can serve as a road map for you as you work to create a healthy emotional bond with your child. I encourage parents to spend a few moments every day recalling their interactions with their children and to write down a few key details while the memories are fresh. Then I ask them to assess their interactions using the eight elements as a guideline. The following descriptions of three different kinds of relationships between parents and children—the emotionally available relationship, the emotionally unavailable relationship, and the apparently emotionally available relationship—should help with your self-assessment.

The Emotionally Available Parent and Child

Emotionally available parents are sensitive and emotionally positive. They appropriately structure interactions and set appropriate limits when needed. They are aware of age-appropriate developmental and safety issues for supervision and monitoring, but such structuring attempts are done in a way that is either welcomed or, at the very least, accepted by the child. Such parents generally are emotional followers of the child except when it is in the best interests of the child to be redirected. Availability as a secure haven to which the child can gravitate is also another key feature of this type of relationship.

Emotionally available children easily "return the serve" and are emotionally engaged in the relationship. They often include their parents in their lives by bringing and sharing toys as an infant, sharing stories as a young child, and generally including their parents in their lives. But they don't always include and gravitate and stay close! The infants move off to explore and then return to make connection. The same dynamic is true at all ages—even teenagers. They move off to do their own thing and then come back to connect. The balance, the circle of connection, is what it is all about.

The Emotionally Unavailable Parent and Child

Parents and children in this category are like ships passing in the night, rarely stopping to connect at an emotional level. Most connections that do occur are at the functional level—for example, feeding, serving, or being sure the children's basic caregiving needs are handled. Often, emotionally unavailable parents are clearly focused on providing for their children (taking them to school on time, checking to see that homework is done, and saving up for college); however, the emotional give-and-take is not there.

In an emotionally unavailable relationship, the parent often focuses on functional "giving" to the exclusion of the kind of emotional giving that is seen in the emotionally available relationship. It is as if the parents are willing to give everything in the name of love or as the expression of love, except the one thing that would be the most direct—feelings. In turn, these parents do not look for expressions of emotion from their children and do not seem to miss or notice the absence of real connection. Babies in emotionally unavailable relationships might seem independent, but it is a pseudoindependence because they are venturing out without their emotional needs being met. Children may indicate that they are in an emotionally unavailable relationship by avoiding their parents or not expressing many emotional needs. They venture out but do not return to make connection in the easy and relaxed way we like to see. The balance is tipped toward "being on one's own" without the clear returns to make connection. These relationships are emotionally vacant.

The Apparently Emotionally Available Parent and Child

In this type of relationship there is much warmth, but the warmth is not always backed up by what is in the best interests of the children. In other words, these parents are nice to their children and interact in warm and caring ways (perhaps because the parents view displaying affection as part of their role), but there are many inconsistencies in these relationships. For example, parents might be warm on the surface but not act in ways that are good for their children's development. There might be preoccupation with other issues that take their attention away periodically or make the parents create a situation of overconnection or overattachment. Infants in this type of relationship tend to be easily distressed because they have discovered that distress is an effective way to keep their parents engaged and connected—it works! As long as they show they are dependent and emotionally hyperreactive to their parents, they have an easier time making inconsistent parents remain engaged with them. Many of these relationships are emotionally vacant as well; although the children might express a lot of distress and the parents might react by attempts to soothe, the "real" give-and-take of emotions is not there.

Whereas there are many ways in which parents and children can be disconnected or even overconnected, there is really only one way in which they can be healthily connected, and that is through their showing of real emotions. Just like the story of Goldilocks and the three bears, what you are looking for is a connection that is "just right" for this child at this stage in his or her development.

#6: TRY TO UNDERSTAND YOUR CHILD'S EXPERIENCE

Recently I met with Don, who was concerned about the way his ten-year-old son, Roger, had talked about him. In my conversations with Roger, the boy seemed to be saying that he didn't like his dad and wished he could get another dad. This was painful to Don, as he loved his son very much. I explained that Roger's comments actually might have nothing to do with Don but might originate with Roger's mother, Dianne. Dianne and Don had divorced several years earlier, and since then, Dianne had had many boyfriends. This created a very unstable living experience for Roger, with a constantly changing cast of characters. It was very possible, I told Don, that Roger might have projected onto him many of his negative experiences with the different boyfriends. We also discussed that Dianne might be bad-mouthing Don (Dianne had overtly hostile feelings toward Don), intentionally or unintentionally creating a rift between father and son.

What you *actually* do isn't necessarily related to your *child's experience* of what you do. No matter how wonderful you might be as a parent, your child's experience of you might include a lot more than just you. There might be "ghosts in the nursery," so to speak. Despite this, you can have an impact on your child by expressing concern about your child's experience, for example, wanting to know what things are like for him or her, and openly discussing what is on his or her mind. By focusing on your child's experience, you are focusing on the most important aspect of development. Your child then begins to understand that you are a parent who cares about what he or she feels and experiences—not just your version or another adult's version, but your child's version. When your child is trusted to provide such information to you, the child learns to trust you with his or her thoughts and feelings and offer them more and more. You then become a communicative parent in your child's eyes, and communicative parents can be approached about both positive and difficult topics, creating the context for sharing of confidences.

#7. SHARE A RANGE OF EMOTIONS WITH YOUR CHILD—AND PLENTY OF POSITIVE ONES

Betsy was the most worried two-year-old I had ever seen in our clinic. The only one more worried than Betsy was her mother, Irene. Irene seemed to relish talking about the problems Betsy was having, as well as the difficulties she herself was having while raising such a delicate child. When Irene wasn't worrying about Betsy, she would talk about Betsy's playmates and their parents, always focusing on what was wrong in their lives, too. Betsy seemed to pick up on her mother's emotions and amplify them. She cried at the drop of a hat and refused to let her mother out of her sight. When the door of the dollhouse Betsy was playing with wouldn't open, instead of trying different ways to open the door herself, she cried until her mother came to help her. The only bond this mother and daughter seemed to share was their common anxiety.

With some guidance, Irene came to understand that her consistently negative emotions were causing her child a great deal of distress. She started working on being more positive around Betsy, looking for ways to encourage the little girl to feel good about herself and her activities. When Betsy came to Irene with a puzzle she couldn't put together, Irene gently guided the little girl to figure out the solution for herself, then praised her for doing such a good job. After several months of observing and feeling positive emotions from her mother, Betsy became far less anxious and clingy. She started to explore on her own more and looked to her mother for affirmation as well as consolation. With greater opportunities for sharing positive emotions, both Irene and Betsy seemed to enjoy their time together and be more relaxed around each other.

Sharing positive emotions doesn't mean you can't share negative ones—far from it. As a parent, you should be able to share a range of emotions. Emotionally available families enjoy a great deal of mutual sharing of positive emotions; however, some families dwell a great deal on distressing emotions. That can set up a pattern with your child of focusing mainly on negativity and anxiety rather than the positive and pleasurable.

To create an emotionally available relationship, it is important to foster an atmosphere of positive emotions and solution-oriented interactions. When your child has a problem, rally around your child to support and problem-solve rather than feed any anxiety the child might experience. When you have conversations with your child at the kitchen table or you're playing together with a new toy on the carpet, focus on the positive, and create moments of mutual pleasure by joining your child's positive emotions.

Sharing positive emotions and a positive approach is easier if you have support in your life. Learn to accept and receive support from others (your spouse, friends, family, or any trusted individual) so you can then be positive with your child. Unless you receive emotional food, it is difficult for you to cook up the same for your child.

#8. BE THE EMOTIONAL FOLLOWER RATHER THAN THE LEADER

Franco was a big, strong guy who used to play football, so it was surprising to me how much he let his three-year-old daughter, Estella, take the lead in their playtime. He would follow her around the playroom, allowing her to choose the toys she wanted to play with, then enter into her pretend world very naturally and easily. When Estella seemed to lose interest in playing with a stuffed bunny, Franco directed her attention toward a toy piano by saying "Estella, what's that?" and pressing a couple keys to make a chord. Estella was easily diverted and immediately went to the piano and started banging on the keys herself while Franco sat back and started to sing along with his daughter's "music."

Being the emotional follower in your child's play keeps you in check with respect to your child's experiences. Allowing your child to lead and staying one step behind your child and following his or her lead in activities is important. One of the best things about parenting is that you can be available without doing anything special. That quality of being emotionally available really comes across in your child's experience. In addition, when your child is given the role of leader, he or she feels empowered and gains valuable experience in exploring the world and making choices. Having that space in interactions also gives your child a "feel" for reciprocity rather than always having to try hard. Such space lets them "feel" that they can be available, by just being "there," rather than always having to do something.

Of course, there is also much that is positive in being a "mentoring parent" or an "encouraging parent"; but it is best to do the mentoring or encouraging and then allow your child to take the lead. Introducing—that is, bringing something new to the attention of your child—is probably one of the nicest things you can do; but then you should step back and allow your child to be the one motivated to pursue further. Occasionally introduce again, but do not take away your child's power to decide and choose. Children who are given more opportunities to lead tend to develop more of a sense of self-action and empowerment.

#9. BE REAL AND GENUINE WITH YOUR CHILD

We find that what matters most to children is not just the expression of positive emotions by the parent but how "real" the parent is in the emotional sense. Smiling a lot, saying nice things, or saying "I love you" are positive only if they are real and not sugarcoating.

> Shirley was always positive. Whenever someone asked her, "How are things going?" she would always smile and reply, "Great. Wonderful." This went on for sixteen years—right up until the moment Shirley asked for a divorce. Was her sugarcoating her situation good for her children? Probably not.

Most children can tell when their parents are suppressing negative emotions, and these children feel that their parents are being dishonest with them as well as with themselves. Denying your own negative emotions is rarely effective and always creates more pain than it is worth. Frankly, no one feels great all the time; by hiding your negative emotions from your child, you can cause your child to think that his or her own negative emotions are bad, too. A lot of parents worry that stress and conflict will be harmful to their children—of course, in very large amounts they can be. But what also gets transmitted through stress or challenging circumstances is your reaction to it. Rather than denying your stress or the existence of conflict, it might be worthwhile to show your child how you can positively cope with such challenging situations.

More important, no matter how stressed you feel, you need to maintain your emotional connection with your child. Don't "drop out" emotionally. When you have problems, don't become uncommunicative or hide your problems completely from your child. Remember that your child might interpret your keeping things from him or her as a lack of love on your part.

> Tammy, a young mother, didn't tell her son Sean that she was dying of leukemia. Instead, she tried to keep an attitude of "business as usual," even though she participated less and less in her son's life as time passed.

Tammy was trying to protect Sean from the disappointment and resentment of loss. But the little boy interpreted his mother's withdrawal from his life very differently. He thought his mother had stopped loving him. Instead of protecting Sean, Tammy had mistakenly caused him many more months of emotional turmoil.

Keeping the lines of communication open during difficult times and being able to express genuine caring and genuine sorrow are all a part of life. Children need to see such emotions in their parents so they will feel open to expressing the same emotions themselves.

Again, it's important that you are engaged in real and genuine relationships with others in your life so you can deliver the same to your child. Parents who have no genuine relationship with others are either isolated from social support (or have isolated themselves) or their relationships are transient and "on the surface." You will have difficulty providing consistent emotional food unless you know how to be engaged in emotionally close relationships with the wider world. It becomes important to do some stock-taking, and that is why parenting is the greatest lesson of our adult lives. In "teaching" your children to be genuinely connected, you learn enormously about what life and relationships are really about.

#10. WORK ON YOUR EMOTIONS, ESPECIALLY DURING TIRING AND STRESSFUL TIMES

The play session with Sylvie and her ten-month-old daughter Corinne had been going very well right up until the end of the hour. Then Corinne tried to pull herself up by using a chair and tipped the chair over on herself. Corinne started screaming, and Sylvie dived for the little girl. Once she ascertained the child wasn't hurt, Sylvie snapped at Corinne, "I told you not to go near that chair! Don't ever do that again!" Corrinne started crying even harder. Sylvie took a deep breath, picked up the child, and finally started comforting her. When I spoke to Sylvie about the incident, she admitted that Corinne had been teething for the last week and neither mother nor daughter had been getting much sleep.

"I don't know what got into me," Sylvie said. "I'm usually a lot better at keeping myself under control."

During nonstressful times, it is easier to create opportunities to share positive emotions. It is also easier to be genuine and follow your child's emotional lead when you are feeling healthy and happy instead of tired or stressed. You look your best to your child when you feel your best. However, life with a baby or young child is an occupation without rest for many parents, and that can create a great deal of stress.

Our studies have shown that hostility (defined as difficulty regulating your negative emotions when you feel them creeping up) is rarely shown by parents toward their children during nonstressful times. But when we videotape parents at the end of a two-hour session, many parents (or their children) "leak" some hostility, allowing small expressions of negative emotions to emerge. Parents who can manage their anger, boredom, and sarcasm (and here, we are talking about managing or appropriately controlling or restraining negative emotions rather than bottling them up) even when they are tired and stressed are more likely to have children who can do the same for themselves. Such children, in turn, have been found to be less aggressive in their kindergarten classrooms, less likely to be victimized by others, and more likely to engage in positive interactions with their peers. It appears well worth it to muster that special energy to get you through such stressful times.

Many of these strategies might seem old hat to experienced parents and obvious even to new moms and dads. These suggestions, however, can make establishing and nurturing strong and healthy emotional bonds with your child much easier. Based on thousands of hours of clinical observation and research, as well as personal experience with my own daughter, I can tell you that putting even a few of these strategies into practice will help deepen your relationship with your child and give you both greater emotional satisfaction and happiness.

Remember, emotional availability is about establishing a high-quality emotional connection between parent and child. It's about doing what you know will make the greatest difference, rather than just being there and hoping for the best. It's about having more fun in the times you spend with your child, and being honest about your own feelings so your child can be honest about his or hers. It's about interacting with your child in ways that will create the greatest connection from your child's point of view rather than yours. Most of all, it's about both you and your child giving each other the gifts of love, trust, and happiness that will last from infancy through adolescence and beyond.

eight

Keeping the Connection While Shaping Your Child's Behavior

"It's not fair!" Susie yelled at her mother, Jo. The eight-year-old had just been told she couldn't spend the night at a friend's house. "You never let me do anything fun. Why can't I go over to Paula's?"

Her mom sighed. "Susie, you know the rules. No visiting on school nights, period."

"But I've done all my homework, and Paula and I are working together on a science project. *Her* mom says it's okay. Why can't you?" Susie persisted.

Jo turned to her daughter and said with exasperation, "Susie, I don't *care* what other people do. Paula's mom can make whatever rules she wants, but in our house, we don't go out on school nights. That's final." And she went back to preparing dinner.

"You're so unfair—I hate you!" Susie turned and ran out of the kitchen. Her mother sighed. She had had such a close friendship with her daughter when Susie was younger, but this kind of scene had been occurring more frequently as the child grew and wanted more independence. Jo felt very strongly that she had to set firm boundaries for her child, but how could she do so without alienating Susie altogether?

Disciplining children and guiding their behavior are some of the most challenging tightrope acts of parenthood. Parents must walk a fine line between staying emotionally available to their children while saying and doing things that might strain that connection. Anyone who has had to put a toddler to bed who doesn't want to go, or made a child do homework instead of talking on the phone with friends, or perhaps even forbidden a teenager from seeing someone who was a bad influence knows how difficult it is to be an emotionally available parent. Yet it is precisely at such times that emotionally available parents can draw upon their "bank accounts" of positive interactions with their children to make tricky situations a little easier for both parties.

Of the eight elements of emotional availability, the two most important in shaping a child's behavior are *sensitivity* and the *ability to structure*. After the child reaches two or three years of age, how a parent structures the child's life becomes a more important aspect of the parent-child relationship. Parents who structure well can say a firm "No" when it's appropriate and lead the child in a positive direction. Of course, sensitivity continues to be important. A parent who is warm, kind, and caring contributes positively to his or her child's development. Structuring, particularly in concert with a parent's high level of sensitivity toward the child, seems to have a profound influence on the child. Sensitivity and structure convey to the child the emotional connection in a relationship. Only when a child feels cared for can he or she accept parental attempts to make suggestions and guide the child toward appropriate and beneficial behaviors. We call such parenting *emotionally available parenting*.

STRUCTURING BY SUPERVISION AND MONITORING

Knowing what your child is doing is important. To structure and guide, you must be involved in supervision and monitoring while at the same time avoiding being overinvolved and/or overly vigilant lest your child rebel. Growing children need space and independence. Studies indicate that up to a certain point, increased parental supervision and monitoring is related to better adjustment in the child. However, at any age, there comes a point at which adjustment actually declines with increasing levels of parental supervision and monitoring.

It is also important to remember that the meaning of structuring changes over time. For a baby, it might mean baby-proofing your house so you're not constantly saying, "Don't go there" or "No" to your baby and toddler. During childhood, the structuring might guide the child toward improving friendship choices and/or providing skills on relationship maintenance. During adolescence, the structuring parent might be ready to discuss tough issues with respect to friends. For example, if a young adolescent is spending time with older peers who might have become sexually active, the structuring parent might intervene and have discussions about sex (even if the parent has done so earlier). A recent University of Minnesota study finds that children who have close relationships with their parents are more likely to begin having sex later rather than earlier in life.

STRUCTURING THAT TAKES ACCOUNT OF THE CHILD'S REACTIONS

There are many different types of parental structuring. The key ingredients of optimal structuring include discovering what type, how much, and in what way you need to reach *this* particular child. Some parents repeat structuring attempts that are not successful (that is, the child resists parental structuring attempts). In the example of Susie and Jo at the beginning of this chapter, it is clear that Jo's attempts at "drawing the line" about school night visits are not working.

If your structuring attempts are missing the mark, try something else. Being emotionally attuned to your child will provide many more clues about how to structure for this particular child than any advice from a so-called expert. If you know your child likes to figure out things for himself or herself, you might state a rule ("No television until homework is done") and then ask a question that will help your child fit within that structure ("Your favorite television show comes on tonight at 8. Do you have a lot of homework? When are you going to get started on it so you'll be done in time to watch the show?"). Successful structuring has a great deal to do with your knowledge of your child's abilities or, more generally, being in tune with your child. The positive in all this is that children love to be included in rule-making, and as you include your child or take his or her emotional reactions into account, you demonstrate that you see your child as a separate individual. He or she will appreciate your granting such autonomy. So Jo could have asked her daughter, Susie, how she would like to handle this dilemma, and they could have been collaborators rather than on different sides of the issue.

STRUCTURING BY DISCIPLINE

The issue of discipline is particularly important because it tests the emotional availability of a relationship. When children sense a parent will not or cannot discipline, they also sense that there is a lack of emotional connection. Discipline is not only related to the quality of the emotional connection; it also can affect the creation and maintenance of the emotional connection itself.

Discipline needs to be delivered in a "real" way. Being emotionally real (from the heart) delivers a different message than saying, "Here are the rules, and I expect you to obey them." Giving the message without the appropriate emotions does not have much impact. Discipline is another opportunity to be emotionally real with your kids.

Discipline delivered with hostility—in the form of yelling or corporal punishment—is never justified. Evidence indicates that children who are slapped, even if it's not to the point of abuse, have lowered self-esteems. Yes, they might stop the annoying behavior for which they were slapped, but other "annoying" behaviors will crop up. Their bodies might not be hurt much, but their feelings might be hurt in terrible ways.

What are the effects of such displays of hostility in the name of the noble cause of discipline? Children who receive discipline with hostility go on to expect hostility in their other relationships, sometimes even setting themselves up to be abused later in life. Parental hostility can produce child hostility, a fact erroneously interpreted by many parents as child hostility leading to parental hostility.

Bill once brought his twelve-year-old son, Jason, to my clinic, complaining that the child was extremely hostile, intractable, and unmanageable. As we explored the history of their relationship, Bill told me he had been disciplining Jason with an "occasional" slap since the child was three. "It was the only way to get his attention," the father explained. "He'd be running off toward the street, ignoring me completely, until I'd catch up with him and give him a smack. What was I supposed to do— let him run into the street and get hit by a car?" Years of being "smacked," however, had caused the child to become hostile himself, especially toward his father. At this point in the relationship, the least little thing would provoke angry reactions in both father and son. From an early age, the child had been "trained" by the father's hostility to be hostile himself.

Studies show that simply threatening to slap or hit can also injure a child's self-esteem. In remembering their families of origin, many parents report that getting their feelings hurt was as bad as or worse than getting hit.

GETTING YOUR MESSAGE ACROSS IN SMALL STROKES

Luckily for parents, it is possible to provide needed structure and discipline in ways that help rather than hurt a child. Your child will listen if you combine appropriate control with your sensitivity. When discipline is combined with warmth and sensitivity, it has positive effects on children. If you have had a good relationship with your child all along, when it comes time to discipline, it is usually done in small strokes rather than huge, sweeping ones. A sensitive parent can get his or her message across with less harshness. There is a connection here that the child would not want to lose, so a slight switch from the established, loving status quo is enough to signal to the child that there is a problem. There's already a "contract" in the relationship; that is, an unspoken agreement exists between parent and child about the shape and quality of their relationship.

It's very important for you to know at a deep level what contract you have with your child.

Studies suggest that this style of parenting—which combines sensitivity with appropriate control—predicts very positive aspects of child and adolescent development in areas as diverse as high academic competence, low incidence of behavior problems, low levels of distress, and low levels of substance use.

> Sam was a single dad with most of the responsibility for parenting his three children. With an ex-wife who abused alcohol and was unable to assume a major mothering role, Sam knew he needed to step up to the plate and "be there" for his children. Yet he also had a demanding professional career as an attorney that drained him emotionally. Although his initial inclination was to have strict rules and regulations and minimal worry about their emotional needs, he eventually observed that the children needed more from him. He continued to set unambiguous rules about good grades, no smoking, no alcohol, and no drugs and good choices about dating, but he also worked at having dialogues with and understanding the children. In this emotionally connected way, he was able to transmit his strict moral values to his children. The children in turn were able to receive these moral values because they had a dad who took the time to understand their emotional needs.

A kind and loving parent who does not structure life for the child (by not setting limits, establishing boundaries, making suggestions, and breaking large tasks into understandable parts, for example) is less effective than a parent who provides both caring and discipline. My very first patient as a clinical psychologist was a child who had serious conduct problems, including truancy, trespassing, and vandalizing the school—for which he was eventually arrested. This child's mother was, for the most part, warm and kind (to an objective individual), but she could not or would not set firm limits. She would set limits and then cave under the pressure of not one but three conduct-disordered sons. The boys interpreted her style as unloving and critical because ultimately she would become exasperated, critical, and rejecting in her talk with them. Being seemingly kind and then abruptly becoming critical and rejecting sends a mixed and inconsistent message to children.

A different kind of relationship is one in which the parent is emotionally *unavailable* due to his or her hostile efforts to structure and control the child's behavior. These parents might be authoritarian or intrusive. They might set limits in a very gruff way without regard for maintaining that all-important emotional connection—the "because I say so" or "my way or the highway" parent. This type of parent seems to care about control but not about emotional connection. It is as if such a parent dismisses the importance of emotions and relationships. Such a parent doesn't think about the child's feelings and in fact might not have access to his or her own feelings. Although this type of parent might do a great deal that is in the best interests of the child (such as getting enough money together for college tuition or taking the child on afterschool playdates), he or she is nonetheless emotionally unavailable because the connection is not there.

Obviously, not all emotionally unavailable parents are cool and distant. Emotionally unavailable parents can also display "hot" emotions of hostility. Research shows that children do not, or cannot, listen to the words that are being said in rage. Instead, they pick up on the nonverbal message— the tone of voice. One of the most important things for parents to remember is that yelling, regardless of the words said, is hostile, and children process the emotion rather than the words. Children simply cannot listen to the words when there is yelling, so it is no wonder that they fail to learn from it; they just become scared or tune out. Our studies indicate that the children of parents who are hostile in interactions with them, even for very brief periods, are aggressive with other kids in school or are victimized by another's aggression. Some children assume both parts of the dynamic and are both bullies and victims, depending on the context.

One of the best examples you can set for your child is to show him or her that discipline can occur without hostility and with emotional regulation. After all, hostility means being out of control. If the parent is out of control, the child becomes scared and out of control as well. There is no container for the child's emotions and no safe haven.

During a research interview, one dad described the ultimate strategy for emotion regulation in his family of origin—one that I hope we can all use because it is such a good example of the highest form of emotional availability. His family had a rule that if something really required discipline, it wouldn't be addressed in the heat of the moment. Instead, the parents would allow a "cooling off" period before they would say anything—not the silent treatment, but a true cooling off that everyone agreed upon. An hour later, they would get together, with parents and children having had time to think through what had happened. Discipline could then happen without the pollution of intrusiveness and hostility.

Kids sense that discipline is hard work for parents. In many ways, overdoing discipline or inconsistently disciplining (trying it out and then caving in when it doesn't work in the short run) are both easier on a parent because they take less effort. To communicate consistently to a child the boundaries within which he or she can operate takes work. It also takes confidence in the relationship; I don't mean just simple confidence in yourself, but confidence that the relationship can withstand it. Similarly, it is easier to yell or slap or insult a child. It is a much more refined art to figure out how not to "fly off the handle." Yes, we all have done that on occasion. But being committed to learning ways to discipline without compromising even short-term emotional connections works best in maintaining a long-term emotional connection with your child.

DISCIPLINE ISSUES AND HOW YOU WERE RAISED BY YOUR FAMILY

In my clinical work, I sometimes find that parents' experiences in the family in which they were raised can affect how they discipline. Studies show that although 30 percent of parents who were abused during childhood go on to abuse their own children, 70 percent do *not* continue this cycle. What we do see in this 70 percent, however, is less-than-optimal parenting. A variety of issues related to emotional availability emerge in this group. Some parents who were abused have such terrible memories of it that they shy away from disciplinary action altogether. Other formerly abused parents might demonstrate less-severe but nonetheless frightening and threatening behaviors toward their children. If you experienced abuse as a child, be sure you handle your own issues with counseling or other treatment. I hope this book will then provide you with suggestions for new and more connected ways of parenting than the parenting you yourself received.

HOW TO HANDLE DISCIPLINARY ISSUES

JOHN: Mom, I'm gonna go over to Chet's house.

MOM: No, I said I want you to do your homework and get to bed early.

JOHN: Forget it, I'm tired of you. I'm getting out of here. *(Storms out, speaking in a bored tone)*

MOM: You come back here! *(Running after him)*

(Later that night)

MOM: John, do your homework now.

JOHN: I already did it.

MOM: *(Checks, and he did not)* I'm tired of all this with you and your brothers. Listen—I'm telling you to listen! *(Yelling, as John ignores her)*

Note that Mom becomes hostile as well as intrusive. She is unable to structure or shape John's behavior. John isn't responsive and certainly doesn't involve his mother in his choices. Of course, they likely have had many instances of breaks in connection, with John moving on according to his agenda and Mom initially trying to discipline but then being out of control and ineffective in doing so. She appears to have little true authority in the relationship. She is inconsistently attempting discipline but without the authority or the emotional connection that can make discipline work.

How can Mom transform the interaction into an emotionally available relationship? Here is an example of how the interaction can move forward:

JOHN: Mom, I'm gonna go over to Chet's house.

MOM: Sounds like a nice idea—Chet's a great kid, and I like the friendship you two have going. And it looks like you're helping him get used to the neighborhood. But what are the rules about weeknights that we've started around here?

JOHN: Oh, that's right. We said I would first do my homework and then get to bed early. But, Mom, can I get the homework done and go over for just a little bit?

MOM: What do you think? Can you get it all done and be in bed by 9?

JOHN: I really want to get to bed at 9, 'cause we decided on that as a rule. Okay, no, I'll wait until Friday and get to have more time with Chet. *(With a smile)*

MOTHER: Sounds like a nice plan, sweetie. You did a good job figuring that out and remembering our agreement for getting to bed on time.

For many parents who have trouble with children seeming out of control and "requiring" discipline, this will seem like a scenario that has little basis in reality. Yet when I have tried it with patients (many of whom have problems disciplining their children), the change in interactions as they begin to place emotional connection in the foreground and discipline in the background is remarkable. Harmony begins to replace previously disjointed, conflictual interactions. It's important to remember, however, that your child will need time to adjust and trust that there will be an emotional connection (which invariably takes their feelings and agenda into account). In other words, an emotional connection is established over many interactions such as those described here. Once it is established, however, this scenario can become a reality.

MARTY: Dad, I'm going out.

DAD: How dare you! Get over here and do your homework.

MARTY: Oh, I thought . . .

DAD: That's the problem. You don't think.

MARTY: But . . .

DAD: I'm not asking you, I'm telling you.

MARTY: All right, Dad. I'll do my homework.

DAD: You sure will; now sit down.

In this relationship, it appears that Dad doesn't trust his son, nor does he give the child much space to have his own thoughts or views. Instead, Marty is told what to do and what to feel. The structuring, intrusiveness, and hostility (all elements of control in a relationship) are turned on to the maximum level, and sensitivity is put in the background. Dad disregards Marty's response, and there is no opportunity for the child to involve the parent. In reaction to this dialogue, Marty (or any child) might feel distressed and angry but unable to express these feelings to his strict father.

Instead, a revised scenario that still includes an appropriate level of control in the context of connection might go like this:

MARTY: Dad, I'm going out.

DAD: So you say, young man. Did you forget something? *(With a knowing glance)*

MARTY: No.

DAD: Okay, let's go through this one more time. I'm saying it nicely.

MARTY: Oh . . . Okay, Dad. Gotta do homework.

DAD: *(Smiling)* I'm so glad you thought of it on your own.

Even though this dad does not back down, he interjects humor into this episode, which then brings about a connection, or reminds both of them of an existing emotional connection. Humor is a great way to say anything. In fact, you can say practically anything as long as it's with humor.

With a few small changes, both of these situations were transformed into greater emotional availability toward the child. Each could have gone in the direction of not being able to negotiate discipline issues with emotional connection. Yet both parents tried a better strategy that had some discomfort associated with it in the short run (because it takes effort) but a great deal of benefits in both the short and long run (because it helps children trust you). These types of transformations hopefully come long before adolescence. One of the beautiful things about the emotional availability framework is that it is simple and timeless. We don't have to think, *What are the things that are right to do for adolescence?* or *for middle childhood?* or *for the preschool years?* or *for the baby years?*

The parent's qualities of sensitivity, structuring, nonintrusiveness, nonhostility—and the child's responsiveness and involvement in re-turn—work at every stage of the parent-child relationship. Mastering the skills of emotional availability will serve you well throughout your own life and the life of your child. Instead, the best time to prepare for ado-lescence (and the issues of discipline that seem to surface during adoles-cence) is really much earlier, when your child is younger than three years old. If your child is past that, it's never too late to start, but do it as early as possible!

A TEACHER CONNECTS WITH AN ADHD CHILD

From the moment he could walk, Carlos would run instead. He was always getting into things and driving his parents crazy. He was diag-nosed with attention deficit hyperactivity disorder (ADHD) by the age of five and placed in a school specializing in hyperactive children. There he was lucky enough to be put in Mrs. Ramirez's classroom. Mrs. Ramirez had the "magic touch" with her hyperactive charges. Within a few months, Carlos was more manageable. He was able to focus on an activity for longer than a minute or two. He listened to people instead of ignoring them. He was still a very lively little boy, but his energy was more directed.

When Carlos's parents asked Mrs. Ramirez how she had worked this miracle, she laughed. "All I do with these kids is love them to start with," she said. "They've got to get to the point where they trust me and be-lieve that I care about them. Once they feel I'm on their side, then we can find out what works best for them in terms of calming them down and focusing them. With most of these kids, they get a lot of attention when they're acting out rather than when they're being good. I try to do just the opposite. I spend time with Carlos when he is focusing and doing something he enjoys. Carlos loves to build things—I noticed that he spent longer with blocks than he did with any other toy. So when-ever Carlos starts getting out of hand, we go over to the blocks and build something together."

Mrs. Ramirez knew that the key to providing structure and discipline with children is first to establish a warm and caring relationship, then to provide structure that's appropriate to the child's age, interests, and circumstances. Even though not technically a "parent," she is a great example of someone who knows how to create an emotionally available relationship with a child.

Furthermore, once you learn how to discipline in an emotionally available way, you don't have to think of how to discipline one child differently from another. In other words, once an adult (or child) masters these qualities of emotional availability, he or she has a greater chance of implementing and using them in other relationships. Certainly, some children are very difficult; nonetheless, it is within the power of the adult-child relationship to rise to the challenge of disciplining any child in the context of emotional connection.

REACTING TO AN UNEXPECTED CHANGE IN YOUR CHILD'S BEHAVIOR

If you normally have a good emotional connection with your child and disciplining or structuring has not been difficult (that is, it is well received by your child), but suddenly there is a change in your child's behavior, you might look at what else is happening to cause the change.

One adolescent—Barbara—who was a straight-A student, began to spend time with the "wrong crowd" and did not listen to reason. Her father, Pete, brought her to me for therapy. He wanted her to "shape up," seeing her behavior as solely *her* problem. In discussions with them, I realized that this adolescent girl's mother had died after a year-long battle with cancer. Pete was so absorbed in his own feelings of loss that he turned to work to ease his pain. He had not realized that he and Barbara had not communicated openly about her mother's illness or the circumstances of her death. (For example, Barbara was with relatives in Europe when her mother died, and her father did not tell her directly of the death.) Pete slowly began to realize that Barbara's "acting up" had a deeper reason and that all the disciplining in the world would not have been effective in this situation.

Children and even adolescents such as Barbara will resist our attempts to set limits and discipline if their behavior is an attempt at "telling us" that there is a bigger picture we need to notice. Usually they are communicating a problem without being aware of the message themselves, and it is up to us to put together the pieces of the puzzle and help them understand.

The important thing to remember is that if you have established an emotional connection early on and you have that foundation, regardless of what might happen, you can reestablish that connection. Your confidence in knowing that you can bring it back is part of the solution.

When you give a lot to have a good emotional connection with your children, you have the right to expect more from them.

- *You will notice that it is easier to structure and discipline in a nonhostile, nonintrusive way if you play with your child about a half-hour per day. Don't worry when you miss a day—this is not a chore, but an ideal time to connect with your child.*

- *When your child knows that you want to connect on an emotional level at any chance you get, and preferably on a consistent basis, your child will instinctively feel that you deserve responsiveness not only during the fun times but also during the tough times. You must make the effort to earn this right!*

- *Giving "real" affection, not just putting in time, makes your child want to respond to you. Underneath your attentiveness, be sure you are not resenting the time you spend with him or her. If that is the case, you might be displaying covert hostility (for example, huffing, rolling your eyes, being preoccupied with work), conveying the feeling that you are missing more important things when you are one-on-one with your child.*

continued...

- *Expect a great deal from your child. Because you are giving a lot, you have the right to expect high standards of behavior, but be sure your emotional connections are there.*

- *Try to understand (or enlist the help of a trusted other in this attempt) if there is a deeper reason for acting-out behaviors, especially if they are a departure from your child's typical personality. Just because your child acts up frequently, don't dismiss the possibility of a deeper reason for his or her behavior. In fact, most children who have conduct problems also have had losses in their lives such as the death of a loved one during childhood or early adulthood, divorce, alienation of one parent from a child by the other parent, or sexual, physical, or emotional abuse. A big dose of simple, garden-variety rejection by one's parents can lead to a child's chronic acting-out behaviors. Explore the deeper reasons for your child's behavior, perhaps through your own introspection or through professional help.*

nine

Supporting Your Child to Have Positive Sibling and Peer Connections

Craig, an Air Force officer, brought his daughters, Marlise (age three) and Laura (age five), to our university lab because the two girls had been having problems in their day-care situation. The observers noted that Craig was very different with Marlise than he was with Laura. He played far more with Marlise, smiled at her more, and in general was more emotionally available to his younger daughter. Although Laura seemed not to care—playing games by herself, selecting a book, and sitting down in a corner to read—she would occasionally try to attract Craig's attention by calling to him or asking him about a word in her book. Finally, frustrated, Laura walked over and hit her sister. Marlise began to wail, and Craig finally turned his full attention on Laura.

When the observer later asked Craig if his relationship with Laura had changed when Marlise was born, he replied, "Now that you mention it, yes. I was away for the first six months after Laura was born, so it took me a while to feel close to her. But I've been around since Marlise's birth. I guess I've always felt closer to Marlise than Laura. She's certainly easier for me to be around."

Laura was caught in a vicious cycle. She had been deprived of her father for the first six months of her life, so they both missed out on a crucial time of emotional bonding. The relationship between them was just beginning to develop when Marlise was born, and Craig transferred most of his emotional availability to his new daughter, whom he felt close to from the start. Laura wanted a relationship with her father, but Craig was unable or unwilling to read the cues she was sending—especially because he was focusing most of his attention on Marlise.

Although it was entirely unconscious on his part, Craig clearly favored one child over the other and bestowed much praise on his favored child. Such differential treatment of one's children has been found to have negative consequences and can lead to what is popularly called "sibling rivalry."

Sometimes the lack of connection with one child might occur due to circumstances beyond your control, as in the case of Craig's being absent when Laura was born. Life situations such as divorce, lack of financial security, and residential instability can cause parents to be emotionally available at certain points but less available at others. For instance, a parent who is highly emotionally available with her other children can still shut down emotionally with her baby with disabilities, perhaps due to lack of experience with physically or mentally challenged children. A problem with emotional availability also can be due to a parent's own emotional problems or difficult emotional history. It can be due to differences in temperament or mistaken expectations on the part of the parent (or of the child as he or she ages). Yet such a lack of connection with one child and the differential treatment of siblings can lead to that child feeling rejected. Such feelings of rejection can then be transferred to the peer group.

STAY OUT OF IT OR DO SOME COACHING?

Many self-help books suggest that parents should stay out of sibling relationships and let the siblings work it out. This approach can backfire. For example, if one sibling bullies the other (for example, hitting, name-calling, engaging in frequent put-downs, or viciously excluding), the bully hones the skills of bullying (or just aggression) in relationships, and the bullied sibling learns the role of victim or being the recipient of aggression. Although siblings might be in conflict, emotionally available families can encourage "friendly" relationships between siblings as a model for future relationships.

An emotionally available parent can encourage sensitivity between siblings by requiring moral behavior. Research indicates that children learn morality including issues of fairness and justice, through their relationships. If one sibling is unjust to another, you can require as part of your structuring as a parent that he or she not only apologize but also make amends. Thus, every time such bullying occurs, that child would be required to make amends, even if it is only saying "I apologize. I was wrong." In this way, the bullying sibling learns to play fair and the victimized sibling receives fair treatment. Having such amends be house rules can go a long way toward correcting sibling conflicts. As long as the overall flavor of sibling relationships is fair, just, friendly, and positive, the occasional outbursts can and should be handled just by the children. However, do not assume

---

Encourage positive connections between siblings.

- *From the start, treat each of your children in a special way. With new additions to the family, continue to make your other children feel special and give them extra time and attention.*

- *Not having a favorite (stated or unstated) among your children is an important beginning. Differential treatment of siblings or preferences can lead to negative consequences in terms of the self-esteem of your children. Often, as in Craig's case, favoritism can be unconscious, and so it takes a lot of soul-searching and open-mindedness to be aware of and then to work through the favoritism. Enjoying each of your children in different ways is not favoritism, but treating them in terms of a hierarchy in emotional closeness is!*

- *Require that your children take corrective actions for any aggressions and not merely apologize.*

it's inevitable that siblings hate each other endlessly and parents are help-less to do anything about it. Positive and emotionally available relationships should be encouraged and nurtured through your skills of emotional avail-ability.

In her well-known and controversial book, *The Nurture Assumption*, Ju-dith Harris suggests that parents matter little—peers are the ones who in-fluence children. For example, Harris states that adolescent drug use is

continued...

- *Look to your own relational skills, or that of your spouse or your ex, to understand where your child might have learned bullying or being a vic-tim. Adults are less likely to tolerate behavior in children that they toler-ate in themselves or in their adult-adult relationships. It is as if adults have a license for such behavior that children have not yet earned. Re-member that bullying is not always about getting into a fight. Bullying can also be more subtle—put-downs, the cold shoulder, silent treat-ment, and constant criticism. Examine your child's network of relation-ships, including those with siblings, to understand and remedy the source of such problems.*

- *Teach your children problem-solving skills (preferably, win-win problem-solving skills so both are winners). They can then work out a lot of their own problems by using tools of reasoning, knowing that there are alter-natives, and most important, that a dialogue can go a long way. Just as you talk to your children, encourage them to talk to one another.*

- *Encourage children to verbally express feelings rather than act out ag-gression and to express such feelings in a nonhostile manner. Encourage such nonhostile behavior by behaving in harmonious and fair ways toward the children rather than aggressive and bullying ways.*

- *Teach your child to express his or her feelings in an assertive, not ag-gressive, way. Encourage your child to express his or her worries as well.*

- *Encourage your children to engage in positive, cooperative activities to-gether to build a positive and pleasurable repertoire in their relationship.*

continued...

- *Encourage your victimized child to feel as if he or she can come and get you. Let him or her know that you will not rescue them, but you will help with the problem-solving that is needed. You might facilitate "making amends." Children feel cared for when they know a supportive person can be relied upon to help them solve their problems—not solving the problems for them, but helping them figure it out themselves. Empowerment is the result. Don't do the work for one, the other, or the relationship. Be an available, nonintrusive presence who can structure life for your children in a sensitive and nonhostile manner.*

- *Read your children's emotional cues correctly and work at understanding the cues of each of your children so you can understand by the look in their eyes what they are feeling. Show your children that you are emotionally connected and available to each of them in special and unique ways. If you have trouble in this area, try building your skills in this area by talking and playing more with your child. As you spend more time with your child, you will be in a better position to understand where he or she is coming from and will more easily read emotional signals and communications. As you get to know your child better, it will become easier to understand his or her emotions.*

- *Nurture in each of your children and through positive interactions between siblings a sense of standards with respect to relationships—inner standards of fairness, justice, kindness, empathy, and other aspects of morality in human behavior. Also, show and describe to them "social causality," that is, "He did this because she did that"-type of thinking. Give them the words to their actions so you help them internalize such views of relationships, even very early on when they do not seem to understand it all. They will, nonetheless, be impressed by the labels, and you will get their attention.*

- *Have playtime with your children, either separately if it is possible for you, or together, designating the "leader" for a certain period of time. Again, such designations are in line with fairness in relationships.*

more influenced by peers than parents. Although the link between adolescent drug use and peers is valid, a "third variable" needs to be interjected to complete the picture: Parents affect the types of friends an adolescent chooses; therefore, parents affect drug use.

Indeed, most child-development research indicates that parents matter a great deal in influencing many aspects of their children's peer relationships, including their children's ability to withstand peer pressure related to drugs, smoking, and sexual initiation at a young age. If a child enjoys emotionally connected relationships with his or her parents, the child is more likely to pick emotionally healthy friends and engage in fewer problematic behaviors, including the risky behaviors seen in many adolescents. Harris's book presents some good information about the importance of peers, but

---

continued...

- Take the responsibility to know if each of your children has his or her emotional needs met by taking the Emotional Availability Self-Assessment for each of them to see if each child is secure in his or her relationship with you. It is easier to resolve issues with these healthy emotional connections with you than without them. If the emotional connection with any of your children needs work, do that work simultaneously—don't sidestep it. Take that responsibility!

- Through your own example and through discussions with your children, help each of them learn to emit appropriate emotional signals (mostly positive) and learn to read others' emotional signals. For example, when a child frequently feels rejected by his or her friends, withdraws from interactions, and cannot talk about it for a long time (and these friends' behaviors do not objectively seem rejecting and/or they try very hard to be inclusive), you might work with your child to try reacting in more appropriate ways, ways that match the intensity of the situation. Instead of sulking endlessly, she can be coached to verbally express, "Hey, I don't like it when you exclude me . . . so please try not to, okay?" and then move on with interactions, rather than being stuck in silent treatment.

---

it excludes critical information about the all-important link of parenting with a child's choice of peers.

It is actually quite positive that parents have so much control over how their children turn out. If children were influenced only by their peers, it would be like "the blind leading the blind." Your relationship with your child, if it is an emotionally available one, is more likely to affect his or her choices of friends, ability to be a leader rather than the follower in these friendships, and ability to leave friendships if they run counter to your child's belief systems.

EMOTIONAL INTELLIGENCE AND EMOTIONAL AVAILABILITY

Emotional intelligence has become such a buzzword among parents and professionals alike that it has become an explanation for why some children do well with people and others do not. The idea of emotional intelligence, defined by author Daniel Goleman as a combination of emotional and interpersonal skills, was a critical step forward in our understanding that intelligence involves more than cognition or the intellect. (In fact, there is now a greater appreciation of multiple intelligences, including musical, artistic, athletic, and so on.) Emotional intelligence has been linked with two important issues: (1) Emotional intelligence can be learned, and (2) emotional intelligence can lead to success in life.

Emotional intelligence as explained by Goleman, however, is considered a quality or trait within the individual rather than a quality of relationship. In fact, for babies, as the well-known French pediatrician D. Winnicott has said, "There is no baby, only a baby and mother." I would rephrase that to include the father, but the idea is certainly correct—the baby does not exist outside a relationship. I would even take this a step further and say that children also exist in a relationship with the parents—that there is no such thing as a "child" outside a relationship. No evidence exists to indicate that being socially related and socially savvy is something inborn or "within the individual." Relationships create the propensity for appropriate relatedness, and people can have an emotionally available relationship with one parent but not the other parent. Or a person might have an emotionally available relationship with a grandparent that makes all the difference.

In contrast to emotional intelligence, emotional availability is a way to understand not only a parent-child relationship, but also how such relationships affect other relationships. Just as there is no child without the parent, the parent-child relationship is the relationship that prepares children for how relationships "feel." As well-known child-development researcher Alan Sroufe and his colleagues have described it, "Relationships create relationships." How parent-child emotional availability "feels" to a child is then carried forward into the child's new relationships with peers.

I would venture to say that we all have some coaching to do with our children in the area of peer relationships, but the foundation for how relationships feel comes from the parent-child relationship. Your child "knowing" at a gut level that he or she needs to be treated well by others, for example, or "knowing" that being enthusiastic draws other children closer or being sad and withdrawn moves others away are all aspects that occur at a subconscious level, gleaned from years of being in an important relationship with a parent or other primary caregiver. In fact, your child probably looks like you, in the sense of emotional expression. If you are enthusiastic and playful, your child is likely to be so as well.

EMOTIONALLY HEALTHY RELATIONSHIPS AT HOME LEAD TO EMOTIONALLY HEALTHY RELATIONSHIPS WITH PEERS

Some very interesting work shows that if we create emotionally healthy relationships with our children, they are more likely to enjoy prosocial, nonaggressive, and nonvictimizing relationships with their peers. In our research on school relationships, we have assessed parent-child emotional availability during the pre-kindergarten year (almost a year before children are in school) and child-peer relationships during the kindergarten year. We have found that greater emotional availability in the mother-child relationship increases the chances of positive, pro-social interactions in the kindergarten classroom and during recess. (We have no reason to think that the father-child relationship is any different, although we have yet to analyze our results on that relationship.)

In addition, we found that children who come from more emotionally available homes are less likely to be aggressive with their classmates (in either words or deeds) and/or be the target of victimization (by either words or deeds). Even though boys are typically viewed as more aggressive than girls, our findings hold regardless of the child's gender—possibly because girls show what others have referred to as indirect/relational aggression with words (name-calling) and sometimes indirect deeds (organizing cliques, bad-mouthing, or gossiping), whereas boys show more direct, physical aggression. In our study, we disregarded the type of aggression shown and included all instances of aggressive behavior, so gender differences were eliminated.

Other research also indicates that, even before kindergarten, children who have had the benefit of secure relationships with their mothers are judged differently by their preschool peers than children who have not had this benefit. An interesting study has found that preschoolers from secure mother-child relationships (as judged by the "strange situation" procedure described in Chapter 2) receive more visual attention from their preschool classmates than do children from insecure mother-child relationships. We infer from this that children from secure, generally emotionally available environments are more attractive in some way to their peers.

Interestingly, one study examined only this issue. Preschoolers were shown pictures of children and asked to rate them on "attractiveness," with no definition of attractiveness provided. Children from secure mother-child relationships were judged as more attractive than children from insecure relationships. The study was conducted with a group of children from regular classrooms with no known bias on attractiveness selection based on parent-child history or any other criterion. Thus, there is something about the presence of children from secure relationships that makes them more visible and attractive to their peers.

Children from secure relationships also are likely to be more "ego-resilient," meaning that neither are they overcontrolled, rigid, and inflexible in their approach to interpersonal issues nor are they undercontrolled and easily "falling apart" in the face of stress.

Another reason for trying to build security into the parent-child relationship is that secure children are more flexible in their relationships with their peers. For example, studies suggest that although insecure/dependent and insecure/avoidant children do not work or play well together, secure children seem to be able to interact harmoniously with all types of children. Although secure children prefer to have their close friendships with other secure children, they are also able to coexist with many different types of children, suggesting flexibility and peacemaking ability as well as (perhaps) the ability to be optimistic about relationships and bring out the best in others.

One of the very interesting facets of secure and emotionally available relationships is that parents don't absolutely "need" to do something to ensure a positive start on peer relationships. Given that most children are securely attached (approximately 70 percent of all children in this country are secure in their relationships with their parents and come from emotionally available homes), it is not surprising that most children do not receive concentrated "teaching" from anyone on social skills with peers. Secure children seem to develop an intuitive sense about relationships from their parents that they then carry forward into their peer relationships. The qualities of emotional availability that these secure children garner from their parent-child relationships—enthusiasm, positivity, optimism, ability to have fun, responsiveness to others, involvement and inclusion of others, and lack of anger and hostility—are then used in other relationships. Notice that these "skills" are "emotion skills" learned by living in an emotionally available environment. Thus, direct "teaching" is not the only means of helping your child with peer relationships.

Emotionally available parents, however, do also offer "coaching." John Gottman, a researcher at the University of Washington, has presented a nice description of "emotion coaching." Such coaching is something emotionally available parents do (for example, "The next time Johnny does that to you, speak up for yourself"). By offering this kind of emotion coaching, parents become more emotionally available. Let me remind you, however, that as a parent you need to create an emotional connection and foundation first, lest your child see your coaching as interfering or you telling him or her what to do.

Best-selling books such as *How to Talk So Kids Will Listen and Listen So*

Kids Will Talk by Adele Faber and Elaine Mazlish also have superb suggestions on how to talk to your child in a respectful manner that evokes positive qualities in the child. I recommend such books with the following caution, however: Although language is an important vehicle for delivering your intents and messages, the emotional relationship needs to be solid before your child will truly listen and respond. Knowing just the right things to say about peer relationships or coaching your child about "playground politics" will barely make a dent if you have not established a secure and connected *nonverbal* relationship before you ever open your mouth. (Remember that most of what goes on between parent and baby during the first year of life is the language of bodily contact, soothing, singing, and the words of emotion.) Of course, speaking in respectful ways and coaching at "teachable" moments can go a long way toward helping you and your child form or maintain emotionally available relationships.

Although emotional availability in parent-child relationships can help enhance the quality of peer relationships, one aspect of peer interaction cannot be taught but can only be experienced: having a happy presence. Studies indicate that popular children have a more enthusiastic presence, and such displays of happiness, or at least contentment, are difficult to teach directly. Rather, happiness is developed on the basis of a happy life. Although children show different styles of being insecure in their relationships with peers—some angry and rejecting; others shy, distressed, or withdrawn—there is really only one style of being secure, and that is a positive, happy presence. Happy children contribute joy or at least positive intent to people and situations. Because they like themselves, they also move away from and/or ignore children who are angry or sad. Happy children create a positive interaction loop, putting themselves in situations where they can contribute happiness and be made happy in return.

Children who are secure and from emotionally available relationships have close friendships, but these close friendships are not exclusive—they have permeable boundaries that allow other children to join in. In contrast, children who are insecure have been shown to create exclusive, possessive friendships, as if they want to or need to keep the friend away from others. Insecure children also show friendships that have a bully-victimization dynamic.

Often, parents see qualities such as sociability as an important temperament quality affecting peer relationships. Studies repeatedly find, however, that it is not sociability that promotes pro-social and positive interactions with peers, but rather how children form relationships. Although more sociable children will seek out peers more frequently, they are not more likely to have positive exchanges unless they have a positive view of relationships, which comes from their prior relationships at home and at school. Simply put, relationships set the stage for other relationships.

Research conducted by Jerome Kagan and his colleagues at Harvard University on a group of "inhibited" children is also interesting in this light. Approximately 10 percent of children are born inhibited, also known as "shy and sensitive." Studies have suggested that inhibited children from secure relationships are very open to forming other relationships, but inhibited children from insecure relationships (particularly of the avoidant kind) are closed off to other relationships. It is as if they came into the world closed down biologically to social interactions and then they become shut down more fully due to the rejection they internalize from their caregivers. The positive message here is that even inhibited children are open to relationships if they have been raised in emotionally supportive environments. Inhibited children raised in an environment that is not fully nurturing, however, can shut themselves off from relationships entirely.

We also know that children who are easy in temperament are no more likely to be secure than children with difficult temperaments, and so the child's nature is not by itself a determinant of the child's bent toward a particular style of relationships. Kagan and his colleagues have found that when such shy and sensitive children are encouraged by their parents to try new things (for example, more playdates with a variety of playmates rather than the old and familiar group of friends) by five years of age, they are less shy and inhibited. Parents can make a dramatic difference in a child's ability to overcome a predisposition to shy away from others. Such parents seemed to know that with some extra help and guidance, their children could become more social and socialized. Left without parental intervention, these shy/sensitive children are at risk for shyness and even a diagnosable social phobia once they reach adolescence and puberty. With parental intervention, however, such children learn to be emotionally available to others and, therefore, have greater confidence in their "people skills." Armed with such skills, they are thus less likely to suffer the deleterious consequences of their anxiety-prone nature. Again, in nature versus nurture, nature is not destiny. Parental interventions of emotional availability can literally transform a child's nature.

> Connie was a shy little girl, much like her mother, Janet. In other words, both were born with an inhibited temperament, at least genetically. But Janet had "liberated" herself from such inhibition during her adult life and vowed to help her daughter grow to be more outgoing than she herself had. She encouraged playdates at their home and later at others' homes, she enrolled Connie in many classes that gave her exposure to new and unfamiliar situations and people, and most of all, she gave Connie confidence in meeting these challenges. By age four, when Janet enrolled Connie in preschool, Connie was already very comfortable around adults and children and was one of the most sought-after kids in her preschool classroom. "Connie doesn't push herself on others," Janet said. "People just respond to her." Janet not only gave her daughter many new opportunities to grow but also framed her "shyness" in a positive light that likely gave Connie a positive image of herself.

DIFFERENCES BETWEEN FATHERS' AND MOTHERS' EMOTIONAL AVAILABILITY

Studies indicate that the emotional availability of the mother appears to be more highly predictive of a child's peer relationships than that of the father. This is a general finding in child development—that the relationship with the mother has more far-reaching effects on children. However, most research has been done on two-parent, middle-income families in which mothers were the primary caregivers. It makes sense that the parent who spends the greater amount of time with the child or children will have the greatest influence on their lives.

But what of the role of the father? And what of the role of mothers and fathers who are single parents or who share joint parenting responsibility? Studies indicate that in two-parent families in which the mother is the primary caregiver, although children are more affected by the relationship with the mother, the father-child relationship also has an important role. *When both parents are emotionally available, children are more likely to show the best possible social outcomes with their peers.* If you are a mother, enjoying a positive emotional relationship with your child already puts your child ahead of the game in terms of social skills. If your spouse also has such a relationship with your child, your child will have an even greater advantage in the world of peer relationships.

What about a divorced family in which the child resides with one parent exclusively or perhaps lives with each parent at different times? (See Chapter 15 for more on divorced families.) No research has been done to help us understand family structures after divorce and the effects on the children, but we do know that a divorced family differs little from a nondivorced family in most ways. We have every reason to believe, therefore, that the quality of relationships with both parents best predicts a child's ability to form quality relationships himself or herself.

Although there is no current research to prove this claim, I will take clinical license here and say that children need only one really good parent to learn to create emotionally available relationships. Most of the time I am assuming—and I want to clearly label this an assumption rather than a research fact—that the residential parent is the more competent and committed parent, and the quality of emotional availability of this parent is likely to be key. If both parents are involved and the child shares residences, however, even one competent parent will go a long way in promoting positive outcomes for the child.

Think for a minute about your own parents. How many of us had two great parents in terms of their emotional availability? In my research on adult women and men, fewer than 30 percent recalled two emotionally available parents in the families in which they were raised. However, 70 percent recalled at least one emotionally available parent. It likely takes one parent to help a child develop a sense or a "feel" for emotional connection as a legacy for future relationships. It makes great sense, therefore, for at least one parent in a family to develop the skills of emotional availability because this one good relationship can pave the way for positive relationships with peers.

If you choose to be the more emotionally competent parent, you can also be instrumental in coaching your spouse to become more emotionally available with the children. Such coaching can have far-reaching effects on your child's peer competence. If your child's emotional needs are met in at least one relationship, he or she then can have a different outlook on the second parent as well as the child's own peers, and he or she will be able to approach other relationships with confidence.

Although supporting your ex-spouse might not work in high-conflict post-divorce families, it is worth the effort for your child's sake.

HOW EMOTIONAL AVAILABILITY AFFECTS A CHILD'S PEER RELATIONSHIPS

What peer skills can be learned through parent-child emotional availability?

- **Emotional expression.** Emotions are contagious. We know that parents who play with their children raise children with whom other kids like to play. Likely, it is the enthusiasm and emotional expressiveness that develops during such playtime that is so attractive to other children.

- **Emotional "display rules."** Given that emotions are so important, attend to your child's "display rules"—the "face work" that is considered appropriate in different contexts. Face work is knowing what face to put on in different social situations. Parental facial expression that is appropriate to particular contexts becomes the ground on which children learn their own display rules. Once, when a client came in with his son, I immediately (and genuinely) commented on the resemblance between them. The dad smiled and said, "He's my adoptive son." Sure, he was right, but I was right, too. Even though they did not share genes, they shared their emotions, and I could literally see the father in the son.

   If you notice that your child does not know the intuitive rules about face work, namely, knowing what face to put on at the play-ground (for example, that being pensive on the swings is not what other kids are drawn to) or knowing how to react to peers from school when they meet unexpectedly at the mall (for example, ig-noring Sally as she runs toward you), some coaching on this all-important area of nonverbal behavior is important. Such "display rules" are more easily learned (or relearned) at a young age. The work is well worth it because children who are judged by children to be "off" (read as "different in some way") do less well with peers, and their overall adjustment suffers. Much of social competence is about having appropriate emotional expressions for the particular context.

· **Emotion coaching.**

Rhonda was generally an emotionally available mother. Although she was very emotionally connected with her son Eric, he had trouble getting other kids' attention on the playground. As a result, Eric was ig-nored a good deal of the time. Rhonda took it upon herself to coach him on the talent of physical communication and appropriate use of body language. She directly taught him to look other kids in the eye in a ro-bust manner and to say what he wanted to say when he was close enough to them, rather than far away. Needless to say, Eric caught on quickly and used the skill. It helped in such a teaching situation that he knew he could trust his mother and that she would be a supportive presence as he tried this new skill.

If your child is having problems initiating interactions with peers and/or joining a peer group, practice some of these skills with him or her in an emotionally expressive and playful manner. We know, for example, that children who successfully gain peer entry stay close to the group and then gradually join in, usually by doing what the others are doing. A child who is more expres-sive and enthusiastic is more likely to get the attention of other children and less likely to be ignored as he or she enters the group.

· **Emotional empathy.** Help your child see the connection between what he or she does and the feelings of others (also known as "empathy"). If bullies could truly feel the emotions of their victims, they would no longer bully. As you interact in an empathic way with your child, your child will feel the importance of empathy toward others by your example. Such empathy can be taken one step further by encouraging him or her to make repairs by apologizing in words or deeds. It is important not only to feel what others feel but also to behave in a just way.

· **Emotional impulse control.** Control your rage, and your child will learn to control his or her own hostile impulses toward peers. Children learn how they should behave toward others from their caregivers' examples and what these adults allow themselves to do. Don't give yourself (or other adults) permission to display hostility when you would never tolerate such behavior from your child. Just because adults are older doesn't give them a license for inappropriate behavior. Don't excuse in yourself (or your spouse, boyfriend, girlfriend, or grandparents) what you would never excuse in your child. Even when there is not physical violence, constant expressions of hostility toward others makes a child not only see the world in a hostile light, but also have difficulties with control of his or her own hostile impulses toward others. Be it toward your child, your spouse, or anyone else in your life—including the check-out clerk—know your point of no return.

· **Set up play opportunities with peers.** As a parent, try to set up opportunities for peer interactions for your child—do not overorganize them, but create exposure and room for experience of such relationships. Research indicates that unstructured activities seem to be the most helpful. Evidence also indicates, however, that children are able to stay with peers in a fun-filled way much longer if they have at least one adult who is "indirectly" structuring (for example, allowing children to lead or making suggestions to avert or sidestep problems in nonintrusive ways). Similarly, encourage and structure your child's peer relationships. Even when you are not physically there, connect and structure at a psychological and emotional level through your discussions.

The following is an example of parental structuring for successful peer interactions:

MOM: How was school today?

JANE: Okay, I guess. *(She seems a little down)*

MOM: I thought you said you were going to study at Claire's house after school.

JANE: *(Glumly)* Claire said she didn't want to study with me.

MOM: Oh? That probably didn't feel very good, did it? Why would she do that? *(Sympathetically)*

JANE: She wanted to invite a couple boys over. I just wanted to study 'cause we've got that big French test at the end of the week, but Claire said I was just being dumb and that we could study and have the guys over, too!

MOM: If you didn't feel comfortable having those boys over, I'm proud of you for saying no. That took courage.

JANE: Yeah, but now I'm afraid Claire won't want to be my friend anymore.

MOM: Honey, you and Claire have been friends for a long time. Do you think there's a way you can talk about this with her so she'll understand why you didn't want to study with the boys there?

JANE: Well . . . she gets better grades than me in French. I have to study a lot harder than she does. I don't mind studying with the guys after school on stuff I don't have to work so hard on. Maybe I could ask her if we could study French by ourselves and then work on history with the guys.

MOM: Would you be comfortable with that?

JANE: Yeah, I think so.

MOM: *(Smiling)* Now, can I be a mom for a moment and ask that Claire's mother be around if these guys come over? Or better yet, do you want to invite Claire and the guys over here to study one day?

JANE: That'd be great, Mom. Thanks.

In this case, the mom left plenty of room for Jane to express her feelings about the situation with Claire. She praised Jane for standing up to her friend and offered the opportunity for Jane to come up with her own solution to the problem. Then she used humor to suggest some options that would give her confidence that her daughter would be properly supervised as she interacted with the boys.

PEER RELATIONSHIP TYPES

- **"Moving toward" peers.** It is easy to spot children who seem at ease in the peer group. They are gregarious and respond with pleasure to their peers and involve them often and in positive ways. The research on peer interactions has referred to such children as either popular or average, the latter meaning that they are socially competent but not necessarily at the extreme of the continuum. Research also indicates that children need to be merely average, not necessarily superpopular to do well in the world of peers. These children are referred to as "moving toward" others.

- **"Moving away from" peers.** Many children, however, seem to shrink from social interactions with others—they "move away." Much of this quality is biological, some children, as we described in Chapter 6, are simply born more temperamentally inhibited or sensitive. One of the nicest things I see most parents naturally doing is embracing the uniqueness of their children—be it temperamental gregariousness or inhibition.

    Genes have a lot to do with temperaments, and parents have a lot to do with later personality—but there is a difference between the two. Help your reticent child join a group by providing some suggestions and structuring. If he or she is wary about going to other homes, don't just say, "Okay." Invite other kids to your home. When your child becomes more comfortable with peer interactions in his or her own home, then encourage your child to take the risk and go to visit a friend. With this type of child, it is easy to cater to the child's needs, to protect him or her from "the big bad world," and to rush to him or her in an oversolicitous way. But such behavior only promotes this type of distressed temperament. Instead, slowly and patiently begin to build robustness in your child, with the expectation that "he [or she] can do it."

A lot of sensitive parenting is about what parents think and expect, not just what they do. Your thoughts get reflected in the subtle aspects of your behavior; you might be transmitting qualities that you do not want to transmit to your child. With insensitive parenting, your highly sensitive child might receive the message that you think he or she is weak or sensitive (in the pejorative sense). In contrast, with sensitive parenting, your highly sensitive child might receive the message that you think it's wonderful that he or she is so full of feeling and has a rich internal life and is, therefore, sensitive (in the positive sense).

Recall the research of Jerome Kagan of Harvard University described earlier in this chapter. Parents who interact in an emotionally available way with their highly sensitive children appreciate the unique quality these children have for observation and intense feeling, and embrace rather than look down on it. It is likely that such parental thinking mediates parental encouragement to engage the world. If a parent thinks that such sensitive temperament is a weakness and, worse yet, a fixed trait, the parent might feel helpless to change it. Without experiences that build social competence, such children shrink from the world and isolate themselves. With successful peer experiences (enjoyed over a period of time), however, these children can and do become socially competent.

· **"Moving against" peers.** In contrast to the natural timidity of the "moving away from peers" child just described, many children are aggressive and treat others in an aggressive way—they "move against." Although such children might have the type of temperament that naturally makes them more aggressive, some of this behavior is also learned in the home. Such girls tend to show what we call relational or indirect aggression, such as gossiping and name-calling, whereas boys show physical aggression. Both types are called bullying.

The parents of children who bully might not bully in the same way. What is intriguing is the more subtle form of bullying that goes on in families. The accusations of significant others can cut to the core. Such put-downs can form the basis for how we reject peers, although we have no idea that we are bullying in this way. For example, the silent treatment a father gives his child when he disagrees with him or her, but would never talk about out in the open, can make a child feel that he or she should not and could not express feelings directly but needs to do so in subliminal ways. Such silent treatment (which can seem like psychological abandonment) can, in fact, seem threatening. With peers, a child might then totally withdraw from interactions with a friend who transgressed.

Another example would be a mother who accepts only positive talk (even when the father has been drinking too much) and does not want to face obvious problems; she is requiring everyone in the family to be in denial with her. Her house rules are "don't talk, don't tell anyone what really happens around here, keep secrets, and pretend." Her children are told, "Dad didn't mean to do that; he really loves you." In this example, children learn that fear is respect and that love is expressed in strange ways; they are required to have distorted views of other people's behaviors. In peer relationships, such a view of relationships can be played out, with the bully being perceived as "having a bad day; when he is less tired, he will be nice to me." A child buys into the dance of walking on eggshells through such family dynamics and can transfer that to peer dynamics.

Living with a parent, two parents, or sibling(s) who show repeated bullying in the form of put-downs, name-calling, manipulative withdrawal can be a form of victimization. And victims (just like bullies) will re-create the family system they came from as they move out into the world.

Talk to your child about appropriate behavior and about the shades of gray in child-child and adult-child interactions, and help feel your child's own emotions and show him or her how to take the perspective of others. Help your child understand that not all aspects of a situation are wonderful and not all aspects of a situation are terrible, but there are textures and shades to our attributions and our relationships.

A key ingredient in improving hostile behavior is to change hostile attributions. The research of Kenneth Dodge and his colleagues at Vanderbilt University indicates that abused children see more hostility in ambiguous situations than do nonabused children. Other research indicates that abused children take much longer to calm down after an altercation on the playground compared to nonabused children. In turn, abused children engage in more hostile acts at school than do nonabused children. They have become sensitized to aggression. Work with your child to create more positive attributions around the "gray zone" of experience.

Let your child know when you notice appropriate behavior, and applaud such behavior. Work out a signal (perhaps even a thumbs-up!) with your child for when his or her behavior gets out of hand that will tell him or her to act differently.

EMOTIONAL AVAILABILITY CAN MAKE YOUR CHILD LESS ATTRACTIVE TO A BULLY

Although bullies generally pick their victims unconsciously, any child can become entangled in a bully-victim dynamic. Thus, every child should be educated about how to respond in ways that "surprise" bullies.

Be it relational aggression usually conducted by girls (name-calling, gossiping, and the like), or physical aggression conducted by boys, bullies want to be noticed. Sometimes ignoring or staying away from bullies is just enough for a child to disentangle himself or herself. Many secure children (who come from emotionally available relationships) do just this because such dynamics are not familiar to them. We all seek out what is familiar. Children who are not used to aggressive interactions move away. I remember one child, Sasha, who was particularly adept at this tactic. When he saw a ruckus in his preschool classroom, he adeptly and quietly stepped over all the toys scattered about to get to the other side of the room. He moved away from what appeared to him to be problematic.

Because children in emotionally available relationships are raised to be expressive, they are not as attractive to bullies. If your child tends to be quiet or does not express his or her feelings, you can encourage him or her to do so by providing support for that effort. Because emotionally available relationships in the home provide an "honest mirror" of emotions, such children do not distort bullying behavior to be "boys just being boys" or "I'm attractive because he just pulled my bra strap." Bullying is bullying even if it is done in a semiflattering way, as is the case with sexual harassment in the schools.

One of the best ways to disarm a bully is to respond in a surprising way—a way that does not emanate from fear or from feelings of vulnerability. Many children (successfully) have clever "comebacks" or directly say that they don't like that behavior in an assertive tone of voice. They show by their verbal and body language that they are not good targets or that they will not "engage in the dance," or they go get a trusted adult who will help. Perhaps one of the best tactics used by children from emotionally available homes is their use of social support. Such children have social allies in school, and these networks help. A child who is socially isolated is a better candidate for a bully than a child who navigates the social world skillfully. Without a willing and vulnerable partner, bullies often look elsewhere.

TEACH YOUR CHILD HOW TO RELATE TO PEERS THROUGH EXAMPLES IN YOUR HOME

As described in earlier chapters, during infancy, toddlerhood, and throughout childhood, it is important that you play with your child as well as offer opportunities for the child to play with his or her peers. Children model their behaviors with peers on their own relationships with their parents. The more expressive, friendly, and playful the parent, the more likely a child is to be the same way with their peers.

By adolescence, your child is more interested in interacting with his or her own peers than in playing, but a little playful banter and humor still goes a long way toward keeping the two of you emotionally connected and conveying the feeling that you not only accept but cherish the time you have with him or her. The playful and accepting atmosphere makes your adolescent feel like coming back to you for a secure base, despite the fact that adolescents are not supposed to "like" their parents too much. The truth is that most adolescents still need and want to be connected with their parents.

It is impossible for parents to be emotionally happy in a consistent and unwavering fashion from a child's infancy to adolescence. Such overoptimistic and overly happy facades are never real; they usually hide a deeper source of unhappiness. For example, in families with at least one alcoholic, such pressure exists to make everything all right both in terms of feelings and in terms of behaviors that children grow up feeling they cannot express their more negative side. Such denial of feelings exists in many families where children learn to present a good front; in some, to the point of psychopathic tendencies, such individuals brilliantly engage in impression management, but in reality have no feeling for anyone.

Emotional availability is about being "real." Showing your vulnerable sides and your mistakes (to an extent) to your child allows him or her to be human. Being able to feel comfortable with expressing good and bad feelings and to have good and bad days gives your child permission not to be "perfect." If your child sees that you have given yourself permission to feel, he or she is less likely to feel compelled to present a false front of happiness and/or deny his or her own feelings.

Although there are some differences, sibling relationships are often the first forays into peer relationships. It is to your credit as a parent to help your children have good relationships with their siblings. Many parents are under the impression that roughness in sibling relationships is the norm, but the fact is that most children work well and play well with their siblings. You have a great deal of power over the quality of your children's sibling interactions. For example, if bullying is going on (for example, from older to younger), you can play an important structuring role in terms of relationship-building between siblings. The bullying child could be trying to get attention in negative ways as well as needing ways to communicate his or her emotions. Although some conflict is "normal" in all sibling relationships, you have the power to help your children create emotionally available and connected sibling relationships.

No parent acts in a vacuum; peer relationships very quickly become important to your child as he or she enters the world. Yet the quality of your relationship with your child is the most important factor in preparing him or her for creating great friendships with others.

ten

Providing Emotional Support for Learning

A great deal of discussion centers on "kindergarten readiness" and "school readiness." No longer are we thinking of children as being ready to learn when they get to a certain age. Many parents are advised by their children's preschool teachers that an extra year before school entry would be in the children's best interests.

HOW EMOTIONAL AVAILABILITY AFFECTS ATTENTIVENESS AND CONCENTRATION AT SCHOOL

We recently completed a project on how emotional availability is related to kindergarten readiness in the sense of social, emotional, and attentional readiness of the child. This project also examined some aspects of learning through use of standardized tests. One of the most important findings to emerge from this study is that the parental side of emotional availability (parental sensitivity, structuring, nonintrusiveness, and nonhostility), as well as the child's side of emotional availability (child responsiveness to parent and child involvement of parent), predicts what we call a child's "readiness to learn." We found that even when we looked at children with similar levels of language competence (measured with standardized testing), the children from more emotionally available relationships were more likely to be attentive to the teacher than the children from less emotionally available relationships.

This study observed parent–child interactions in a laboratory at the university and then observed the children's attentiveness at school. The observers of the laboratory-based interactions were different from the observers of school attentiveness—what we call "blind" to other aspects of the study. This blind type of study ensures that observers don't mistakenly give higher tallies of attentiveness at school because they have seen a positive interaction in the laboratory or vice versa.

In the laboratory, we set out some Playmobile toys (knights and princesses) and ask the children (usually prekindergartners) and parents to play as they normally would. The play session lasts about twenty minutes, and we film the interaction. We also ask the parents to play with their children with an Etch-A-Sketch, where the parents operate the vertical dial and the children operate the horizontal dial. They are asked to create a house and then a boat (we give them a sketch to work from). This Etch-A-Sketch session lasts approximately five or six minutes. We then score these interactions for the dimensions of emotional availability that I have described in this book: parental sensitivity, structuring, nonintrusiveness, and nonhostility, as well as child responsiveness and child involvement. We have found that for parents and children who seem to be more emotionally connected as judged by these six dimensions, the children are the most attentive to the teacher in the classroom.

One mother, Carla, seemed anxious and worried. During the Etch-A-Sketch exercise, she drew most of the house and boat, giving her son Ricky little chance for autonomy. He looked sad, but rather than acknowledging his emotion signals, Carla continued to do her best to perform the tasks she thought were expected of her in this situation. It increasingly appeared that this was Carla's job. In the Playmobile aspect of the observation, however, Carla began to take a backseat and then completely checked out of the interaction. She provided little structure for Ricky, and he seemed mostly bored. In fact, Carla started to yawn and read a nearby newspaper. Ricky seemed unable to stay with the task of creating a story with knights and princesses without his mother's help and only moved the pieces back and forth somewhat.

At school, Ricky was one of the loners. He had some fleeting interactions with another boy, especially during recess, but otherwise was on his own. In the classroom, when the teacher was teaching the class reading, he was distractible. Ricky's eyes moved across the room and back, and he sometimes turned his head to see other aspects of the room. Ricky's eyes looked glassy, and he sometimes even looked sleepy. He almost seemed to have checked out, except that he was not disruptive in any way. Ricky, therefore, seemed to fit right in, and although the teacher stopped the disruptiveness of other children, she barely noticed Ricky.

Peggy and her mom, Carrie, have an emotionally available relationship with one another. Carrie is spontaneous, animated, and light in her interactions with her daughter. In the laboratory, she allowed Peggy to lead with the Etch-A-Sketch and responded positively to her daughter's constructions with a little verbal encouragement in a light and fun atmosphere. Their relaxed style with one another and their rapport suggested that this really *was* how they played together and was not an act for an audience. Peggy was having fun, giggling, and including Carrie in her play. Carrie was not overly cheerful, but just appropriately so. What was striking was that she seemed to stay clearly available and present with Peggy, never seeming preoccupied or psychologically unavailable.

At school, Peggy was one of the most popular children. She had so many friends that there was even some "disruptiveness" that the teacher needed to address, but such episodes never lasted long and seemed to just be exuberance. The teacher easily controlled such exuberance, and only one reminder was heard during the school observation. When the teacher was teaching, Peggy showed focused, even rapt attention. Peggy seemed genuinely interested and engaged with the teaching and with all other activities—she visually touched base with her friends during transitions from one activity to another but was otherwise well controlled. Carrie's structuring during play showed itself in the way that Peggy could remain contained in the classroom. Peggy's face moved quickly to a smile, and she rarely seemed overserious or emotionally checked out of the classroom. She was very engaged and ready to take in the day—with gusto!

> By being emotionally expressive and playful with your child, you are showing attention. By being "emotionally fed," your child is then able to turn his or her attention to the outside world of learning. Pay attention to your child before he or she needs obvious attention.

The study found this link between parental emotional availability and classroom attentiveness to be strong at the transition point into kindergarten (within the first one to two months of kindergarten). Less classroom attentiveness translates into the need for greater repetition before the child will take in what has been taught. Such a link is "readiness to learn." Parents who want to prepare their children for kindergarten serve them well by having an emotional connection long before kindergarten!

IS YOUR CHILD SECURELY ATTACHED TO SCHOOL?

What makes some kids "attach" to the school as an important and significant influence in their lives while other kids see it as something to be endured? To answer this question, we need to conduct studies on the qualities of schools, the qualities of families, as well as the qualities of children that create a positive and secure context within the school. Some children are bullied in school so they dread each day. One study in New Haven indicated that one-third of school-age children were afraid that they would be bullied that day. Schools must strive to combine competence and nurturing qualities within their walls and become aware of the corrosive effects of bullying and victimization, self-esteem issues of learning-disabled children, and the many other deleterious events rendering our children vulnerable. When the environment is positive and safe, children will potentially "attach" to school and want to continue on a positive trajectory, rather than feel as if the school is a negative environment. One of our studies indicated clearly that children begin to form impressions of school liking and school avoidance (for example, not wanting to go, not having friends) as early as the kindergarten year.

We used to think that school was about cognitive pursuits. We now are realizing through research that there is an "emotional" component to learning. Thus, learning itself as well as the contexts of learning at home and the school environment should be framed in an emotionally positive light. For example, you can use your emotional communication to impart to your child that math is fun, that the teacher is interested in the students, and that you have confidence in your child's ability to master the material—with some support if necessary.

Help your child "attach" to school and school relationships. Children have an attachment to school just as they have an attachment to the family system and to the peer system. You can help make that attachment a secure one.

- *Be involved with the school. When parents are involved in school activities, children feel more connected to the institution of school and see it in a positive way.*

- *Nurture positive interactions between yourself and the teacher(s). Do some emotion brokering on behalf of your spouse in this respect as well. Although no teacher or school is ideal 100 percent of the time, a positive frame and an open-minded, constructive, and nondefensive attitude can help the teacher, the parents, and the child find positive solutions to even challenging situations.*

- *Try not to express hostility about the school or the teacher(s) if the school is "stepping up to the plate." Such hostility would easily translate into less positive attributions about school on the part of your child. It's important to stay positive and optimistic and to frame issues in a positive light. If you are concerned about your child's learning, see the next section.*

WAYS TO MAINTAIN CONNECTION WITH THE SCHOOL
IF YOUR CHILD HAS LEARNING PROBLEMS

Research indicates that parents need to be emotionally available in different contexts. That a parent is emotionally connected during early feeding does not immediately translate into that parent being emotionally connected around learning. In fact, our work indicates that there are even cultural differences on this issue, with Western-culture families showing greater concern about a child's happiness at school and Eastern-culture families being very concerned about academics. How does the emotionally available parent balance academics with a child's happiness?

When their children begin to have learning problems, many parents find it difficult to be attentive to their children's happiness (or the happiness of the family). Many educational psychologists have described "classroom trauma" as a type of post-traumatic stress disorder in children. Children with learning problems are an at-risk group for such classroom trauma and require adult interventions to keep anxiety at manageable lev-

continued...

- *Help your child have a nonconflictual and nondependent relationship with the teacher. Learn whether he or she relies on the teacher in a dependent way (for example, moving toward the teacher and away from peers perhaps) or conflictual way (for example, moving against the teacher as well as against other kids). Help your child engage instead in an emotionally available teacher-child relationship, one that is based on positives rather than neediness or conflict.*

- *Help your child create a "secure base" from which he can explore by having at least one or two school buddies. Peer relationships are very important in the community, but a child will find it difficult to get enthused about learning if he or she is a loner who does not have others at his lunch table or a buddy at recess. Toward this end, make your home a place that is welcoming to other children.*

els and keep self-esteem afloat. Numerous families in my private practice, in which I specialize in the assessment of learning disabilities in children, are traumatized by the education of their children.

If your child is having trouble learning letters, playing pig Latin (there is a link between pig Latin and dyslexia), or creating rhymes, do consult with a specialist around language issues—just in case. One of the nicest interventions and how-to techniques I can suggest is to get the help of a professional in your community. Your child needs testing to understand the cause of his or her learning difficulties. Although it is customary to wait a few years in school before children are diagnosed with reading difficulties, my practice is to see children as early as the kindergarten year or first grade to assess their development. I then recommend a remediation specialist to help with their specific learning difficulties. The earlier the better! Although preschool or prekindergarten is too early to diagnose reading difficulties, many harbingers such as difficulty playing pig Latin, difficulty rhyming, and difficulty learning letters and colors might indicate a potential problem.

Some children show social skills deficits and fall prey to depression. It is important to read your child's signals and communications (for example, that he or she is having difficulty making friends or that he or she has difficulty with self-esteem). Reading emotional signals (for example, knowing when your child is sad or when the sadness has become pervasive) and reading them accurately is the first step in your processing of emotional information. When well-intentioned parents can do this, I would venture to say with great confidence that most will try to do something positive about it. Where parents go wrong is in not knowing that they have to read their children's signals and communications beginning at a very young age, and that they must continue doing that. Read the body language, and respond!

Children who show signs of social skills deficits and/or depression might also have a disorder related to reading (dyslexia), math (dyscalcula), or handwriting (dysgraphia), or another disorder. That "other" might be a "nonverbal learning disability." It is possible for your child to have a right-hemisphere difficulty that creates the context for difficulty in interpreting emotional information; such children also have difficulties with math concepts. This is an important social disability and should also be assessed by a psychologist, as should other difficulties related to social interactions.

Asperger's Syndrome, for example, is a disorder in which a child shows normal cognitive and language development but has difficulty with the social context of language—called pragmatics—and with social interactions. Such children often need to be taught many implied aspects of social interactions as, for example, rhetorical questions, jokes, and the like. Because these children have difficulty with emotional information, their lives in school can be difficult. Many such children might go to college, but they will have difficulty with the social and emotional aspects of college life. It is difficult for them to be emotionally available to others and, hence, they suffer in silence. Intervention programs are designed to help such students with the inferred aspects of social intercourse.

Continue to honor your child's self-esteem around areas in which he or she is good (for example, nonverbal/spatial objects such as puzzles). One child who could hardly read in the fifth grade could nonetheless build a car with his dad, and, much to their credit, his family applauded his unusual engineering talents. Using the self-esteem he garnered from his talent, he was able to remain strong in the face of his learning disability.

Help your child's self-esteem by having him or her contribute to others in some way, be it raising money for charity, helping a younger kid, or some other positive offering. When children have the chance to give of themselves, they realize that we all live in an interdependent society where we share our strengths. Such giving is one way he or she can find a "strength."

Be sure your child's teacher is emotionally available. Adults sometimes feel that they have the license to bully children, and many teachers, unfortunately, still bully children (for example, humiliate or belittle them by saying "You're just lazy" due to their own learning issues). Further, make sure you are not projecting your frustrations about your child's learning issues onto the teacher and school. Maintain a positive partnership with the teacher and school. Focus on solutions rather than doling out blame.

The school years are particularly difficult for children with learning problems. Research indicates, however, that as adults, most such individuals find their niche and are well adjusted within it. When we help our children maintain a positive self-image and encourage the strengths in their academic, social, or other areas, we help them find that positive niche, rather than allow them to wallow in self-blame and other-blame. Helping our children find ways to diffuse and resolve "classroom trauma" (which can be long-lasting if unrecognized) is part of being emotionally "there" for them.

Ted was a shy child who had had a terrible year in kindergarten. Although he was a whiz with numbers, he was not learning to read easily, and the relationship with his dad in particular had become very strained. The family, however, decided to create a positive experience for everyone. They "shopped around" until they located a small, private school specializing in individualized education (with small classes and lots of attention given to each child's individual needs). Soon, Ted's emotionally available teacher, Phyllis, recognized Ted and his "book buddy," Aaron, for doing a great job together. Their quality reading time was recognized publicly at the "Friday morning meeting" (conducted every Friday at 8:30 with the whole school present). Ted was beginning to securely attach to school and not experience the trauma he had experienced in

Stay sensitive and attuned to your child's learning.

- *Take responsibility as a parent not to buy into negativistic thinking at school, should it exist. Create a culture of optimism and resilience in your own home that will provide an example for your child.*

- *Don't blame or shame as a way to encourage your child to do more work.*

- *Do structure work space and teach work skills, but do not do your child's work for him or her.*

- *Reinforce the road to success; that is, take small steps to the goal. Help your child break down apparently insurmountable or overwhelming tasks into smaller sizes. If your child is afraid to be in the school play, have him or her practice first to the family. In this way, your child can experience success.*

kindergarten. With many other such events, Ted began to feel comfortable and secure enough to learn. Six months into first grade, Ted was loving every minute of school, and the problems of kindergarten were a distant memory. He felt good about himself and was engaging in his work at the pace that was right for him.

"PERFECTIONISM" IN CHILDREN WITH RESPECT TO SCHOOL

Parents are understandably thrilled when a child shows achievement in school. We know that parents who are warm *and* have high expectations of their children have children who are achievement-oriented in a positive, perfection-oriented, but nonanxious way. Their achievement motivation comes from an inner sense of security, and they have the motivation to succeed. They get into a flow with work, and such "flow" (interest, engagement, and intense motivation to know more) sustains them to get to the heights of knowledge in a particular area.

---

continued...

- *Read your child's emotional signals about school and friends, and help make school and learning a fun (rather than always a serious) situation.*

- *Enter into a positive partnership with the school and with the teacher(s) and other professionals (for example, remediation specialist) in finding solutions to your child's learning difficulties. Be your child's advocate in finding a professional who can diagnose and remediate; schools have been known to respond to positive parental pressure to hire professionals for remediation once they are sold on it by a psychologist. Children with learning problems can be helped. The keys are early intervention and remediation geared toward the specific difficulty.*

- *Keep in mind, and highlight for your child, his or her strengths. It is through believing in those strengths that a child with learning problems will become resilient. Be his ally in keeping a positive self-image afloat.*

Other children, however, are achievement-oriented but with a perfectionistic edge. The difference here, of course, is that perfectionistic children have a "need" to be perfectionistic. Such children usually achieve (or overachieve) out of a need to prove themselves, and significant anxiety accompanies this need. Parents of such children are usually cool, critical, and/or hostile in their behaviors, perhaps subtly so beneath a warm demeanor.

> Dana had a cool and distant relationship with her mother, Ingrid, but Ingrid had an especially close and special relationship with her other daughter, Emily. Dana naturally felt rejected by her mother. To get attention in the family, she sought to get attention at school. The more Dana excelled in school, the more she felt good about herself. She felt that she had to be perfect for her mother to notice and accept her. Interestingly, Ingrid barely noticed Dana's achievements (or overachievements). She was still mainly concerned about Emily, who was the less attractive, the less bright, and the less promising of the two girls. Interestingly, Dana became valedictorian of her high school class. However, once she got to college, she was crushed by her first B and plummeted into the depths of depression. Dana had no way to cope with her own imperfections. Ingrid did not notice this change in Dana's behavior—she was still mainly connected with Emily. It was up to Dana and Dana alone to pull herself out of her rut, and she succeeded to do so. Dana was a participant in one of our research projects, and to my knowledge, the story was a positive one in that Ingrid and Dana became close as adults. Ingrid realized that she had not been much of a mother to her daughter during her childhood and adolescence, and tried hard to make up for it when both were adults. It's never too late!

Perfectionism is an escape from reality, as children anesthetize themselves from the world by throwing all their energy into the world of work. Studies indicate that perfectionism is related to teen suicide risk as well as many other problems such as anxiety, depression, and eating disorders. Perfectionism has even been empirically linked with denials of unwanted pregnancies by teenagers. Teens from loving homes are sometimes reluctant to disappoint their parents and even fail to tell them (and fail to tell themselves!) that they are pregnant until it can no longer be denied. Many cases of infanticide have been linked with such perfectionism or, more correctly, the pursuit of perfectionism. Therefore, parents preparing their children for the adolescent and teen years should be concerned about that balance between wanting to raise children who achieve and creating a situation so their children achieve for the wrong reasons.

Don't push your child. Some parents are so concerned about learning—even in their babies—that they use flashcards and other gimmicks to give their babies a "head start." In the earliest years and during preschool, the best type of learning is through naturally occurring experiences that take place in an emotionally positive atmosphere. Remember, an important aspect of emotional availability is the quality of "being there" as a nonintrusive presence and being able to follow your child's lead, rather than "taking over." Children whose cues are followed (rather than overwhelmed by their parents' suggestions, activities, and needs) get the message that they can make a difference in the world and become encouraged to further try out their skills. By hanging back a little, you give your child permission to learn about the aspects of the world that interest him or her.

Also, be aware of whether you are or have been pushing your child toward success and perfectionism because you have a need (related to how you were raised) to have grandeur in your life. You might be making your child perform by projecting your own needs onto your child. Don't "achieve by proxy" or, worse yet, "proxy by distortion" (project onto your child what you did when you were a child, what your own parents wished you had done when you were a child, or what you wish you had done when you were a child but did not get to do). Before you push and shove your child to the front of the line (clearly intrusive, but so noble, once again), know that a child put in such a situation generally burns out sooner than other kids and becomes "lazy."

Separate your own needs from what is in the best interests of your child. Be sure you know where that line of separation is. You are then showing good boundaries, one of the hallmarks of having worked out your own issues about how you were raised. Examine whether your parents had difficulty letting you differentiate from them in becoming your own person; if these issues remain unresolved, you might have such difficulties with your own child. The goal to have a high-achieving child is so noble that it is not always recognized as a problem. You can be intrusive with your child and overstructure for the most well-meaning reasons. You must recognize, however, that to be truly emotionally available to face the world, your child needs to be seen and treated as separate from you and needs to be seen not only in one way (for example, as a talented child) but with his or her age-appropriate needs for security and emotional connections. If given the choice, rarely will a child push himself or herself toward perfectionism unless the child took some funds from one "bank account" (the account of "real feelings and emotions") and put it into another "bank account" (the one with "cognitive and intellectual pursuits"). Your perfectionist child is really overdrawing from the emotional availability bank account to please you or others. Emotional availability is about parenting with a heart and head, rather than parenting with only the head.

Related to the need to be perfect, your child might be feeling that he or she is not living up to his or her standards. Even a talented child can fall prey to feelings of failure and depression. Read the signs of depression in children—which look different than in adult depression—because it can manifest itself as irritability and "acting out" (along with lack of pleasure, sleeping or eating difficulties, and/or feelings of hopelessness). Talk to and "be there" for your child. Many such children have high standards for themselves and identify a "failure" as emanating from a stable, fixed quality rather than a quality that can be changed easily. Try to work with your child so he or she begins to view difficulties as correctable, rather than as fixed personality or intellectual deficits. Being interested in your child's internal life is a gift, and moving your child from all-or-nothing thinking or catastrophizing to having more positive perceptions is also a gift you can give your child. This is another opportunity to show your child that he or she can trust you during the tough times. Your child can use you as a "secure base" from which to tackle difficult times.

Also, talk to your child about what he or she is thinking and whether he or she has ever thought about ending his or her life. By doing this, you will not put ideas into your child's head, but you will demonstrate your sensitivity to his or her emotional and physical safety. If your child has been thinking about suicide (and even if not), professional help might be needed because suicide is the third-leading cause of death for adolescents, and it can also be a risk for children. I have seen elementary school–age children with such thoughts, which sometimes lead to suicide attempts.

THE IMPORTANCE OF AUTHORITATIVE PARENTING IN SCHOOL PERFORMANCE

A large number of studies have been conducted on authoritative versus authoritarian parenting, typologies developed by the well-known Berkeley psychologist Diana Baumrind. Although these terms sound sim-

---

Learning and exploration cannot proceed without mistakes and an accepting atmosphere in the learning process.

- Rather than seeing your child's faults or noting his or her shortcomings, dwell on your child's strengths. (Some mistaken parents have said they need to criticize so their children can improve.)

- Teach your child skills of resilience by rewarding and being in awe of a "comeback" after a difficult task. Take notice of behaviors that are not helpless but mastery-oriented, where your child is optimistic about a learning goal or how far he or she has come in some area. Reinforce the fact that, in life, the challenges are just as important as what comes easily. Such rewards can occur in the context of sensitive discussions that help structure and shape (and perhaps help rebuild) your child's ego.

- In demonstrating that you are emotionally connected to your child (not just saying "I love you" and then yelling at him or her), you give your child the message that he or she is "loveworthy." In this way, you let your child know that being perfect is not the only way he or she can be seen by you. Make sure your child is visible to you—literally—rather than having him or her feel invisible. If you truly see your child and delight in what you see, your child would not need to have indirect means to show his or her need for attention.

ilar, the difference is in the types of control used and in the level of warmth.

Authoritative parents combine warmth with an appropriate degree of structuring. Authoritarian parents show little warmth in the context of strict control. Another difference can be seen in what happens to the children of authoritative and authoritarian parents. Children from authoritative homes do very well in school because positive performance is encouraged in a warm and friendly manner, and life is structured to support school-related behaviors such as study habits, getting to school on time, involvement with the teacher and the school, and so on. The children of authoritarian parents also do well in school, but the difference is the level of distress these children endure. Many children of authoritarian parents who do well also harbor distress, anxiety, and depression within themselves, and their A's cover such feelings, at least on the surface. Although children (and adolescents) from both types of homes do well in their schooling, only authoritative parents appear to take into account the emotional life of the children.

continued...

- *Spend time talking with your child. The average American parent speaks to his or her child for 12.5 minutes a day, and most of that time it is critical comments.*

- *When you care to read your child's signals and feelings (rather than assuming he or she must be feeling what you feel or dismissing that your child is entitled to his or her own feelings rather than needing to be an extension of your own), you become less likely to "peddle a product." Your child is not your object.*

- *Be sure you take a second look at your own thinking and behavior when you overschedule and "overencourage" your child toward the heights of success. Read your child's experience and look for signs of stress (fatigue, irritability, or depression). Be sure your child is emotionally with you before you forge forward.*

Other types of parenting styles have also been investigated in child-development research, particularly the permissive and indulgent types. Permissive parents show little warmth and lax structuring, and indulgent parents show warmth with lax structuring. Neither of these styles appears to be beneficial for children's learning. You should think twice before you "cave in" to your child's needs to test boundaries and limits. You should hold your own, not as dictators but as part of the same team—being on your child's side emotionally and understanding his or her experiences of the family and of the world.

LEARNING AS PLAY AND PLAYFUL LEARNING: A PERSONAL STORY

I'd like to end this chapter with a few personal words about play and the importance of play in motivating children to greater heights of atten-

---

Help your child's school adjustment (both academically and socially) by creating an environment in your home that has structure. Do this in a positive, emotionally expressive way.

- *Have activities that occur at predictable times (for example, homework is done as soon as your child gets home).*

- *Help your child create an organized learning place for homework and related activities.*

- *Be sure your home does not have excessive rules or is not excessively lenient. If your child lives with you as well as with your ex but open communication is not possible, be confident that your children can switch between expectations of them in each home.*

- *Examine whether there is intense stress in your home and/or whether your child has been subjected to intense stressors in his or her life. If your child is having trouble concentrating in school, could it be because he or she is concentrating on problems instead?*

tion and cognitive work. One summer, I wanted to devote more time to teaching mathematics to my daughter, Erin. She had shown some interest in the subject, and I wanted to give her a gentle "push" so she would have an easier time in third grade. I know, however, that Erin likes play! For example, if I tell her to practice piano, the response is dawdling. If I tell her it's good for her, the response is more dawdling. So I knew we had to make math *fun!* We opened our *Pizazz Schoolhouse* last summer—just the name was juicy enough for her. We put on our Southern accents and got to work on fractions, counting money, long division, multiplication tables, and many other math skills that she thought were all part of a "game." It was fun, and she was responsive. Frankly, I was more convinced that this was going to be important for her than she was, but she was willing to go along with it because it was fun. Her school also uses this approach. Erin, in fact, thinks that she goes to school to have fun every day—what a treat for her! Science is taught by creating songs, and there are fun "tricks of the trade" for learning multiplication tables. If all learning in the early years could be couched as fun and games, fewer children would experience classroom trauma.

---

continued...

- *Do not be overinvolved with homework, actually doing it for your child, but do support him or her by being physically and emotionally available for "consultations."*

- *Express in your home an open and democratic atmosphere in which you reason and allow your child to reason and debate different viewpoints. Reflect and share in your child's enthusiasm in different topic areas, rather than viewing your role as checking up on your child.*

- *No matter what, maintain a positive emotional climate in your home. It will help clear your child's mind.*

eleven

Keeping the Connection When It's Time to Talk About the Tough Issues

Parents are connected with their children in myriad ways; sometimes being able to openly communicate and connect around the tough issues is very revealing about the quality of the relationship. Does your child or adolescent feel comfortable approaching you with a tough issue? Or is he or she most able to connect with you when the topics are easy to discuss? Does your child turn away from you and rely on himself or herself or peers when the going gets rough? When there is teasing or bullying, does your child come to you and reveal his or her vulnerable self, or does your child hide what is going on and not want to be exposed? How comfortable is your child in seeking you out when there is a problem?

The key to keeping the connection in tough times lies in the evolution of your relationship with your child over time. Certainly, during the baby years your child will not be coming to you for comfort about teasing or asking about sex. Such tough topics will likely not surface until your child is able to talk and has a wider social world. Yet the foundation for "the talk" or other tough topics is built during the baby and toddler years. If you are beyond the early years of your child's life, don't worry. Just as foundations in homes can be rebuilt, relationships can be reconnected and repositioned, although it is common sense that "getting it right" at the beginning is easier and better for all concerned.

You can do a great deal during your child's baby and toddler years to set the stage for being a parent your child can approach when times are tough. During the earliest years, it is most important to give your child a sense of security. Such security is built during your everyday interactions with your young child.

One of the nicest ways you can give your child a sense of security is through physical interaction. Many cultures go so far as to carry their little ones around on their backs during these early times. The exercises in Chapter 7 were designed to give you and your baby and toddler time to experience one another in a physical, "here and now" sense. Music, hugging, and especially the two combined are nice ways to be present with your baby. Close and affectionate hugging that is welcomed by both sides gives your young one a sense of physical security. The physical connection during hugging, bath times, and diaper changing will make your baby aware of his or her body and how others react to it. When you touch in a gentle, caring way (as opposed to being rough, hurried, and impatient), you create calm, nonanxious emotions for your baby, and your baby learns to experience the world in the context of contentment.

In my dissertation study at the University of California at Berkeley in 1987, I found that some mother–infant interactions showed a considerable degree of mother or baby or both moving slightly away or seeming uncomfortable in close bodily contact. Much earlier research indicated that such "physical rejection" by the mother was predictive of insecure attachment to the mother of the child. Many other studies emphasize the physical aspects of the parent-child relationship and the importance for a baby's development of relaxed and caring bodily contact that gives the baby the sense of being supported rather than rough-handled.

Once you have built a base of comfortable physical interactions, you can continue this kind of appropriate physical closeness throughout your child's development. A child who feels he or she can hug a parent or be hugged usually experiences a greater closeness to that parent than a child who is not comfortable with parental physical contact.

Just remember that your sensitivity to your child's emotions and needs is critical when it comes to physical closeness. Sometimes your child needs a hug; other times a hug can be intrusive. As a parent, it's your job to read the cues your child is giving as to his or her emotional state and whether a hug or a caress is appropriate.

SEXUALITY EDUCATION

Experts in the area of sexuality education believe that the foundation for a child's sense of his or her bodily self begins during bathing, changing, and being carried around during babyhood. In fact, the Sexuality Information and Education Council of the United States (SIECUS) believes that sexuality education begins with babies feeling comfortable with their bodies and parents feeling comfortable with their infants, naming body parts and treating the baby's body in a gentle, nonintrusive way. Much of sexuality education, SIECUS believes, starts before babies and toddlers can talk. Nonverbal messages about holding, touching, and comfort with one's body are all learned at this time.

As children become more verbal as preschoolers, it is important for parents to name body parts and answer questions in an age-appropriate way. One preschooler in our research asked where babies come from, and the mother began a long discussion about the miracle of birth. After a few minutes the child said, "Mom, I just want to know whether all babies come from California." The child had gone to California to visit her grandparents and thought that, because her parents were from California, all children must come from there.

During the school years, many children are very interested in and are subjected to a great deal of sexual information. Sigmund Freud thought that children were very disinterested in sex at this time and, therefore, he labeled this stage the "latency period," but this couldn't be further from reality. Children are very interested in sexual information long before adolescence. Despite what some journalists and pundits would have us believe, children still obtain most of their information about sex from their parents. In fact, it is best for children to obtain such information in the home.

It is crucial for parents to be available to answer questions and help their children feel comfortable as they ask about sexual topics. An emotionally available parent is sensitive in physical contact and is flexible in terms of adjusting his or her behavior and discussion to the context at hand. When your child sees that he or she can have small discussions with you on this topic, your child will feel it appropriate and comfortable to have bigger discussions with you later. A young child might ask questions such as, "What's in that lady's stomach?" (pointing to a pregnant woman), or "Why does David have a penis and I don't?" or "Why can't I sleep with you and Daddy all the time?" The small questions are usually "testing the waters," and if the interactions feel fine to your child, he or she will feel good about asking the big questions later. As a parent, you should know whether your child finds you emotionally available in this area. Many adolescents feel that they can talk to their parents about almost everything *except* sex. It is important to create the type of emotional availability that makes you, in your child's eyes, emotionally available in this area as well.

Studies suggest that the "big talk" is much better handled as a series of smaller talks. There is no need for that dreaded single talk that covers all topics and then is brushed under the carpet and never referred to again. A series of ongoing, open discussions about sex is far better. Age eight is a great time to begin these talks because children at this age are very open to new information and are still very connected to their parents. Here's an example of such a discussion with a preadolescent child:

TREVOR: Hey, Dad?

DAD: Yeah, Trev?

TREVOR: Why do girls have breasts?

DAD: What brought that up?

TREVOR: I dunno . . . I just wondered.

DAD: Well, both girls and boys have breasts. But when girls grow up and become women, their breasts get bigger so they can feed milk to their babies. Men don't feed babies from their breasts so their breasts stay small.

TREVOR: What makes breasts grow?

DAD: When girls and boys become teenagers, their bodies produce chemicals called hormones that make them grow up and turn into adults. Girls and boys produce different hormones; that's why they look different when they become teenagers.

TREVOR: Oh. Thanks, Dad.

If Trevor had wanted further explanation, the dad would have continued the discussion. But Trevor was satisfied with his father's answer, and the dad was careful not to overwhelm his son with a lot of information the boy didn't want at this point. These small discussions on specific questions, whether initiated by the child or the parent, can make communication about sexuality easier for both parties.

Contrary to popular myth, the need for communication and connection with parents continues into adolescence. Most adolescents are not disconnected from their parents but show a nice balance between autonomy and connection. Also contrary to popular myth, parents, not peers, remain the most important source of sexuality information for adolescents. Unfortunately, either because they have subscribed to these popular myths or because they feel uncomfortable discussing sexual issues, many parents neglect to provide their children and adolescents with correct information about sexuality. Their children and adolescents then turn to their peers for enlightenment. Peers, however, often deliver information that is not totally correct (for example, the first time you have sex you can't become pregnant, and sexually transmitted diseases can't happen the first time), sometimes with disastrous consequences.

A new study has shown that when mothers enjoy a close and openly communicative relationship with young adolescents, particularly their daughters, the daughters are less likely to engage in sex at a young age. Given the significant and positive relations between age of sexual initiation and the number of sexual partners, and between the number of sexual partners and higher occurrence of sexually transmitted diseases (STDs), the value of the emotionally available parent-child relationship becomes obvious.

Here's an example of a conversation about sex with a young adolescent (about twelve years old):

PATTY: *(Walking in the house after school)* Hi, Mom!

MOM: Hi, honey! Hey, who was that boy walking you home?

PATTY: Oh, just a friend . . . David.

MOM: He looks a little older than you.

PATTY: Yeah, he's fourteen.

MOM: I saw he had his arm around your waist. Do you like him?

PATTY: Yeah, I guess.

MOM: I'm glad you like him, honey. You're old enough now that the boys are starting to notice you. And you're noticing them, too, right?

PATTY: Well, sure.

MOM: Sometimes it can be kind of confusing, those feelings. I'll bet you and your girlfriends giggle about it a lot.

PATTY: I guess.

MOM: That just means you're turning into a young woman, and you're developing the beginnings of sexual feelings about boys. Sometimes those feelings are nice, and other times they feel really strange, don't they?

PATTY: Yeah. I mean, I don't think about having sex with anybody yet, but some of my friends are already kissing and making out and stuff.

MOM: The question is, how do you feel about kissing and making out?

PATTY: We talked about that—that I shouldn't do anything that makes me feel uncomfortable.

MOM: That's right. And you have to use your good judgment when it comes to being sexual.

PATTY: Mom . . . David tried to kiss me yesterday.

MOM: What did you do?

PATTY: Well, I liked it for a moment, but then I thought I wasn't ready. So I told him to stop.

MOM: Good for you, honey. I'm glad you followed your instincts and used your good judgment. When girls grow up, it's easy for them to feel pressured by boys and by their own hormones to be sexual even though they aren't really ready. But I have confidence that you'll make the right decision when it's right for you. And I'll always be here if you ever want to talk about anything.

PATTY: Thanks, Mom.

It's clear from this conversation that the mother already has laid much of the groundwork for an open and honest discussion about sexual feelings with her daughter. She trusted her daughter to make the right decisions when it came to sex; even more important, she trusted that she and her daughter had a strong enough relationship that Patty would feel open to bring her questions to her mother. The mother was emotionally available without being intrusive, and the daughter responded in kind.

Of course, there is no reason to think that because a parent is emotionally available, he or she will have all the answers to all the questions their children might present. Being able to handle false starts and discomforts is all a part of the journey of parenting, and children rarely notice if parents have to struggle to find the right words. If you feel at a loss to respond to your child's question, just take a break until you've had a chance to think about it, but then be sure to address it later. Admitting you don't know the answer is fine, too. Making mistakes in communication and feeling comfortable about the process of finding the right information, or mishaps, is a part of emotional availability—it implies that perfection in communication is not the goal. With the tough topics, open communication and emotional connection are far more effective than scholarly perfection.

As demonstrated by the conversation between Patty and her mom, an important aspect of sexuality education is transmitting your own family values to your child. Studies again suggest the link between the values of the family of origin and the child's own values. However, sometimes parents have trouble clarifying their values. For example, if the parents grew up in the 1960s and subscribed to the value of "free love," they might feel awkward now about subscribing to the value of "virginity until you get married." A great deal of soul-searching is needed to clarify the family value system, not only for yourself but also within the parental unit (husband and wife, spouse and ex-spouse, parent and stepparent). Once parents are clear on the family value system they want to adopt, the best route to transmitting those values is to be clear and direct. The greater the clarity of parental messages (both verbal and nonverbal), the greater likelihood of concordance between the two generations.

If you are divorced and are uncomfortable with your ex's values, then very clearly communicate to your child the differences between the value systems in the two homes. Studies indicate that children, particularly daughters, are not very clear on their fathers' views of sexuality. It might be that fathers leave the sexuality education of daughters to the mothers, whether in single- or two-parent homes. Where value systems in the two homes differ dramatically, however, it behooves parents to speak to their children about the pros and cons of the different, perhaps unstated, value systems. As children approach adolescence, they will be able to not only appreciate but also cognitively understand different realities and will be able to engage in cause-effect reasoning. In emotionally connected relationships, discussing tough topics is just one more area in which the relationship grows and deepens; open and direct communication and open and direct expressions of feelings—rather than subliminal agendas—are familiar to the child.

Parents must remember, however, that their behavior is a better determinant of their values than their words. One of the best things parents can do is to live their own value system. This can sometimes lead to difficult choices for parents. If, for example, you want to promote the value of sexual abstinence until marriage, then allowing your sister to sleep with her boyfriend when they come to visit sends a mixed message. If you teach your child that sex is a beautiful and sacred part of a relationship, but you're uncomfortable discussing sex with him or her or expressing affection with your spouse around your child, again you are teaching your child one thing while living another. Once you are clear about which values you want to hold for your family, it is up to you as a parent to be the best possible example of those values for your child.

HELPING YOUR CHILD AVOID SUBSTANCE ABUSE AND READING THE SIGNS OF DEPRESSION

Another popular myth in our society concerns the effect of peer culture on drug use and abuse in our children. Although peer culture can have a great deal of influence, again parents create the seed for their children's interest in drugs as well as selection of a peer group. One very interesting research study indicated that although adolescents from more emotionally connected families did experiment with smoking and drugs, they were less likely to *abuse* either. This intriguing finding suggests that adolescence is the time for exploration; children from secure environments do a great deal of that, but they are less likely to have such exploration and experimentation lead to heavy use or abuse.

One of the eight elements of emotional availability is structuring. As children grow into teenagers, part of the structuring parents provide is to teach responsibility. Therefore, children from emotionally available homes usually have been taught about personal responsibility and they are less likely to engage in truly risky behavior. In fact, research indicates that when parents combine warmth with appropriate control, their children are less likely to be involved with drugs and, in addition, have lower levels of other problem behaviors such as delinquency.

Throughout this book, I have emphasized the importance of reading your child's verbal and nonverbal signals and communications. Reading the nonverbal signals, however, is not limited to the years before our kids start talking. Nonverbal communication begins during early infancy but continues throughout life. Language is added to but does not replace the need for reading our children at a nonverbal level. And being able to read our kids' nonverbal signals is of great importance when it comes to the issue of depression, which sometimes can lead to or can be otherwise linked with drug abuse. Obviously many children and adolescents can be depressed and never use drugs, but many who do use drugs are depressed.

An emotionally available parent should be attuned not only to the obvious signs of problems such as intense anger and hostility, but also to the more covert signs of depression such as a "blue" or "down" mood that does not disappear. Some of the signs of childhood or adolescent depression include:

- Changes in physical appearance

- Minimal smiling or pleasure in everyday activities

- Changes in friends or lack of interest in friends

- Easily putting down others

· Physical or other bullying of others

· Slipping of grades, truancy, or other school-related problems

The most important indication of potential depression is a clear change from what the child or adolescent has been in the past. Because our children and adolescents sometimes don't know that they are depressed, they cannot tell us how they feel; but signs of hostility, unsmiling faces, boredom, and a clear change in their demeanor can all be telltale signs. Certainly, if children and adolescents are taking drugs, there are some additional indications, such as vacant eyes, smelly clothing (if they are using inhalants such as paints or glue), stains on clothing, changes in financial needs, and friends who seem to show many of the same characteristics.

Talking to your child or adolescent about drugs, including tobacco and alcohol, is important, and such talks should begin early. As in the area of sexuality education, smaller talks are far better than one big talk. "Teachable moments" occur all the time: a discussion of a friend or family member who smokes or drinks, for instance, or seeing a drug bust on the nightly news or another television program. Remember, these moments should be discussions rather than simply saying, "Don't do drugs." If these discussions are held in an emotionally available way, your child will feel free to bring his or her questions and challenges to you when faced with drugs, cigarettes, or alcohol.

IF YOUR CHILD IS TEASED, REJECTED, OR BULLIED

The emotional availability framework is valuable because it can be used in so many different contexts. However, as your child grows, you will probably discover that being emotionally available is easier at some times than at others. A parent who is emotionally available during the baby years might find it challenging to exercise enough discipline and appropriate control during the preschool and school-age years. In a similar vein, the parent who is emotionally available in the context of school and learning might not be fully supportive when a child is feeling socially vulnerable. Similarly, a parent might find it easier to be emotionally available to a daughter than a son or vice versa.

Children, however, don't divide their worlds into different contexts. If you let your child down by being emotionally unavailable in a particular area (or differentiate on the basis of gender), he or she might feel vulnerable across the board. Even if you feel uncomfortable in some situations, it's up to you to do the best job you can to be emotionally available. This is especially true when it comes to your child's social interactions. Parents are often great at supporting their children academically but unsure of how to help them if they're having trouble socially. The problem is that the social aspect of children's lives impacts their cognitive skills and vice versa. Children who feel a lack of parental support when it comes to their social lives are less likely to feel supported in their academics no matter what their parents do.

Many parents simply do not respond to their children in any special way during times of need. It is not as if such mothers and fathers exhibit hostility toward their children in these situations, finding fault or belittling them for their lack of social skills; they simply fail to address their children's experiences. These parents are not disconnecting from their children, but they are missing key opportunities to connect emotionally at times when their support is needed the most. Such empathic failures leave the children "hanging," so to speak, and are often seen with children who are insecure in their relationships with their parents.

To keep the emotional connection, you must make a commitment to support your child's social development. This means you must take a very clear-eyed look at some of the most painful aspects of childhood. When your child isn't looking perfect in his or her own eyes or in the eyes of his or her peer group, what is your reaction? Do you embrace and support your child's difficulty, or do you find fault? Everyday events such as teasing (or at the extreme, being bullied) at school or not being invited to parties or playdates can be devastating for a child. Later in a child's development, rejection by potential boyfriends or girlfriends could be similarly devastating, particularly if it occurs as part of a pattern. These social and emotional aspects of childhood can have severe consequences for your child in terms of schoolwork, social skills, and even aspirations. Your reaction as a support figure can be the presence that makes the greatest difference for your child.

So how can you support your child during tough social situations? Recall the eight elements of emotional availability—parental recruitability, sensitivity, structuring, nonintrusiveness, and nonhostility, and the child's recruitability, responsiveness, and involvement. Utilize *sensitivity* in support of your child. Sensitive parents can detect problems in their children's lives. Merely knowing that tough situations are out there is part of sensitivity to children's issues today.

It can be difficult to read your child, however, if you do not know what topics you should be "reading." Two such topics to be on the lookout for are teasing and bullying. Part of reading your child is knowing the telltale signs of teasing and bullying, such as the following:

- Reluctance to go to school on a regular basis

- Slipping grades

- Signs of traumatic reactions (difficulty sleeping, nightmares, fear of new places or people, or intense anger)

- Bruises, cuts, or torn clothes

- Missing possessions

- Frequent trips to the school nurse

If your child faces difficulties, your empathy toward him or her helps your child learn empathy toward others. A child who is the bully at school rarely thinks of the feelings of the victim. A parent's empathy with his or her bullying child, however, is likely to have the consequence of "opening up the empathy possibility" toward others. Instead of "Now you cannot go to school for a whole week," a response of "You must have been feeling awful to do something like that. Let's talk about it together and figure it out. Can you help me understand?' can go a long way. In fact, such incidents can be opportunities for change.

If you believe your child is being bullied, you can utilize one element of emotional availability—*structuring*—to help your child handle the situation. A structuring parent makes suggestions and sets appropriate limits for child behavior. The issue of teaching your child appropriate boundaries is a key task of the structuring parent. Ask your child if there is a problem. Look at your child's face closely before he or she has a chance to minimize or deny what might be going on. Preferably long before any bullying or teasing incident or acts of similar rejection, talk to your child about these tough topics and prepare your child for the possibility. One of the best ways to coach your child for such events is to teach him or her that bullies need a victim and that by not acting like a victim, he or she will not fulfill the role that bullies need. Structuring interactions with your child so he or she knows the appropriate boundaries with you and with others is an important contribution to your child's life.

The *nonintrusive* parent is one who gives the child enough room to grow and develop. You cannot fight your child's battles on the playground or elsewhere. In fact, you need to empower your child to handle his or her own issues as he or she grows older. By structuring, as described above, you provide your child with the tools he or she will need to set boundaries. By being nonintrusive, you provide your child the space to use the tools you have provided.

The *nonhostile* parent is one who does not react with a put-down to his or her child's behavior. How you react to your child facing these issues (or even the possibility of such issues) will be very important. A parent who interacts with a child in a hostile manner introduces the idea of bullying in everyday interactions. Consider this exchange between father and son:

DAD: Hey, John, how's that model coming you're building for science class? Did you fix that thing you messed up yesterday?

JOHNNY: *(Happily)* Yeah, I managed to mend the side of the rocket.

DAD: Well, I'm glad you're not all thumbs . . . But isn't that due tomorrow?

JOHNNY: Yeah.

DAD: Don't you still have a lot to do on it?

JOHNNY: Yeah, but I was kinda hoping you'd help me.

DAD: *(Angry)* Well, you can forget it. I've told you time and time again you have to get these things done earlier. How could you be so dumb to leave it to the last minute?

JOHNNY: It's not my fault—it broke!

DAD: "It" didn't break, *you* broke it. Now you're just going to have to fix it on your own, young man. And don't go crying to your mother for help, either. You should have started this last week.

In conversations such as these, the parent teaches the child that hostility is acceptable. Such behavior and interactions can be so insidious that the child "feels" that all relationships are like this and, therefore, doesn't know how to "bullyproof" himself or herself, because, in effect, this child has been raised to be a victim. Because of familiarity with this dance, such a child unwittingly becomes the target of others' bullying behaviors. As a parent, you need to be very careful not to "leak" hostility when it comes to your interactions with your child. How you treat your child will teach him or her how he or she deserves to be treated by others. If you treat your child with sensitivity and respect, he or she learns self-respect and is far less likely to stand for being bullied by others.

The child's side of emotional availability includes responsiveness and involvement. When your child is emotionally available to you due to the trust and care you have helped create, he or she includes you in his or her life and is emotionally responsive to what you have to offer in terms of feelings, suggestions, and advice. As you engage your child in sensitive, structuring, nonintrusive, and nonhostile ways, your child becomes more responsive and involving to you. Because emotionally available children are by definition happy children, they are less likely to be consistently in the victim role. Many children have been victimized by a bully; 30 percent of sixth- to tenth-graders report having been bullied at one time or another.

Emotionally available parents don't send their children off to school psychologically unprotected for very long. As children describe what happens at school, these parents either help arm them with skills to neutralize bullying behavior or enlist the help of professionals in this endeavor. Teach your child how to respond to name-calling to nip in the bud the impression that your child is easy prey, which is what bullies look for. The following situation is a good example:

LYNN: *(Crying)* Mom, Karen called me a dummy on the playground today! Then she pushed me and told me I couldn't play with her and her friends!

MOMN: Gosh, sweetie, I'm so sorry that happened. Are you okay?

LYNN: Yeah, but she shouldn't have done that!

MOM: No, she shouldn't have. That wasn't nice of her at all. What do you want to do?

LYNN: I want to hit her back!

MOM: Well, that's one idea, but is that going to solve your problem with Karen and her friends?

LYNN: No—but why don't they like me?

MOM: Sweetie, maybe Karen was just in a bad mood. The main thing is to figure out how you can act around Karen and her friends so maybe they won't do that again. Will calling them names or pushing back work?

LYNN: No.

MOM: What about if you found someone else to play with on the playground? Is there another friend you'd like to get to know?

LYNN: I could play with Daisy—I like her.

MOM: What if you and Daisy were to go to recess together tomorrow? Could you have fun doing that?

LYNN: Yeah.

MOM: And if Karen and her friends bothered you or called you a name, what could you do?

LYNN: I could tell them that Daisy and I are playing and to leave us alone.

MOM: That's right. And maybe you could just ignore them and concentrate on playing with Daisy.

LYNN: Yeah—who needs them?

MOM: And I'll bet that if you look like you're having a great time with Daisy, Karen and her friends might even want to join in your game at some point. Would that be okay?

LYNN: Well . . . as long as they were nice to Daisy and me.

Lynn's mother has helped her daughter come up with her own solution for dealing with a bully. She has demonstrated all the traits of the emotionally available parent—recruitability, sensitivity, structuring, nonintrusiveness, and nonhostility. In return, Lynn was recruitable, responsive, and willing to involve her mother in her life. Both mother and daughter have resolved a tricky situation in a way that has strengthened their emotional connection.

When it comes to bullyproofing your child, one of the most important things to remember is that happy children are rarely bullied for long. Happiness creates a robust aura in children that makes them less desirable as consistent victims. The more you can do to help your child be happy with himself or herself, happy with his or her life, and happy in his or her relationships, the better your child's social interactions will be at every stage and every age. The best way to help your child be happy is to be sure your child's relationship with you is happy, strong, and emotionally available.

Make these tough issues not just a part of your child's life but a part of the connection you have with him or her.

- *Show your child by your actions (particularly your nonverbal behavior) that you are in a relationship with him or her and that you will emotionally support your child through tough topics and events. Through the experiences you have had together, your child knows that he or she can use relationships to work on tough issues and he or she is not left alone to deal with tough events.*

- *Discuss with your child the issues surrounding these tough topics and events. You have shown that you are easy to talk to, and you already have a problem-solving approach you have started with your child. Assure him or her that you will continue through the tough topics.*

twelve

Being Emotionally Available Even If Your Child (or Adolescent) Isn't

Sometimes our children seem less emotionally available toward us. Regardless of the age of the child (infant, toddler, child, or adolescent), we look for the "degree of responsiveness toward the parent" and "degree of involvement of the parent" as the emotional barometers. Lower levels of emotional availability can occur for a variety of reasons.

"CHASE AND DODGE"

Psychologist Beetrice Beebe at Columbia University has identified a style of interaction between babies and their parents that she calls "chase and dodge." She and her colleagues conduct painstakingly detailed observations and scorings of sequences of young babies interacting with their parents. It can take years to score and analyze such interactions! In this style of interaction, the parent initiates interactions, trying too hard, and the baby turns away and away. Many new parents do not realize that young babies need interaction followed by time to decrease the arousal that they feel from such delightful exchange. Too much delightful exchange is just that—too much of a good thing. Because so many of these parents have not cared for a baby before, it is tough for them to know how babies typically respond.

Although we use a different scientific paradigm to understand children—namely the overall index of emotional availability—we also see parents and infants being out of rhythm with one another, where the parent is constantly initiating, sometimes with the parent reporting, "All he does is close his eyes" or "He won't look at me."

In a face-to-face situation, four-month-old Emily was interacting with her mother. Her mom poked her belly, then her cheeks, while little Emily squirmed, as if in discomfort. Noticing that Emily was not interested in this interaction, her mom began to sing a lively tune. Still, Emily was not enchanted and looked away.

Compare to this interaction just two weeks later, with some video viewing with mother:

In the same face-to-face situation, four-and-a-half-month-old Emily was interacting with her mother. Her mom poked her belly, then her cheeks in a playful way, but little Emily squirmed, as if not enjoying this interaction. Noticing that Emily was not having a good time with this, her mom just touched her cheek soothingly and sat back. Emily looked at her mother and smiled. Mom smiled back and began to hum a soothing tone.

Note how well Emily's mom began to match her baby's affect! Matching can give a baby (or child) the feeling of joining in rather than being pushed and prodded. We all respond to those who join us better than those who directly want to lead us.

Such behaviors on the part of a baby signal a need for space and a pause from interaction. Because babies cannot tell us verbally what they need and desire, they tell us at a nonverbal level. As parents, to understand our babies at this nonverbal level is one of the most profound gifts we can give to them throughout their lives. So giving some space and becoming an available but nonintrusive partner will give babies a chance to "return the serve." When we give this type of feedback to new parents, the behavior and the whole style of connection can change—sometimes in ONE session! The baby becomes more seeking of interaction with the parent, and the parent does not have to "chase" the baby.

Although a good deal of such "chase and dodge" occurs in interaction with babies, because it takes time to adjust to a new baby, it is important for parents to be aware of this style throughout the life span. Sometimes, if we give some space, our children will come to us, rather than be unavailable to us. We need to be aware of the nonverbal level of communication with our young, preverbal ones, but we also need to remember this aspect of communication even after our children are fully verbal.

POSSIBLE DISRUPTIONS TO ATTACHMENTS FOR CHILDREN

Loss can take many forms in the lives of children, including divorce of one's parents, being taken into foster care and away from one's parents, as well as loss by death. In our clinic, we often see young children who are having difficulty when their parents divorce because they are faced with continual separation experiences—for example, one week in one home and the subsequent week in the other home. Psychologists Judith Solomon (Early Childhood Mental Health Program, Richmond, California) and Carol George (Mills College) have reported that babies who live with one parent and have overnights with the other might have difficulty establishing a sense of security with both parents. They reported that two-thirds of the twelve- to eighteen-month-old babies who lived with one of their parents and visited the other on an overnight basis were found to have disorganized attachments as compared to a married comparison group. In other words, they had difficulty in trusting parents and handling stress of separations and reunions and did not turn to parents to help them handle stresses. They seemed to be living in a state of fear. These overnights seemed to be particularly difficult for babies when families argued a lot and used the baby as a bargaining tool.

Particularly with babies, who typically need physical stability, it might be best to try overnights on a trial basis and be sensitive to how your baby is reacting to transitions. Containing hostility is particularly important. Allowing enough time to warm up to a parent at the time of the transition is also important. These transition times are difficult for children, and being sensitive to their (sometimes inward and sometimes outward) distress but not intrusive is crucial. Preparing your child for a transition by words and deeds is also helpful to them and is an aspect of structuring. Being attentive to your child's cues of responsiveness toward you and of involvement of you not only over the course of the divorce transition but also afterward is important as well. Remember, for babies or for older children, their responsiveness toward you and involvement of you (although shown in slightly different ways) are signs that your child is coping well.

Other possible disruptions of attachment for a child can involve being physically separated from caregivers for long periods of time (through one parent moving away and having limited physical proximity, foster care placements, or loss by death). In any situation that taxes a child's sense of security, caregivers need to stay the course. Sometimes emotional availability is not easy to sustain when the child (or children) are not being responsive and involving. It is much easier to have a great relationship when you're getting something back from your partner! Suggestions in chapter 14 offer many ideas on how to remain emotionally available when your child is not.

ADOLESCENT ISSUES

A common thought used to be that adolescents go through inevitable turmoil—"storm and stress," as some refer to it. Increasingly now, we are recognizing that many adolescents don't go through that level of upheaval. Although the popular media has sensationalized the lives of adolescents involved in drugs, sex, and rebellion from parents, we know that such issues do not necessarily characterize adolescence.

Another misunderstanding is that adolescents move away from parents. On the surface, this common observation appears to be a fact, but the reality is that most adolescents strike a balance between what psychologist

Karen Horney calls "moving toward" and "moving away" from parents. Just as secure babies move toward and away from their primary caregivers—exploring the world but returning for doses of love and attention—adolescents continue the same kind of behavior on an expanded scale. In fact, most secure adolescents like to involve their attachment figures (usually their parents) in their lives as they continue to gain increasing autonomy from them. The balance between connection and autonomy indicates the level of security adolescents experience in terms of their relationships with their parents. Teenagers who pursue independence without an accompanying need for connection are in the minority and represent an insecure form of gaining independence. Similarly, parents who are still combing and washing their adolescents' hair or helping dress their adolescents are equally rare and represent an insecure form of connection; this type of parent-child relationship has not enabled the adolescent to establish age-appropriate autonomy.

Emotional availability during adolescence has a great deal to do with what has happened in the parent-child relationship prior to adolescence. In fact, the best way to prepare for adolescence is in the earliest years of life, just as it is best to prepare for the transition to school in the earliest preschool years. This is not to say that major changes in the parent-child relationship cannot be made later on. There can be an incredible forgiveness in parent-child relationships throughout our lives, particularly during adolescence.

One of the reasons parent-adolescent relationships hold a great deal of promise is that adolescents achieve what the well-known Swiss psychologist Jean Piaget called "formal operational thinking." This means that teenagers are able to imagine a different reality and life from the one they have known. This ability is a blessing in terms of healing relationships. If the parent-child relationship has not gone well until that time (possibly due to major stressors in the family such as a nasty divorce, the death of a parent, conflicts in stepparenting, and so on), adolescence can allow a reworking of the parent-child relationship.

For example, many fathers who did not have custody of their children tell me that they had a minimal role in their children's lives until adolescence. At this point, their children could step out of the "reality" they have constructed from their own assumptions about the divorce and or their father's lack of connection and begin to imagine other possibilities at work. Fathers can then talk to their children, correct any misconceptions, and reestablish healthy new relationships based on what both the parent and adolescent want the relationship to be.

> Julio loved his son Claudio very much, but his marriage had fallen apart by the time the boy was five years old. In the divorce settlement, Claudio's mother had been awarded sole custody of the child and had promptly moved to another state, so Julio saw his son only once or twice a year for a week at a time. Whenever the two were together, Julio made a point of doing everything with his son, but within a year after the divorce, Claudio had completely changed toward his father. He was hostile, uncommunicative, and seemed unhappy with all Julio's efforts to get close to him. (Julio later found out that Claudio's mother constantly badmouthed her ex-husband to the child and told the little boy that the divorce was all Julio's fault.)
>
> By the time Claudio was fourteen, Julio had almost given up. But that summer, when Claudio came for his annual week's vacation with his dad, Julio sensed a new maturity in the boy. Claudio asked a few questions about the divorce and why his dad had left. While doing his best not to put his ex-wife in a bad light, Julio was able to explain why he felt he had to leave the marriage and why he thought divorce would actually be better for Claudio than being stuck in the middle of parents who were constantly fighting. For the first time, Julio could share his pain over having to leave his son nine years earlier and be separated from the boy for most of the year.
>
> Claudio was floored. He knew his dad cared for him in a distant kind of way, but Julio had never communicated these kinds of feelings before. Now that he was older, Claudio could understand that the stories his mother had told him about the divorce might not have been the only version. More important, he was able to accept his father's expression of emotions and desire for connection as genuine. By the end of the week, Julio and Claudio were closer than they had been since the divorce. Julio had seized the opportunity provided by Claudio's increased emotional

maturity and understanding to heal the long-standing breach between them and to create a new relationship that would serve both father and son well through the years.

Although teenagers might not seem to want to think reasonably or rationally, they are usually fully capable of doing so. Your adolescent has the capacity to talk with you about the past, present, and future in terms of what he or she would like to envision for your relationship. If there have been problems in your relationship in the past, adolescence actually can become a time of healing—but only if the communication begins. It is not about love or lack of love, but about communication with your adolescent about your feelings and thoughts. Your teenager cannot know how you feel or have felt without communication from you.

TEENAGERS WANT CONNECTION EVEN WHEN THEY SAY OTHERWISE

Once a physician who found out that I was a child psychologist immediately told me, "I've got three children—seven, ten, and fifteen. The seven- and ten-year-olds think I'm the best thing since sliced bread. The fifteen-year-old thinks I'm a jerk. And the fifteen-year-old thought I was great when he was ten." He implored, "What do I do?" Despite the promise that the period of adolescence holds, many parents view teenagers as emotionally unavailable. Certainly adolescents do a lot to create that collective image.

However, adolescents can appear emotionally unavailable even when they desperately want to connect with you. There can be a true difference between inner and outer reality for an adolescent—something that is not true for an infant or young child or, to some extent, an older child. Although there might be a real difference between how they *appear* to feel and how they really *do* feel, the needs for emotional connection are still there for *every* adolescent. All adolescents need emotional connection, but they certainly resist it, and many even militate against it.

Basically, adolescence is a time when children change their views about their parents. When children are young, parents seem omnipotent. As children become teenagers, that view changes—they start to see parents in life-size proportions or smaller. They start to notice parents' foibles and follies; they judge their parents by their own or their friends' standards; and they're not afraid to tell parents when they are found wanting. This changing perception is part of a teenager's self-discovery and assertion of autonomy. As a parent, you must be prepared to lose your status as "perfect" and learn to develop a relationship with your child based on your humanity. Acknowledging changes in your relationship and giving your adolescent the space to explore these changes in feelings and perceptions can be a great way to connect and reconnect, because it gives credibility to your adolescent's feelings.

Remember, however, that in the same way parents provide both autonomy and opportunity for connection with secure babies, parents of teenagers must balance freedom with love and a secure base for the teenager. I would suggest allowing your adolescent his or her space but creating an invitation for connection by being more physically available. Many parents think that adolescents want and need more space and, therefore, they supervise less. They might feel that older kids no longer require constant supervision. Some parents feel a need (or desire) to return to work now that the kids are "old enough." However, your physical availability can be the thread that keeps the connection between you and your autonomy-seeking adolescent. Although physical availability in and of itself is not a guarantee of emotional availability, physical *un*availability certainly precludes emotional availability.

Although many parents might be unable to be physically available to their teens on a continued basis, awareness of their needs for connection is important. Your comfortable and comforting presence at the times you've indicated (or better yet, the two of you have decided) will go a long way in providing your teenager with an emotional connection.

Another reason for parents to make physical availability a priority concerns legal parental responsibilities. One recent groundbreaking case concerned a single mother whose daughter hosted a party for about sixty teenagers at their home. The mother closed one eye (or both eyes) during the party. Unfortunately, the partying involved a great deal of alcohol, and two of the teenaged party guests died in car accidents on their way home. The mother was put on trial for manslaughter. The mother asserted that her daughter had lied to her, telling her there was no alcohol at the party, but the prosecution argued that the mother had to have known about the drinking. The mother was convicted and sentenced to fifteen years in prison. Similar reasoning has led to the lawsuits against other parents of high school students. The question asked is, "Why didn't these parents know what their teenagers were doing in their own homes?" Issues of the physical and psychological availability of parents are more important than ever, whether viewed through the lens of emotional availability or legal responsibility.

THE IMPORTANCE OF NONINTRUSIVENESS AND STRUCTURE DURING ADOLESCENCE

The biggest threat most parents feel is that their formerly open and available children will start adopting dangerous behaviors during adolescence and then hide them from them. The teen years mark the time when children start doing drugs, joining gangs, drinking alcohol, engaging in risky sexual activity, developing eating disorders, and so on. Nonintrusiveness is one of the eight key elements of emotional availability, but many parents of adolescents would take issue with this credo during adolescence and change the terminology to *seemingly* nonintrusive presence. In fact, many effective parents of adolescents practice "snooping"—that is, going through their children's rooms or possessions or talking to the parents of the children's friends without their children's knowledge. Parents who snoop believe that in this way they can learn about the private lives of their children without making them feel a lack of space. You need to determine your own views on this issue and balance your child's autonomy with the need to know if your child is engaging in risky behaviors.

Although it is important to refrain from obviously intrusive and hostile behaviors, it also is important to continue your attempts to provide structure for your teenager. In my private practice, I have seen many parents who were afraid to structure lest the emotional connection with their teenagers be threatened. They were afraid to say that they didn't like their children's girlfriends or boyfriends, for instance, although they saw obvious problems ahead. Such parents think that to intervene would be intrusiveness, whereas such interventions actually fall into the realm of structuring.

One of my patients realized that her nineteen-year-old son was in a relationship with an older woman who was using street drugs. Neither parent knew what to say to their son or how to say it, and so they said nothing. Eventually, they came to the realization that they should not remain silent in their disapproval.

Parents might not always be heard, but it is important to try to speak up about important issues. Sometimes parents will lose their children if they *don't* speak. As a parent, you cannot let your child develop in a vacuum. Independence and "letting go" are never total. The balance between connection and autonomy is one that must be maintained throughout your child's life.

Here's an example of providing structure for a teenager while doing your best to maintain the connection:

CAROL: Mom, I'm going to a party at Frank's house on Saturday night.

MOTHER: Wait a minute, honey. Who's Frank?

CAROL: You know—he's my friend Paige's boyfriend.

MOTHER: Carol, you know I don't like the crowd Paige runs around with. They're much too rough.

CAROL: Oh, Mom, it's just a party!

MOTHER: Where's this party going to be?

CAROL: At Frank's house, on Forsythe Street, over on the east side of town. His parents are going to be there, so you don't have to worry.

MOTHER: Carol, that's not a good neighborhood. I'm sorry, but I don't want you over there after dark and at a party, even if Frank's parents are there.

CAROL: Mom!

MOTHER: The only way I'd feel right about your going to this party would be if I went with you and stayed the entire time. Would you like that?

CAROL: *(Horrified)* No way. Why won't you treat me like an adult?

MOTHER: Sweetie, you're certainly old enough to make a lot of your own decisions, but I'm worried about your safety. You're welcome to have some friends over here, and there are a lot of parties I'd be happy for you to go to. But you're just going to have to miss this one. I'm sorry.

Lack of parental structuring during adolescence can lead to an adolescent making many choices that have a lasting impact. For example, adolescent girls who smoke (particularly before the age of sixteen) are more likely to get breast cancer as adults. Inhalant use among adolescents can lead to permanent brain damage; use of other drugs has similar consequences. Many adolescents are not well informed about sexually transmitted diseases (STDs). For example, one of my early adolescent patients believed that if she remained in the missionary position during sex she would not get AIDS. Risk prevention and management of risky issues is more important than ever for parents to recognize.

Although learning from experience is the credo of the adolescent, too much learning only through experience can lead to disastrous conse-

---

Although adolescents don't behave as if they want to be close, they still want the emotional connections with you.

- *Be physically available—even at odd times or hours—so your adolescent has the chance to ask for your support and advice.*

- *Continue discussions and dialogues, especially when your teenager is not braced for it, for example, in the car as you are driving your adolescent somewhere.*

- *Continue the tradition of playing with your child (for example, board games, card games). The playtime can now be long conversations or talking in the car on the way to ballet class.*

- *Do not be discouraged by the occasional negativism of your adolescent or the demands for increasing independence. Continue your emotional availability to your child.*

quences. Parental structuring can provide infusion of wisdom without seeming intrusive. Creating a climate in the home that is safe for discussions and emotional connection is probably the best place to begin. Even if you have never done that before, your adolescent will respect you for your courage in trying a new route. Your teenager might even acknowledge that you are human, too.

---

continued...

- *If your relationship has needed healing, know that adolescence is a great time for mending a less-than-good situation. Adolescents' increased cognitive abilities enable them to imagine a changed future.*

- *If your ex's relationship with your adolescent has needed healing or has not even begun healing, remember again that adolescence is a time of new possibilities, perhaps in that relationship or in your adolescent's understanding of that relationship.*

- *Know that your emotional availability and involvement or reinvolvement can help. Studies have found that closer connection during adolescence is associated with less incidence of risky behaviors, including early sexual debut.*

- *Continue helping your adolescent with problem-solving, perspective-taking, and the subtleties of thinking (in contrast to all-or-none or black-and-white thinking). Such thinking will lead to greater emotional understanding of the self and others.*

- *Be sure your adolescent knows (and hopefully has known all along) your values. If you are a single parent and see the children only part-time, and you and your ex do not share the same value system, try to have some interparent communication on this topic with your ex so that your adolescent is not confused by differing messages. If this is not possible, then make the "better" (better for your adolescent) value system very explicit. Do not be ambiguous about this. Children and adolescents take on the values of their parents, provided they know what these values are. Sometimes the parents do not know themselves. Therefore, it is important for you to clarify your own value system so you can transmit it.*

The balance between connection and exploration is tipped toward exploration during adolescence, but how can you nurture the connection without seeming intrusive?

- *Be physically and emotionally available in the "right" places—for example, at night when they come home or while driving them to soccer practice.*

- *Many families of adolescents speak to the importance of "playtime" with an adolescent—real floor time, playing cards, playing board games, and the like. Or talk to your adolescent as you are driving him or her around, and let that be the playtime. Playing with your adolescent is as much a possibility as playing with a younger child. Just connect with what your teenager finds interesting. Think of how playtime makes a child more receptive to everything else about the relationship.*

- *Support your adolescent in making good choices by enlisting the help of third parties. Although an adolescent might seem as if he or she does not want to hear some information from a parent, he or she might be more receptive to hearing it from another adult, such as a doctor or a friend's father.*

- *Adolescents might seem as if they don't listen and they don't hear, but continue talking with them because they will absorb a great deal of your values and your style. But when you talk to them, it is often helpful to "describe" ("You dyed you hair purple"), rather than always being critical or prohibitive.*

thirteen

Dual-Income Couples—
A Neat Balancing Act

Many people assume that being part of a "traditional" family (with a breadwinner father and stay-at-home mother) is good. The dual-earner family is still looked on with some skepticism. In fact, as I chat with my undergraduate students—mostly in their early twenties—I hear references to the need for a stay-at-home mother, such as:

> "My greatest wish is to become a wife and mother."
> "Why have kids if you're going to put them in daycare for most of the day?"
> "I can see the difference between me and my sister—my mother didn't have to work when she was raising me and she had to work when raising my sister because my parents divorced soon after my sister was born."

I certainly think there is nothing wrong with being a stay-at-home mother. But is there something wrong with being a partner in a dual-earner relationship? The statements from my students certainly indicate that there might be something remiss in this modern solution. But psychologist A. Gottfried, as well as others, has found that two-parent families in which both parents work are *not* putting their children at risk. Children from such families do not show any evidence of less-optimal adjustment. In fact, his research indicates that when mothers are highly satisfied with their outside work, their children actually do better than if such mothers stay at home to raise the children. Some women might just need to have challenge in their lives, and work provides such a challenge. The positive attitudes of these women then become part of the emotional lives they create for their children. Research by Ann Easterbrooks of Tufts University indicates that children from dual-earner families have as much a chance of being securely attached as those from single-earner families.

OPTIMAL TIME TO RETURN TO WORK AFTER THE BIRTH OF A CHILD

Based on the work of Mary Ainsworth and her colleagues, as well as my own clinical observations, I believe that a parent's schedule for going back to work should be based on the particular family. Some families adjust to a new family member easily; others take more time. I took a full year off after my daughter was born. My obstetrician had induced labor with each of her babies and then went back to her private practice within two weeks. Today, her children as well as my own seem to be doing very well socially, academically, and in family relationships. So in answer to the question, "Is there a 'best' time to go back to work so the parent-child relationship doesn't suffer?" the answer is whenever it feels comfortable and proper arrangements for child care can be made. (I would say the best possible arrangement is one with an emotionally available caregiver, either in the home or in a center.)

The time a parent chooses to start back to work depends very much on the care arrangements made for the child. If parents can arrange for in-home care by a grandparent or other relative, a baby-sitter, a nanny or an *au pair,* then (like my obstetrician) they might be able to go back to work right away. The choice to put a new baby in out-of-home day care, however, might be more problematic. As discussed in Chapter 2, babies have the need to form attachments with primary caregivers, and some studies indicate that starting day care in the first year of life may have emotional consequences for children. (There are other studies, however, that find no link between early entry into day care and problems for children.) Likely, the best time to start work in terms of leaving your child in out-of-home day care might be after your child is at least two years old; prior to that time, an in-home caregiving arrangement is best. At that point, studies indicate that there are few, if any, negative effects of day care in terms of creating insecurity in the parent-child relationship.

In some circumstances, day care actually might be a better choice for the child than a stay-at-home parent. Studies conducted by the NICHD Early Child Care Research Network indicate that for some lower-income families and families in which there might be insensitive caregiving, early entry into day care can be a benefit for a child—even an infant. Day care can provide many positive caregiving role models that some children might not have at home. Similarly, if the home environment is not sensitive to the emotional needs of a child, time in day care also can be of benefit. In fact, day care and preschool have many positive effects for *all* children, as long as entry is not too early. I usually recommend that parents place their children in a quality day care or preschool by age two or three. Such settings expand the child's world of social contacts, give him or her opportunities to relate to many people, and help the child grow mentally, socially, and emotionally at an accelerated pace.

HOW TO BE SURE FATHERS ARE EMOTIONALLY AVAILABLE, TOO

Much emphasis in parenting is on mothers, and not infrequently on mother-blaming. Certainly, as my generation was growing up, mothers assumed the lion's share of parenting responsibilities and were seen as the "emotion brokers" in the home. "Don't tell your father" or "It'll upset your father" are phrases many of us heard while we were growing up. Interestingly, I still see some of this even when both parents are working away from the home. Despite equality of tasks outside the home and "job-sharing" at home in the area of parenting, women do more home and child care than men. This finding has been replicated in study after study. Yes, fathers do more than they used to, but women typically take on more of the responsibility for home and children. Gender equity has yet to find its way into the area of parenting.

Many mothers know intuitively that they also have a role in fostering emotional availability in their spouses. Some will actively coach their spouses in being more emotionally open to the children. Other mothers simply try to be sure the home is an emotionally welcoming place and their spouses are generally happy in the marital relationship. In fact, studies from my laboratory indicate that a father's emotional availability toward his children is highly associated with his overall feelings about the marriage. Men who are happier in the marriage interact in more emotionally available ways with their children.

Interestingly, the marriage is the seat for maternal emotional availability as well. Women who are respected and supported by their spouses are more emotionally connected with their children. A mother of a child patient of mine recently was diagnosed with breast cancer and subsequently had surgery to remove her breast. We noticed how her spouse supported her through and after the process. In watching this family, I told the father, "The best way you can support your daughter as a father is to stay emotionally connected with your wife—even during the tough times."

Although some research, such as that by Gretchen Lovas at the University of California at Davis, indicates that the father-son relationship is the lowest in terms of emotional availability toward one another, much work also indicates that fathers can be very nurturing with their children. When husbands and wives work different shifts so the father has more independent parenting responsibility, or in a divorced family when the father has time alone with the children, most fathers can do everything mothers do. Yet in two-parent families in which both parents work, fathers take a backseat to mothers in terms of parenting. Women come home from work and assume a "second shift" of family work, whereas fathers are able to take a little time off. Certainly, much of this style is based on specific families; families that have been able to negotiate and release themselves from such traditional roles have much more equal division of responsibility and sharing of emotional connection with children.

If nothing else, we should give fathers a chance to express their emotional availability to their children and negotiate their own terms, rather than assuming that fathers need to be "monitored" or giving them permission to be the less-important parent. Finding and expressing one's emotional availability takes space, and women might need to step back and share a bit of their territory. I admit that I certainly have a difficult time taking the backseat to my husband (by being physically available but allowing my spouse to express his own emotional availability in his own way). Most women still feel that they are better than men at emotional availability. But this is just an assumption with no basis in reality. In our research, we see many dads with exquisite rapport with their children—sometimes much better than the kids have with their mothers.

The real secret for all parents—whether you work outside the home or stay at home, whether you're a single parent or part of a happy marital relationship, whether you're the mom or the dad, whether you see your kids every day or only on weekends—is to make emotional availability a priority. Don't let yourself get caught up in the admittedly important task of providing for your child's physical needs. What do you recall the most from your own childhood: the times your parents changed your diaper, fed you, or wiped your nose, or the moments when your mom kissed you good-night or your dad read you a story? Making the emotional connection with your child is as important as feeding and clothing your child or putting a roof over his or her head. So use the elements of emotional availability as your guide, and make the most of the moments you spend with your child. It doesn't matter if you are with your child all day long or only after you return home from work. In terms of emotional connection, the quality of your time together is more important than the quantity. Make your time with your child rich emotionally, and you and your child will reap enormous rewards.

Emotional Needs of Foster and Adopted Children as Well as Children with Special Needs

Throughout this book I have been describing so-called "normal" parent-child relationships. But many families find themselves in extraordinary circumstances. What if your child has disabilities or attention difficulties? What if you adopt a child or are raising a foster child? How do you create an emotionally available relationship with such children who might have very different needs? Our studies have found that emotional availability is even more important in these exceptional families to create greater emotional strength and resilience as well as to strengthen the bonds that will support the child's later development. However, exceptional circumstances might require exceptional strategies for creating emotional availability. Take heart; you can establish emotional connection through "therapeutic parenting" or other parental intervention techniques.

Certainly, when it comes to exceptional children, parents must be extraordinarily creative in developing and maintaining an emotionally available parent-child relationship. They might even need emotional support themselves in the form of counseling and/or "time off" from the constant care of a difficult child (called "respite care"). Taking care of an exceptional child is not easy, but if you know and can use the elements of emotional availability to create a strong, healthy, emotional connection with your child, I believe the parent-child relationship can be far more satisfying and rewarding for both parties.

BECOMING A "THERAPEUTIC PARENT"

As a child psychologist with an active practice, I see many exceptional children. Their parents bring them in for counseling because of the child's behavioral, emotional, and psychological problems. My job is to provide professional expertise about the child's difficulties, suggest solutions and guide both child and parent into implementing these changes. Although I (or any other professional counselor, psychologist, psychiatrist, or social worker) might be able to help the child and the family through a difficult diagnosis and suggest a treatment regimen and/or psychotherapy, such work is usually of a temporary nature. At some point, the professional relationship will end.

I have found that enabling parents to become guides of the therapeutic process with their children is a valuable part of therapy. I use the term *therapeutic parenting* to describe emotionally available parenting with a child who has problems. Such parent interventions can help just as much as the interventions of a therapist. Lillian Stover (who pioneered what is called "filial therapy") and others have shown that "nontraditional therapists" (such as paraprofessional counselors) can be effective in achieving therapeutic goals. Indeed, a child's most enthusiastic therapist is sometimes the parent. A family wishing to continue the gains made in professional sessions or in jump-starting the change process needs to think about therapeutic parenting.

Although your task as a therapeutic parent is to continue to help your child process his or her feelings and make progress, it is also important to know when to work in conjunction with a professional. If nothing else, professional counselors and therapists probably have had a great deal of experience working with other exceptional children like yours. They might be able to suggest strategies and ideas for your child based on their knowledge of what has worked and what hasn't. I believe parents should avail themselves of any and all resources possible to help their children live better, happier lives. However, parents also should remember that one of their primary responsibilities is to provide emotional connection and support to their children—and that is a job no therapist can fill.

USING THERAPEUTIC PARENTING WITH YOUR CHILD

One of the best ways to "parent" therapeutically is through play therapy. Play therapy is not the same as playing together; there are subtle differences between playing with your child and doing play therapy with your child. The goal of play therapy is for your child to be able to work through and problem-solve his or her issues right during play. Play therapy can help children express withheld emotions, process feelings they cannot handle in other ways, and face challenges and create solutions in a safe, nonthreatening environment. Playing with your child in this way builds the emotional relationship, and all problems are more easily weathered in the context of a relationship.

Children above the age of two (with no real upper limit) are good candidates for play therapy. I recommend that play therapy sessions should happen weekly, for approximately thirty to forty-five minutes per session. (Even if parent and child are having a great time, the session should be stopped at the designated point to make the "session" distinct from normal, daily routines.) The designated time should be free of any interruptions or intrusions from other family members—in other words, it is strictly your time together. The child also should try to go to the bathroom prior to the session so there is no interruption.

The Play Environment

The same environment and the same materials should be available to the child at each session. Such predictability and boundaries will help you and your child look forward to the next session. Particularly nice for play therapy purposes are toys such as a dollhouse, a toy gun, a rubber knife, animal figures, tanks, planes, people figure puppets, and blocks. Children can use these items to act out situations from their world, expressing both positive and negative emotions. With older children and teenagers, you can play cards, games, and other activities together. The point is to have dedicated time with your child on a regular basis in an atmosphere that focuses on *them,* rather than on you.

From an emotional standpoint, the environment should be free of criticism, judgment, or direction. It also should be an environment in which you, as a parent, refuse to react personally to the events or topics arising in the course of the session. Providing a warm, accepting, and reflective climate will help your child find his or her resources for independent problem-solving.

The overall protocol for play therapy sessions is as follows:

- The parent should sit relatively close to the child but not in oppressive proximity.

- The parent follows the child's lead during the play. The parent is not the boss. (I discuss this in greater detail in the discussion that follows.)

- The parent's comments should reflect and speculate on what the child is doing. The comments are "descriptive." (I discuss such descriptions in greater detail in the discussion that follows.)

- The parent is warm and accepting.

- The parent doesn't ask questions.

- The parent doesn't give the child the feeling that he or she has to do something specific or that the parent feels any anxiety about these sessions.

- The parent should describe one clear rule to the child: "You cannot be destructive or hurtful to yourself or others." If this kind of behavior occurs, the session is terminated.

Be the Follower in the Play

To get a sense of how to do this successfully, pretend you are going to play with your boss. You sit on the floor, ready for play, and your boss says,

"You go get those animals," "Our task is to have this dinosaur kill the other dinosaurs," "You get the other animals now," "No, not that," "Now, put that here . . ."

Now, sit back and ask yourself how you would feel playing with this boss. Would you go the extra mile for this boss? Would this boss have won your heart and made you want to outperform yourself? Just as you are unlikely to like such a boss, you need to not be a "boss" and to let your child lead. Be the follower in play.

Refrain From Asking Too Many Questions

One of the most difficult things during play therapy is to refrain from asking questions. If your child is pretending to bang one doll against the other and you ask what's going on, the child might say, "I don't know" and stop banging the dolls together. However, this stops the process of play (and the therapeutic process) in its tracks. When children say, "I don't know," in such circumstances, often what they mean is that they don't want to describe what they are doing—they are avoiding the parent's question.

But if, instead of asking a question, you comment, "You want to bang this doll against that one." Your child might answer or not, but the process is not stopped. And if your child does answer, you can gain a sense of what your child is going through. For example, your child might say, "Yes, this doll has been bad and is getting punished," which might reveal some of what he or she is thinking and feeling. When feelings are expressed in a safe and secure environment, they can lead to feelings of calm for a child.

Sometimes, parents are appalled at the aggressive feelings expressed in play and say things such as, "Don't do that!" or "Don't hit that doll!" But such comments can cause children to inhibit their aggressive displays and prevent them from working on the very issues that caused the aggression. Again, reflective comments such as, "That doll is mad, isn't he?" or, "He's angry at Sally," and so on are likely to give your child a safe haven for the expression of *all* his or her feelings. Of course, in real life, you can nip aggression in the bud, but not in play. In the context of play, nonjudgmental, nonintrusive, reflective comments provide a structure and safe haven for expressiveness.

Do Not Suggest That Your Child Is in the Play Itself

It also is important for you *not* to talk as if your child is in the play, as for example, "You are beating up that doll." Rather, *reflecting on* or *describing* the feelings expressed by the objects—by saying, for example, "That doll must be angry at the other doll"—is more likely to lead to greater expressiveness on the part of your child.

Be Close—You Do Not Always Have to Describe

You can also just be with your child as he or she colors or otherwise plays, allowing the child to just enjoy the closeness. You do not need to feel compelled to reflect or always say something. But it is wise to indicate by your demeanor an *emotional* presence and availability. Double-check yourself to make sure you do not seem preoccupied or otherwise psychologically inaccessible to your child. (Our children pick up on whether we are paying attention to them. More than once my own daughter has said to me, "Mom, you didn't hear what I said!"—and she was right.)

Emphasize the One Important Ground Rule

The one ground rule for the play therapy session is that the child cannot be destructive or hurtful to himself or herself or others. An example of how to set limits and boundaries during a play session follows:

Scenario: After twenty minutes of a play session, Mike begins to get aggressive and doesn't abide by the limits his father is trying to set for him.

MIKE: *(Throws doll at the wall)*
FATHER: Sally the doll is angry at something.
MIKE: Yes, she's picking on all the kids at school. *(He throws the gun and the doll at the wall)*
FATHER: That will damage the wall. If you throw anything more at the wall, you know we'll need to call it a day.
MIKE: *(Continues to throw things at the wall without heeding the father's admonition)*
FATHER: Okay, that's the end for today.

By setting clear boundaries that prohibit destruction but allow the child to express his or her feelings freely, you can set a feeling of safety within boundaries. Within these boundaries, you help your child feel that his or her feelings, even those of aggression, are accepted. Being able to express aggressive feelings is different than acting them out and being destructive. Such feelings can be allowed in the play session at the same time the destructive behavior can be limited or banned.

Dealing with a child's aggression is something all parents need to master. Instead of automatically redirecting a young child's aggressive play and communicating (even if in subtle ways) your disapproval of such expression, you should see and hear it differently in the context of play. What is your child telling you? What is your child showing you? What is your child asking of you through his or her play? Such feelings are "just right" in terms of the emotional availability framework because sensitivity combined with appropriate control is essential. A framework that consistently combines sensitivity and structure will make it more likely that, over time, your child will become appropriately responsive and involving during play and then will generalize such emotional availability during the play sessions to the day-to-day interactions in your life.

Be Patient with the Process

You will likely become closer to your child after play becomes a regular routine. Parents in play therapy usually report that they begin to feel closer to their children even after the first session. Realistically, however, it will take time to see the benefits of these play sessions. In the early stages, many parents feel that they are not being effective and the sessions are going nowhere. This, in fact, is how many professional therapists feel in their initial sessions with patients. It takes children some time to warm up to the context and to feel that they can open up during these sessions.

Be the Parent, Not a Peer

Throughout all these sessions (as well as other activities in this book), remember that you need to be the therapeutic *parent,* not the friend or peer, and limit-setting is part of your job. Interestingly, many children and adolescents say they have other friends and do not want one in a parent. This is not to say that you can't be both a parent and a friend. But there is a distinct difference between being a parent and a friend (a desirable situation) and being a peer. Solely being a peer deprives children of the boundary-setting and leadership qualities of parents—the very qualities children need so much from their parents.

Your task as a therapeutic parent is to help your child process his or her feelings and make progress.

- *Help your child become more logical in his or her thinking. Such logical thinking will enable your child to understand the world and to understand that it is in many ways a predictable world and that relationships are predictable in many ways.*

- *As part of such work, engage your child in long conversations to extend his or her logical reasoning as a coping strategy for life, so your child does not fall back into more primitive ways to express himself and interact with the world (for example, tantruming, hitting, or other dysfunctional strategy).*

- *Don't insult or force your child to be more logical. There is no room for blaming or shaming—instead, listen with empathy and try to help your child to logically move from one point to another, perhaps saying, "Hey, honey, I got lost . . . you were telling about . . . how did that then happen?" Your questioning is a nice way of structuring your child's thinking, and such questioning can help organize and make his or her thinking more coherent.*

- *Be a participant of the drama—you don't want to merely watch your child's play—but also do not take over. This is the time for you to get to know your child.*

- *Be patient. Don't feel that you are not accomplishing anything*

FOSTER CARE AND ADOPTIVE FAMILIES

A challenging circumstance can occur when a new child—an adopted or foster child—joins a family. The parent in such a family is in a particularly interesting and difficult position because the child comes to the relationship with a degree of responsiveness and involvement that has nothing to do with the new parent.

Many adopted children adjust to their new families with no problems related to healthy connections. For such children, then, using the principles of emotional availability already described in this book makes sense.

On the other hand, sometimes foster and adopted children have difficulties connecting with their new families. Many of these children are diagnosed with "reactive attachment disorder," which suggests the possibility of abuse or neglect sometime during their first five years. Although a diagnosis in the *DSM-IV* (Diagnostic Statistical Manual for Mental Disorders), this disorder is in fact treated by clinicians as a continuum, meaning that it can vary anywhere from mild to severe, depending on issues with connecting with the children's caregivers.

A child might come into a new relationship less responsive and involving than a child who has been in a caring environment. After all, the child doesn't know that the new environment will be any different than the old one, so the child continues his or her emotional *unavailability*. At times, such a child might seem to want to trust the new parent; at other times, he or she might seem cool, avoidant, almost suave in his or her seeming disregard of any form of emotional connection. "How do I get my child to trust me?" is the question most asked by foster or adoptive parents. But why should the child trust these parents when other parental figures haven't been trustworthy? Thus, the dance with only one partner starts out—unless the foster or adoptive parents can learn to be emotionally available in the face of apparent child unavailability.

On the other end of the continuum, some foster and adoptive children enter the new family hungering for connection. These children might be overly responsive, seeking to fulfill the family's slightest wish to make sure the family will want them to stay, or they might demonstrate a constant need for the new parent's emotional attention. Even if they have other children, parents of a foster or adoptive child are faced right from the start with different circumstances—either the child's emotional unavailability and unresponsiveness, or an inappropriate degree of responsiveness and need for availability.

Some of these children, in addition, show many of the symptoms of ADHD, with irritability and hyperactivity being fairly common. Others might show severe fluctuation in their affect (indicative of bipolar disorder). If these children have been neglected and or abused, they might show the mistrust and anger of maltreated children; they might also show many symptoms of trauma and have a full-blown post-traumatic stress disorder (for additional explanations of traumatic reactions, please see Chapter 16). Thus, adopted children who are given the diagnosis of "reactive attachment disorder" due to their difficulties with responsiveness (either over- or under-responsiveness), might in fact have additional issues, such as ADHD and mood problems, as well as issues related to maltreatment and traumatization.

If problems arise in the relationship with foster or adoptive children, what does the parent do? An option well publicized in the media and elsewhere is "holding therapy." I am seriously against these types of options. Parents are sometimes at their wits' end with such children, but it is a mistake in my professional opinion to physically constrain children and make them emotionally and physically surrender, which is what "holding therapy" is all about. Rebirthing and restraining techniques, also called attachment therapy, are part of this holding therapy model and are to be avoided. There is no scientific evidence that they are good solutions for any child. Such experiences are traumatizing for the child and only result in the type of bonding that occurs with one's enemy or captors, that is, traumatic bonding through regression, sometimes called the Stockholm Syndrome. In fact, it is unfortunate that the term *attachment therapy* is often used here because the research on parent-child relationships and security of attachments does not support this therapy framework. It should be avoided, even in the face of feelings of helplessness with a child diagnosed with reactive attachment disorder. What you want to strive for is a more benign and emotionally available relationship—one based on true give and take, rather than emotional surrender.

In addition to seeking professional help early, rather than when the family has experienced "secondary trauma," including depression and loss of energy (from caregiving of a traumatized child), the parents can become "therapeutic parents," as described in the previous section. Although your child will see the professional therapist for only one or two hours per week, you will be with your child on a daily basis and can help set the stage for additional gains.

Additionally, families and/or professionals should try not to separate the child from the family, unless absolutely necessitated in a time of crisis, such as for inpatient treatment. Such repeated separations during childhood are part of the reason for the reactive attachment disorder. However, families should have access to "respite care," which is a way for such families to get some needed time off from parenting. Respite care (for example, through contracting with other foster or adoptive families, perhaps for the weekend) is an absolute essential for such families to reenergize. The new foster or adoptive family is not to blame for this child's history, and to be a part of this child's future, the family needs to have some time off.

It is essential for families to have a professional specializing in reactive attachment disorder involved in their lives—early—rather than after becoming traumatized themselves. (A professional at a mental health center treating many foster and adoptive families is best because the approach is usually a team approach.) A professional skilled in this line of work will contact a child advocate, who can provide suggestions to the school on how to educate such children. For example, in school the child might be charming and delightful, but at home there might be a great deal of acting out. The school might then blame the parents for being part of the problem because they themselves do not see the problem behaviors. Or there might be "acting out" at the school as well as the home, and the children might manipulate the teachers to provide special exceptions for them (for example, to be excused from writing a report). The advocate can help advise the school that such exceptions are not in the best interests of the child and that consistency is important. Holding the line is key for both the schools and the families. Such professionals would also refer the child for medication evaluations, as many of these children need to be put on medications for their secondary diagnoses (such as ADHD or bipolar disorder). In addition, in case of crises (such as when there is a serious and angry outburst), someone on call can go out to the family to deescalate the situation. There are many safety considerations in such situations, and a team approach is what is most advisable. Waiting to enlist the help of a professional until much later only makes the family treatment more difficult.

It is also crucial for both parents to give similar and consistent messages to such a child, as such children have a knack for making one parent the good guy and the other the bad guy. As partners, you need to support one another, rather than providing different communications. It is particularly important for the primary caregiver to have a lot of support from the partner or spouse because these children have a tendency to dump on the person they spend the most time with and schmooze the other, so it is difficult for the nonprimary partner to see beyond the manipulation.

Use Emotional Interactions in Play

You can help your adoptive or foster child with the world of emotions by being the type of individual who can feel comfortable in that world. Your being able to express feelings in appropriate ways is often the invitation for your child to express his or her feelings.

In the context of play, aggressiveness might be one theme you'll need to address. If this is an issue your child is working on, you might have a box of animals available to let him or her act out aggressive fantasies. If your child picks out dinosaurs, also pick the same, so as to have a "family." As you pick out the same (preferably also the same number) of dinosaurs, say, "Bet you can't get me," getting into his or her world and feeling playful and comfortable in it. Your child is then likely to act aggressively and kill the animals. Let him or her do that, and announce, "You're the winner!" In this way, you can build self-esteem. Many of these children not only love to win (like all children), they absolutely have to, lest their self-esteem take a nosedive. You might make such comments as, "You're too strong for me," or, "You're too smart for me." Regardless of what your child does, try to have him win. His self-esteem will start soaring.

Another theme that might need addressing is "early starvation" because some of these children might have been malnourished. Kitchen food and pans will be good props. Still other children might respond to the theme of "doctor" using doctor kits because they might not have been taken care of in those early years. Remember, except for destructiveness to you or to himself or herself, this is the world of play, and any emotion is allowed. What most parents see over the course of time, and sometimes even in the first session, is a child moving toward benign themes.

Make a Poster of "Family Rules in Our Home" Together

Many of these children need very clear-cut structures and rules because the means of survival has been to fend for themselves. Tell your child that this poster will help with safety and feeling loved. Include here all the rules in your household, including the following:

- Relationships with siblings

- Relationships with pets (if pet safety is an issue, you might have a rule that your child will need to stay one foot away from the pet)

- Off-limit areas (example, your desk)

- Issues of space and physical boundaries between people (for example, getting too physically close to a family member or friend is not allowed)

- Not okay to hurt any person or any animal

- Other rules of your house

Do Some "Cognitive Restructuring"

In your interactions with your foster or adoptive child, you can take the child's perspective and discuss with him or her that the way he or she acts and reacts has a great deal to do with what happened early in his or her life. Point out that it is a good thing that your child turned out the way he or she did—because he or she survived! (Many of these children have been exposed to severely traumatizing experiences, and to survive, they have had to dissociate feelings from the pain inflicted on them. Had they not dissociated the feelings from the event, they might not have survived the event—as for example, of physical or sexual abuse.)

Do some "cognitive restructuring" so your child can see that the old actions that helped him or her survive are not helping in this new home. Assure your child that he or she is not bad, but merely a child who had to survive, and just as he or she learned those survival behaviors, he or she will need to relearn other behaviors more appropriate to the current environment. Assure your child that you will help him or her survive in this new situation without those old "survival behaviors." But now your child has a different life! By doing such cognitive restructuring with your child, you can help him or her make sense of his or her behavior.

You can also explain that your child might have been hurt and endangered by those who were close to him or her, and that is why he or she now feels distrust of close individuals. That is why the child can be so nice to a stranger but be scared of loving again. Say, "I love you anyway," but explain that this behavior is causing the child to have a consequence. In these ways, you help your child do a mind switch and begin a new life view about grown-ups—one in which his or her "broken heart" is taken into account. The story of Tin Man from *The Wizard of Oz* is usually helpful here to describe to your child someone who does not have a heart and is used to taking care of himself. This type of understanding also helps you, as the parent, so you do not personalize the problem behaviors.

Professionals trained in EMDR (Eye Movement Desensitization and Reprocessing) would use this type of cognitive restructuring to help such a traumatized child reprogram his or her brain to accept these messages. Such training is specialized and can actually change brain-behavior connections in traumatized children so the brain becomes more ready to accept new behaviors.

Help Your Child with Coherent Self-Expression Through Play

Indeed, many adoptive and foster children have had such disorganized lives that they are afraid to "let go" of reality to engage in imaginative play. They will engage with only a minimal imaginative quality. For example, such children might find it difficult to elaborate on any play theme and move aimlessly from one toy to another without developing a theme at all. Simply continuing the routine of play sessions in a consistent and predictable manner will enable your child to feel the emotional safety needed to move into imaginative play. Such play is usually the first sign that your child is ready to express the anxiety within and rechannel it into productive directions.

By being a part of your child's play, you can also help if he or she fragments easily in play or easily gets into chaotic themes that he or she cannot later reorganize (for example, if there are earthquakes or floods and everyone ends up dead). Such lack of coherence is not a sign of lack of intelligence, but merely a sign that the child's life has been disorganizing in some way. When one child was asked to tell a story with a beginning, middle, and end (or lesson) about why the cup in a picture was broken, she said that she had broken the cup (beginning) but told her mother that the cat had done it (middle). The end (or lesson) was that cats do bad things. Many children have difficulty creating coherent stories. Rewarding your child (for example, with different-color glass beads) for each part of the story that makes sense can help him or her create more logic in chains of events. Bruce Perry has described that children who have been traumatized often show disorganization because their brain becomes disorganized from early trauma. Such exercises help the brain reorganize.

Although some professional help might be necessary if your child's play shows such fragmentation and disorganization, you can also help as a parent by being empathic ("It must be scary to have that happen") and hanging in there with your child so he or she feels secure expressing such feelings. Over time, your child's play should become more organized. Certainly, one of the qualities of secure children who are also emotionally available is the ability to come back to a reality orientation. Escaping into fantasy, particularly fantasy of a destructive nature, is cause for concern. Professional consultations might be needed.

Use Alternatives to Praise

Because children with reactive attachment disorder view themselves as "bad," it is difficult for them to receive direct compliments. Many of these children have very low self-esteem. Praising them sometimes does not work. Instead, describe what your child is doing, for example, "You did the dishes, Andy," or "You're home on time." Be a "sportscaster." To your child, it will feel like praise or approval.

Complimenting indirectly by writing notes such as, "I love the way you gave me a hug when you came home" works better than directly saying it. Of course, try the direct route, but if your child shrinks in response, try this indirect route, which usually works well.

Build Empathy by Emphasizing Feelings

Particularly if foster-care placement or adoption occurred beyond infancy, your child might have trouble empathizing with others and knowing that others have feelings. To build empathy, play games related to feelings. Many professionals have such games available. In addition, spontaneous games can include everyday interactions in which you say to your child, "Guess what the cat must be feeling," or ask, "Do you remember what Mom was feeling in that situation?" Such children hear the feeling but often have difficulty remembering the feelings of others. Some practice can help. You can start the game by offering your own answer so your child has a chance to have a model of what you mean.

Maintain a Flair for "Inconsistent Consistency"

All children benefit from surprises, and when children have come to expect that grown-ups will not understand them, one of the nicest strategies is to surprise them—time and again. When your child violates one of the family rules, instead of having a detailed diatribe about it, say for example, "Okay, I need my kitchen floor cleaned in five minutes!" Or when your child least expects that you will comfort him or her when he or she has transgressed, say, "Let's go see a movie. It looks like you've had a hard day." As your child gets into one scrape after another, having a bag of surprises often gets his or her attention in a way that the age-old, repetitive prohibitions will not. Given that many of these children also are diagnosed with ADHD, they respond well to novelty and might be impressed by it. So at the same time that you maintain a consistent household and remain consistent with your partner, also maintain a flair for "inconsistent consistency."

Don't Push

As a parent of an adoptive or foster child, being nonhostile, nonjudgmental, nonevaluative, and nonderisive can go a long way toward creating a strong emotional relationship. Many adoptive or foster children have received a heavy dose of hostility and often "push limits," as if seeking that as a sign that life is familiar. Being available without being intrusive, feeling the need to take over, or feeling the need to perform are also part of being a therapeutic parent. Just sit back and see where things will go. That's a part of confidence and emotional availability. In the case of foster and adoptive children, not pushing is very important. You must allow your child to come to trust you. Even after a child trusts, there can be lapses of trust, but as long as you continue to be consistent in your own behavior, the child's trust will grow over time.

CHILDREN WITH DISABILITIES

Nowhere is the need for emotional connection between parent and child clearer than when the child is disabled. Many parents of children

---

Help your child make connections.

• Just like you are making connections—such as between past and present or your view of your child and your behavior—help your child make connections, too. Such connections in the context of conversation with your child can help him or her see the world in a logical, predictable fashion and will discourage distortions of reality.

• Therapeutic parenting is crucial for foster or adoptive children.

• Don't push. Allow your child to trust you.

with disabilities find themselves inhibited, often not knowing how to connect or even that they need to connect. They're confused, saddened, and often in mourning so much that they freeze emotionally or they put the focus on themselves rather than on their relationship with their child. A parent who has unresolved issues related to other losses in his or her life might face a challenge in understanding and relating when it comes to his or her disabled child. In fact, studies have indicated that if a parent has had other loss issues and has not resolved the grief related to those losses, he or she will be emotionally disconnected from a child with a disability, which is yet another loss—the loss of the perfect child. For example, having been rejected by a parent in the family of origin is a loss, and if a parent has not "earned security" related to such a loss (see Chapter 3), he or she might have difficulty interacting with a child with disabilities.

Autism

Establishing and maintaining emotional connection with children with autism, where there is less responsiveness toward the parent, can be especially difficult. I want to make the point clearly that years of research have proven that autism is a biologically based difficulty, not one that is "created" by parents. No amount of emotional unavailability will lead to childhood autism or Asperger's Syndrome. Nonetheless, we have important evidence that some autistic children seem more emotionally connected to their parents than others. It is thought that the parents' ability to read the autistic child's signals and their understanding of the syndrome and empathy toward the child can help foster an emotional climate where the autistic child can form relationships with his or her parents.

Cognitive Disabilities

To create emotionally available interactions with a child who has cognitive disabilities, take care not to focus only on your child's language or cognitive difficulties. Focus as much as possible on emotional communications. In one study, children who were hard of hearing or deaf were found to make greater gains in language development if their mothers were emotionally available, even after taking into account these children's earlier language development. What does that mean? It means that among children with similar levels of language competence when they are toddlers, those who have had emotionally available relationships make greater gains in language competence. I have watched numerous hours of tapes of hard-of-hearing and deaf children, and I am struck by the creative ways that some parents have been able to elicit lively, enthusiastic, and enjoyable interactions. Such emotionally available mothers show animated facial affect and create playful give-and-take with their children. In many, I would never have known that the child had a disability because the interactions look very similar to other emotionally available parent-child interactions.

Believe in the importance of emotional connections with your child with disabilities. Although your child might have a disability, he or she also is a whole child, with the same needs as other children. The disability is only one facet of your whole child.

- Learn as much as you can about your child's particular disability, and focus on the possible obstacles to emotional connection. For example, children with autism have trouble with social responsiveness and are, therefore, less emotionally available to their parents. In return, the parents might feel unrewarded in interactions. Work with yourself to read your child's cues. Although they will be difficult to read, you have the best chance of responding in an emotionally available way if you can interpret some cues. Children with Down's syndrome are difficult to read emotionally because their cues are not clear-cut. Again, learn about the disorder and your child's muted cues so you can make gains in reading his or her signals.

- Do not focus solely on cognitive or intellectual improvements. Focus as much on the whole child and the rich emotional connections you can establish with your child.

- Find other ways to communicate your emotions if your child's disability keeps him or her from understanding your expressions.

In a home setting, I watched a blind toddler and his mother. She seemed to make her voice as varied and melodic as could be. She was very eloquent in communicating her love through the verbal channel. Also, her focus did not seem to be on overcommunication of dangers in the environment but rather on emphasizing her enthusiasm for his new travels about the house. In turn, he seemed to enjoy his newly developed skill and delighted in his navigational skills. Similarly, a mother of a very fragile infant nonetheless engaged in robust physical play with her, as if she trusted that her daughter was strong and vibrant.

My goal here is to give hope to parents of children with disabilities that such children can form emotional bonds, that parents' attachments don't have to remain one-sided, and that no matter what a child's disability, he or she has the potential for connecting with a parent who loves the child and is willing to be emotionally available to him or her.

ATTENTIONAL/DISRUPTIVE PROBLEMS IN CHILDREN

Several studies from the University of Minnesota's renowned Institute of Child Development indicate that infants, with more intrusive mothers, even when the children have similar levels of distractibility, are more likely than others to be diagnosed with ADHD by the time they are in kindergarten. By more intrusive mothers, I mean a scenario something like this:

> A toddler moves toward an object of interest—say, a crystal vase. His mother comes from behind him and grabs the child, attempting to redirect him away from the vase. The toddler, feeling physically restrained and maybe even violated, becomes tense. After a short time, he moves toward a nearby plant and starts batting at its leaves. The mother again comes from behind the child and grabs him, this time yelling sharply, "Don't! I can't trust you for a minute!" The child now feels uneasy about trying anything new and starts running around the living room, batting at anything and everything in sight.

Parental intrusiveness is combined with hostile behavior. However, the parent seldom recognizes this combination of hostile-intrusive behavior in himself or herself. Such behavior might even seem normal. One dad (incidentally, married to a hostile-intrusive mother) told me, "I don't know if you have kids, but they can drive you crazy!" Another parent told me, "All my life, I wondered how parents can abuse their children. Then I became a parent, and now I am wondering why there isn't more child abuse." Comments such as these point to the normalization of hostile-intrusive behavior on the part of parents as they speak with other parents or adults.

Practitioners (and obviously parents) also know that ADHD children are tougher to parent. What works with your non-ADHD child often does not work with your ADHD child. Research indicates parenting with sensitivity as well as clear rules is the key to success with ADHD children. It is easy, however, to seem intrusive (even to yourself) as you parent an ADHD child. Here are important considerations so you do not tip over into intrusiveness:

- Particularly with your ADHD child, make the rules crystal clear.

- Also make clear that there will not be arguing about the rules, nor will there be discussion and debate of the rules. "Rules are rules."

- Explain that there will be clear, positive consequences for staying within the boundaries and clear, negative consequences for not.

- As you say, "Don't do that," to your ADHD child, it is crucially important for you to build pleasurable times as well. Make sure rewards include some one-on-one time with you that builds and rebuilds your rapport so your child "feels" that you like him or her. Such children are at very high risk for depression and low self-esteem.

- Recognize ADHD symptoms in your daughter as well as your son. ADHD is often thought not to exist in girls because they do not show the hyperactivity boys show. Although there is some controversy on this matter, girls with ADHD might be prone to anxiety, depression, low self-esteem, and helplessness.

- If your child has need for additional parental intervention techniques, consider some of those described earlier in this chapter. Be aware that many foster or adoptive children might also have a diagnosis of ADHD.

As a therapeutic parent, being available—that is, joining in your child's life in a positive way without feeling the need to "do" something—is sometimes the best thing you can do for your child. Being a positive "emotional follower" is very effective in signaling your availability. Be available when your child initiates interactions and creates pleasure. You can't force your child's gaiety or pleasure, but certainly you can join in it when it occurs! Sometimes *not* trying so hard is the best attempt you can do as a parent. Wait for signs of responsiveness in your child and then reward those signs by joining in with your child and sharing positive emotions. And when your child involves you in interactions, show pleasure and interest. Above all, *listen* to your child. These are behavioral ways in which you can reward your child for initiating interactions with you and for being responsive to you. The goal of emotional availability is connection and a sharing of emotions, not just one-sided positive emotions for either you or your child.

In all these exceptional situations, the parent's responsibilities for initiating and maintaining emotional availability is greater than ever. Parents with exceptional children quickly learn to celebrate the smallest movement, the smallest improvement in their children. But sometimes parents miss the improvements in the emotional relationship with their exceptional children, and those deserve to be recognized and celebrated, too. When your ADHD son sits still in your lap for a minute, or your autistic child smiles at you, or your foster child asks you for advice—these are moments of emotional connection that let you know your efforts are succeeding and you are giving your children the emotional sustenance they need so much.

Supporting Your Child During Your Divorce and Remarriage

The divorce transition is undoubtedly one of the most stressful events in anyone's life. For many, the shock of an impending divorce is delivered suddenly by the soon-to-be ex, beginning a process of loss for the entire family. For others, the process is prolonged, and there is much anticipatory loss even before the transition occurs. Many would call divorce an "ambiguous loss" because the person is not dead, the relationship continues in some form (especially if children are involved), and feelings can remain unresolved for a long time.

Although divorce dissolves the marital bond, children also can be very affected by the realization that the parents are no longer married, as well as the changes this causes in their own lives. One child said to his mother, "Will you still love me?" Another child asked her parent, "Will you die soon?" suggesting that she feared more unanticipated changes in her life.

For many parents, the process of divorce means "minimal parenting": As the parents try to sort out the different pieces of their lives, they can have a difficult time managing to take care of their children's most basic needs. Coping with the feelings of distress, anger, conflict within the self, conflict with the soon-to-be ex, and fear of the unknown looms large for parents at this time and, as a result, parenting can take on a lower priority. However, if you are in this situation, it is important to remember that your child is experiencing many of the same fears and feelings as you are, and he or she often has fewer emotional resources with which to process those feelings. The key is to focus on what your child wants most during this time, which is your emotional connection. If you can reassure your child of your love and your connection, if you can make your child feel he or she is still an emotional priority in your life, then your child is more likely to weather the difficult times of divorce in an emotionally healthy way.

THE NOTION OF A "GOOD" DIVORCE FOR CHILDREN

If emotional connections are healthy prior to the divorce and efforts are in place by both parents to keep those connections solid, then divorce is unlikely to be obviously harmful to the children. But is it possible to have a "good" divorce with few negative effects for children? Are there times when children actually experience benefits from divorce? These are very tough questions for families to ponder. For the first question, the answer is yes and no. If the emotional ties are kept healthy, divorce will probably have few effects on children. Of course, "few" effects does not mean that there are no effects. Research by Judith Wallerstein and Joan Kelly shows that divorce can have a long-term impact on a child's or adolescent's sense of trust in relationships. A child also might generalize this lack of trust to his or her view of romantic relationships. Divorce, therefore, can affect aspects of life other than parent–child emotional availability. Even in "good" divorces, children can grow up to have issues related to intimacy and commitment.

In some cases, however, divorce is actually helpful to the family's emotional health. In situations that involve intense conflict (up to and including spousal and/or child abuse), divorce can be a relief. One mother said, "I don't know why everyone said 'sorry' when I told them about my parents' divorce—it was the best thing for us." Hers was a family in which there was much violence toward the children. Constant bickering also might lead to a sense of relief when parents separate. Many children can feel happy that there might now be some peace in the household. The benefits of divorce usually are in direct proportion to the problems in the marriage that led to the divorce. For most children, a "good" divorce is infinitely better than living with parents who have a bad marriage.

PARENT-CHILD EMOTIONAL AVAILABILITY IN DIVORCED FAMILIES

A huge misconception is that divorced families need to do something different with their children for them to succeed. It certainly can be tougher to maintain emotional availability over time in a divorced family, if for no other reason than the "resource" problem (parents now provide care and connection singly rather than as a team). Nonetheless, what still matters most is for parents to find as many ways as possible to nurture emotional availability in the parent-child relationship.

If you have less time to be with your children after the divorce and seem to be spending a great deal of that time in basic care (picking up the children, getting supper on the table, and so on), you might have less playtime to connect. However, play is an important aspect of connecting and staying connected. Therefore, I suggest that parents find ways to incorporate playing with children with taking care of their needs. Any amount of playful exchange as you are preparing dinner or picking up the children from school at the end of a long day can be valuable. Play "I Spy" when you are driving your child home. Allow your child's doll to "help" fix dinner. Encourage your son to make up stories about Mr. Dish and Mrs. Spoon as you clear the table. Adopting a more playful style in general when it comes to parenting may go a long way to compensate for the lack of actual time spent in one-on-one play.

In the area of play, I also would suggest that parents be proactive. By this I mean that *you* suggest play before dinner. Simply saying, "Let's play for a few minutes together with those dolls you just got" (and then following through) can go a long way toward preventing behavioral problems. Children often seek negative attention because they think they will not receive any other kind. When parents are proactive, children don't need and seek negative attention, and when you offer them the extra focus of proactively seeking opportunities for play, you are actually preventing problems from cropping up. Because disciplinary issues are important aspects of single parenting, and particularly single mothering, I highly recommend the proactive playtime approach with your child. Single or married, you certainly can squeeze a few minutes out of the day to play with your child.

Studies from my laboratory indicate that it is not the amount of time we spend with our children (as a single or married parent), but the quality of that time that is crucial. I also believe, however, that parents do need a certain amount of time to be able to display and have their children experience their emotional availability. "Knowing" our children occurs in the context of spending time with them. Therefore I not only recommend that parents focus on spending high-quality time with their children, but I also emphasize parental physical availability. By physical availability, I mean being around and available to your child—not necessarily focusing all your attention on the child but not ignoring him or her, either. Sitting in the living room, reading a newspaper, or going through mail while your child plays close by can give your child the reassurance of your physical presence. And when your child glances your way and sees you are noticing him or her, the child feels an emotional connection with you even if you do nothing else in that moment.

What is the "right" amount of emotional and physical availability? Your child as well as your relationship with him or her are the barometers for the "quality versus quantity" question. Look to the experience of your child. After a long period of close connection (during a family vacation, for example), it might feel fine for you to have long workdays. But if your emotional connection with your child is frayed, invest more time in the relationship. After all, how a relationship "feels" to your child and to you determines whether you are involved in an emotionally available parent-child relationship.

EMOTIONALLY AVAILABLE SINGLE PARENTHOOD

A friend of mind whose husband went out of town for four days and left her with two preschoolers said, "No one should have to do for this more than a weekend." A single dad told me, "It's so hard to do everything all the time." Indeed, single parents have limited time and limited resources as they try to meet all of a child's (or children's) needs, with no reprieve in sight. Limited time and limited emotional resources are two important factors that create stress for single parents. Indeed, relieving their own emotional stress is a vital skill for single mothers and fathers. When a parent's negative feelings (called hostility in the emotional availability framework) can be released elsewhere, then children are less likely to be exposed to it—a huge plus. Be it within support groups or through old or new friendships, single parents need to have outlets to dissipate any buildup of hostility.

Being a single parent can mean you are geographically far away from your ex-spouse and, therefore, you must rely only on yourself to be physically available—to pick up the kids, supervise playdates, help with homework, and so on. It's a tremendous strain when you cannot rely on anyone else to "fill in" for you in a physical sense. Therefore, it is important for single parents to accept support when it's offered or when it's available. It is also important to *ask* for it. It's remarkable what others will do for you if you simply and directly ask them to—for example, "Could you have the kids over for a playdate this week?" Being able to receive others' emotional availability is a reflection on one's sense of trust of others.

John Bowlby, the British psychiatrist who described the importance of the parent-child bond and its effects on later development, recounted stories of individuals who are "compulsively self-reliant." Such individuals are self-sufficient in most aspects of their lives, including the personal, and do not rely on others. Bowlby viewed this quality as similar to the profile of the insecure/avoidant infant and child who does not believe that he can trust another to support him in times of need. Thus, to be able to accept support from a trusted individual is a nice sign of interdependence, what Bowlby referred to as "self-reliance." Such individuals take care of many aspects of their lives in a competent fashion yet know that at times they need to rely on others. Such individuals were likened to the secure infant, who is competent and independent but knows that he or she can come back for connection with a trusted caregiver.

No matter how much time and energy single parents expend in physical availability, however, I firmly believe (and studies support the fact) that beyond a certain point, emotional availability is more important than physical availability. One single mother, Linda, told me, "My husband was so disconnected from the kids and from me for the last seven years of our marriage that it has been easier to single-parent the kids than to parent them together." The emotional differences in the two spouses can be such a strain in parenting that it can be easier (and less confusing) for the children to see each parent separately. Nonetheless, creating emotional availability is still an important goal, whether in single- or two-parent homes.

There is good news, though, for single parents: Research by E. Mavis Hetherington of the University of Virginia shows that as long as parents are sensitive to their children's emotional needs, family structure has only a small effect on child adjustment. Of course, it's more difficult to be consistently emotionally available as a single parent, but, as Linda just stated, many single parents do a better job now than they did when they were married. It is increasingly recognized that family structure by itself is not an important predictor of an emotionally available home. If parents can maintain emotionally available relationships with their children, then children from single-parent homes do not look different from those from two-parent homes.

THE QUESTION OF JOINT PARENTING AFTER DIVORCE

The issue of having an ex-spouse in the picture is clearly a difficult one. Many parents want to forget that they ever married or had children with their ex. In a recent divorce transition of a low-conflict, sixteen-year marriage, the mother became highly combative in the divorce process and refused to have any contact with the father, even around the children's day-to-day activities. "Contact me by e-mail or phone only in bona fide emergencies, and nothing else," she said; she didn't even want to know what medications the children used or what school-related events transpired while the children were with their father. She already had started a new relationship and wanted to ignore her prior marriage altogether. Certainly, for her not having an ex-spouse in the equation made her life smoother, as her new relationship didn't have the intrusions of an ex.

The children suffer in this type of situation, however. High conflict in a family is the single most important indicator of childhood maladjustment. High conflict usually means that there is little interparental communication. In this case, some communication would have helped the children; for example, when there is something as mundane as pinkeye, it is helpful to know how long a child needs eyedrops. With no communication (except for bona fide emergencies), the children were caught in the middle. It is difficult to be emotionally available to your children without taking the full context of their lives into account. More important, if you are unable to create nonhostility in the marriage and/or the divorce, the children will feel your hostility and will be affected by it. Hostility is obviously detrimental to emotional availability.

In the case of single parents, each parent's emotional connection with the children is better when there is less conflict in the divorce situation. At the very least, single parents should avoid saying anything negative about their ex-spouses directly to the children, or even when the children might hear them. Children need to feel some positive things about each parent, and hearing negative comments makes them feel inadequate about themselves. As one child put it, "When my dad talks that way about my mom, it's as if one half of me is bad and not lovable." Thus a good divorce, just like a good marriage, can help paternal (as well as maternal) healthy emotional connections with the children.

In spite of whether you and your ex-spouse now share parenting responsibilities, you *have* shared in the creation of your child, who now will be affected by your attitudes toward each other. For the sake of your child, you and your ex-spouse need to come to some sort of agreement about how you will treat each other and talk about each other. Any feelings of hostility on either side should be handled through counseling. Remember that hostility can "leak" into your relations with your child and affect your emotional connection in a negative way. Especially if both you and your ex-spouse continue to be active in your child's life, you owe it to your child to treat each other with courtesy.

HELPING YOUR CHILD TRANSITION FROM ONE
PARENT TO ANOTHER

Emotional availability is a dynamic quality of a relationship. If you attend to it and nurture it in yourself, and attend to it and nurture it in your baby or child, you begin to have more of it. However, circumstances beyond your control can affect your emotional availability as well as that of your child. For example, if you share parental responsibilities with your ex-spouse (an arrangement formerly called "joint custody"), the emotional aspects of the separations and the residential instability need to be negotiated and renegotiated with your child. If you don't see your child on a day-to-day basis, for instance, you need to reestablish a connection after each transition. The transition period, in fact, is a specific point in time when parental emotional availability matters greatly, even in the face of a child's apparent emotional unavailability to the parent.

Some children show avoidance upon reunion with a parent after they have been with the other parent by turning away, not talking or answering questions, and so on. Such avoidance might not be a rejection, but merely a sign that the child is reserved after the separation. If you can help your child during the transition period, rather than seeing it as an active rejection of yourself, the quality of the emotional connection in your parent-child relationship will be enhanced in the long run. What is important is for you to be sensitive to the dynamics of your child's feelings in such situations and to do your best to apply the elements of emotional availability to reconnect with your child after a period of time apart.

Stephen, a physician in Colorado, shared custody of his six-year-old son, Joseph, with his ex-wife, who lived on the other side of town. Whenever Joseph would return from spending a week with his mother, the little boy would go straight to his room and play computer games. He would avoid his father completely for a day or so, no matter how hard Stephen tried to involve Joseph in conversation, play, or other activities. Stephen felt frustrated and saw Joseph's behavior as a personal rejection.

When Stephen talked to me about this situation, I pointed out that Joseph's avoidance was not personal and could simply mean that the child needed emotional space to make the transition from one parent to the other. I suggested that Stephen signal his emotional availability to Joseph by telling Joseph how glad he was to have him home, being available but not forcing his son to relate until the little boy was ready, then offering opportunities for emotional connection that the child felt comfortable accepting. Stephen told me later that by giving Joseph a chance to reestablish his emotional connection with him on Joseph's own time, their relationship was easier and actually closer than before.

One of the nicest things you can do to facilitate the transition is not to immediately ask your child about time with the other parent. Many children sense that they need to protect one parent (perhaps the parent who didn't want the divorce) and might report negative events in an attempt to please the parent. Be the follower here as well, and wait for your child to describe his or her time with your ex.

DISCIPLINE IN STRESSFUL TIMES

Certainly stressful life circumstances (divorce, unemployment, or illnesses) might make it difficult to start off on an emotionally available footing. Such events also can derail an already emotionally available relationship. However, discipline in the context of emotional connection is still possible, even under stressful circumstances. For example, studies by E. Mavis Hetherington show that single mothers find it more difficult than single fathers to discipline in a consistent manner. Yet the children of single mothers who are able to discipline with emotional connection are better adjusted that those without emotional connection. Thus, the same principles apply in two-parent as well as single-parent relationships. Discipline is good for children, and disciplining in an emotionally connected way is good parenting, be it in a two-parent family or before, during, or after divorce.

Families of divorce must understand that because emotional availability is about a relationship, each parent can establish his or her own rules with respect to disciplinary issues. Although inter-parent communication about discipline as well as many other issues is ideal, in the absence of such communication, each parent can establish the quality of emotional availability in each household. Discipline—being an aspect of the relationship—is negotiated. Children do have the capacity to keep things separate and to respond in a way that is relationship-specific. Thus, emotional availability—emotional connection in the context of discipline—can be your trademark even if it is not your ex-spouse's trademark. Certainly our research indicates that when parents show more emotionally available qualities in the context of discipline, children respond. And when parents change their level of emotional availability, either through therapy or through a personal reawakening that such a change has to happen, children respond in turn.

SUPPORTING YOUR KIDS WHEN YOU FORM A NEW FAMILY

"We're so happy we're getting married—except for all the problems we've been facing with the kids!" This is an all-too-common statement when parents remarry. A parent's remarriage often causes a rise in children's behavior problems at school and other settings. Over time, however, children's adjustment generally improves. This is not to say that remarriage isn't problematic as far as the kids are concerned. Hetherington's research indicates, in fact, that children from single-parent families are better adjusted compared to remarried families.

Does that mean you should not remarry? No. But it does mean that being particularly attentive to your child and listening to his or her experiences is an important part of forming new attachments. As a parent, be sure your child feels welcomed and included in your new life, and be sure that you remain open to communication and discussion with your child. One undergraduate student remembered that her father was so focused on making his new relationship work that he spent a great deal of energy "keeping things happy." In truth, what keeps a relationship together is communication, not extraordinary efforts to keep things positive. The student said later that communication was always missing from her relationship with her father. A lack of communication often can be the real reason for the breakup of a marriage, the difficulty with the children, and the difficulties in the remarried family. Open and meaningful communication can be helpful at all levels.

CREATING EMOTIONAL CONNECTION WITH A NEW SPOUSE'S CHILD

One of the most important aspects of remarriage is that as a new spouse you do *not* attempt to replace the father (or mother). Many new spouses make the mistake of assuming that they should walk into the shoes of the ex-spouses and discipline their spouse's children. But this, in fact, is the very act to which a stepchild reacts negatively. *Joining* with your "new" child at an emotional level is more effective. Over time, your relationship with your stepchild may grow to include a certain amount of control—hopefully structuring with minimal intrusiveness and hostility. Starting with an attempt to control is almost always a mistake. Keeping discipline in your spouse's court might be the very thing that helps you bond with your new child.

Fortunately, when a new spouse is emotionally sensitive to the feelings and needs of his or her stepchild, and when the new spouse is smart enough to go slow and allow the relationship to develop at its own pace, the stepchild can form a strong attachment with him or her. When recalling their families of origin, many adults remember stepparents as an important part of the equation. Many report that their stepparents were closer to them than their biological parents were. The possibilities for emotional connection exist in stepfamilies, but they need to grow over time rather than being viewed as an instant connection.

It is true that children are a main reason for the fragility of many remarriages. Older children and adolescents are particularly difficult to convince of the importance of their parent's remarriage. (Younger children are generally more accepting of a new parent.) Emotional availability with your stepchild need not feel different than emotional availability with your own child. The same elements continue to be important, except for the disciplinary compo-nent. When it comes to discipline and structure, it might be wise to think of yourself as a mentor rather than a parent. Children react well to an adult men-tor and report that stepparents have been very effective in teaching them im-portant habits and life skills. Until you have spent a lot of time with your stepchild, it might be worthwhile to see yourself as a mentor.

CREATING AN EMOTIONAL CONNECTION BETWEEN A NEW SPOUSE AND A CHILD

The same rules apply with your new spouse and your child as for you and his or her child. The new spouse should take his or her emotional cues from the child, just as you do. It also is important for your blended family that neither parent speaks negatively about the ex-spouses. Evidence sug-gests that a remarried family is at risk for "parental alienation syndrome," in which the remarried couple forms a coalition against the ex-spouses. Evidence indicates that children are very negatively affected by such at-tempts at parental alienation. If you cannot be friendly, at least be cordial and civil about your ex-spouse. Such civility will actually help nurture bonds within the new family unit. In addition, listening, communication, and trying to understand the experience of the child through this process are all important aspects of the new family relationship.

"BLENDING" A FAMILY

Blending two families into a new family group after remarriage is al-most always a challenge. But the key, as always, is to do your best to keep the emotional connections you have had with your own child while nur-turing new connections with your spouse and stepchild. Use the elements of emotional availability as a shortcut to creating relationships when you can. Ultimately, it will take time for these relationships to develop. Be sat-isfied with small wins in the short term. They will add up to strong rela-tionships and a happy, blended family in the long run.

Keeping the Connection
in Times of Crisis

The terrorist attacks of 2001 affected everyone in some way. After September 11, many parents felt helpless and hopeless trying to reassure and comfort their children about peace and harmony in their lives. With additional terrorist threats and attacks, including anthrax, sniper shootings, and so on, what can parents do to help children feel safe in a terrorized world? How can we reassure our children especially when we ourselves are feeling uncertain and fearful?

Emotional crises also are personal. Most families must deal with personal crises such as accident, death, terminal illness, trauma, and violence at some point in their history. How can a family reorganize after a grief-related event such as death, illness, or trauma? If there is only one parent remaining after such an event, how can the remaining single parent help his or her child deal with grief?

In today's world, it is far too likely that children themselves will be the victims of violence or other trauma. Many children are exposed to violence in their schools, in their neighborhoods, and in their families. The closer the violence is to their own backyards, the greater the traumatic impact on children. Sometimes children actually witness such violence, which results in greater traumatization than if the children had simply heard about it. Sometimes trauma is not the result of violence but of accidents—car crashes, in particular. We now know that children experience trauma long after being involved in a car crash. How can parents help their children process their fears of being hurt, injured, or killed themselves? How can parents help them feel safe again in a world that we cannot deny is a dangerous place?

Caring for your child is not only your territory as the parent. Such caregivers as teachers can help children deal with crises or trauma occurring both at home and in the outside environment. What is the role of additional caregivers (in day-care centers or preschools) and teachers in helping children in times of personal or world crises? What can caregivers do for children who show signs of emotional difficulties? How can they help children in day-to-day ways cope with what appears to be an unsafe world?

Whether national or personal, in times of crisis, your emotional connection with your children becomes even more important. All the traits of emotional availability, but in particular sensitivity and nonhostility, will help you keep a strong, connected relationship with your child when things are difficult. Your child needs to know you are there for him or her, and that even if your child is uncertain of everything else, he or she can count on the security of your love.

UNDERSTANDING YOUR CHILD'S SIGNALS AND COMMUNICATIONS

How can you show your sensitivity to your child's signals and communications? The following suggestions should help you.

- Try to understand your child's fears and provide a safe haven in facial expression, tone of voice, actions, as well as words. Make eye contact with your child as often as possible. Eye contact gives your child a sense of connection rather than the distance that often accompanies trauma.

- Pair the nonverbal with verbal. During trying times, children need words ("I love you," "I will make sure you are safe") and actions (hugging, holding). Such pairings can be reassuring to children—even the youngest children who are preverbal.

- Be openly communicative by putting words to your own feelings as well as your child's. Words help organize the world and provide a filter and lens for feelings. Help your child recognize and label his or her feelings (sad, worried, scared, nervous, mad, and so on).

- Especially in times of crisis, you will not spoil infants and toddlers by giving them "too much" emotional attention. Meeting your child's emotional needs helps him or her become more confident and secure with you. Such feelings of security then generalize to the outside world. Even though the world is not secure in all ways, particularly now, children need to learn to live as if they are in a generally secure world.

- Even when it's not true, behave as if your interactions with your child are going the way you would like. When you go to pick up your child and he or she turns away or seems withdrawn, pretend as if he or she is looking at you and hugging you. If your child feels that you have a positive expectation of him or her, any "shutdown" behavior your child might demonstrate can be modified.

- Play, especially vigorous play (see Chapter 7) helps children bring up big feelings and "work on" those emotional clouds. Engage in physically active play (exercise and creative movement) with your child—such play can be particularly important during times of stress and crisis.

- Play with your child using the therapeutic parenting principles described in Chapter 14 and be sensitive to any traumatizing themes. Help your child release the anxiety by acting on such themes in play. Joining your child in such imaginative play is exactly what emotionally available parents do. You need not end each of these sessions on a positive note through problem-solving; over time, however, the chaos of traumatic play usually becomes more organized.

- Even if you yourself are crying from your own grief and trauma, telling your child that you love him or her even though you are in distress provides relief.

MAINTAINING STRUCTURE AND "BEING THERE" FOR YOUR CHILD

How can you be sure that you are maintaining enough structure in your child's life after a crisis or trauma and that you are "being there" for him or her?

- Keep to your routines as much as possible. Continue any family rituals, such as kissing your child good-night, reading a story at bedtime, going over homework, or playing with a certain toy. Predictability acts as a security blanket for your child (and you!) in troubled times. Although it is normal for a child to "act out" his or her emotions during times of stress, be sure your child understands that the family rules of conduct continue to apply.

- Be predictable yourself. It's important for your child to see you as consistent and predictable—someone he or she can take for granted.

- Spend extra time being close to your child. Kids communicate when *they* are ready, not when their parents are. When your child seems ready, slow down to listen and notice what he or she has to say.

- Do activities that your child chooses. It will help your child feel in control.

- Follow your child's lead. When children are feeling out of control, it becomes even more important to give them a sense of control by following their lead and joining them in whatever they want to play or whatever they would like to talk about.

CONTAINING HOSTILITY AND NEGATIVITY

You can contain hostility and negativity in your home by enacting the following suggestions:

- Find avenues to vent your own anxiety so you can be calm and less irritable for your child. Because young children look to adults to help them organize what the family is experiencing, adults need to recognize and manage their emotions (although they need not and should not deny their own negative feelings). It is important for your child to know that you are in control, but that does not mean that you cannot show your feelings. Most important, your child must know that he or she is not the cause of your feelings of distress.

- Maintain a peaceful culture within your home. Limit your child's exposure to media and adult conversations about crisis or disaster (which repetitively show violence or other terrifying events), and be sure your child spends ample time with calm and reassuring adults.

REGAINING EMOTIONAL AVAILABILITY

When children are experiencing the effects of crisis or trauma, their behaviors often change. Some kids become whiny and clingy; others become remote. Here are some key things to look for when your child is in crisis and ways to respond that will help your child process his or her feelings more quickly:

- Know the language of young children. They absorb the tension, fear, and hurt of the people around them. Even the youngest babies react to the distress and depression of adults, and they show their distress through their behavior—clinging, crying, and being contrary.

- Do not act as if your child's traumatized behavior is a personal insult. When children are traumatized, they often avoid or move away rather than moving toward caregivers. Infants and toddlers might do this by looking away, turning away, kicking, and screaming. Older children might do some of the same, or they might be quiet, closed to discussion, or even aggressive. They might use rejecting and aggressive language toward their caregivers. Such behaviors are the expression of traumatization and terror; they are not a personal rejection of you. Continue being nurturing and caring, and over time, your child will respond, especially when such behaviors do not drive you away.

· If your child becomes whiny, clingy, or has tantrums, be prepared to "stay through" such times. Although it is very difficult to stay and soothe a child who shows such reactions for a prolonged period, remember that, as a parent, you are the "container" that can help your child feel safe as he or she expresses such feelings. Such reactions combined with your calming and supportive presence help a child work through grief and other trauma-related emotions.

· Encourage richer thinking. When children are particularly anxious and fearful, they might have more trouble being reassured that life will be fine and that their family and friends will be fine as well. What can help these as well as other children is getting them accustomed to thinking about "different possibilities." Even though they do not have the cognitive wherewithal of adolescents to truly hypothesize about different realities and possibilities, all children benefit from a richer texture to their thinking, and adults can provide the modeling for that. For example, these children can speculate with adults that either this will happen or something completely different, or maybe even something that is a surprise. They can be taught to have richer thinking, which is helpful as a coping strategy for all children in all spheres of their lives.

· Ask your child to draw pictures and talk about them. Have your child draw pictures of negative feelings and then of positive feelings. Ask your child to think about and talk about the differences between the two pictures.

· Ask your child to draw a family map, especially showing the distance and closeness of family members. Encourage your child to talk about what makes him or her feel the closeness and the distance.

TAKING CARE OF YOURSELF

It is important to remember that you also need to take care of your own emotional needs in times of trauma and crisis in the following ways:

- Be aware of how your past might be affecting your reaction to terror and crisis. Early experiences in people's lives shape how they deal with stressful events. For example, a woman who was raised by her mother after the unexpected death of her father recalls that her mother seemed emotionally distant throughout the woman's childhood. Under stress this woman now becomes emotionally remote and numb herself, rather than being able to be emotionally connected.

- Take time to express and release any feelings that might weigh you down and make it difficult for you to play with your child. As a parent, you need to disperse the emotional clouds gathered over your own head and life. If you must cry, do so. It is time well spent and will help you on the road to recovery.

- Try to have more listening time with others. Sadness and other feelings of grief need to be communicated. When you are listened to as a parent or caregiver, you will be able to listen to your child. Such communication and support by others can give you "staying power" to help your child at a later time. There is a parallel between helping yourself and the help you can provide to your child; caring for yourself is a start in caring for your child.

STRENGTHEN FAMILY BONDS

Times of trauma and crisis also can be moments of opportunity to create stronger, deeper emotional bonds. Families who have weathered crises often report they are closer to each other than ever before. As a parent, it is up to you to help your child turn crisis into opportunity—to help your child grow stronger, happier, and more appreciative of the love you have for your child and the love your child has for you. If you are a caregiver, you also can help your charges learn from life and take the best possible meaning from difficult circumstances. No matter what age or level your child is, you can become closer to him or her by offering support in the difficult moments. And you will feel more supported yourself as a result.

Conclusion

Emotional availability in the parent-child relationship is important because it can help a child feel an enduring sense of security in the parent-child attachment and, consequently, make a child feel more secure in this insecure world. Some parents will easily connect to these ideas and the scientific evidence that supports such work. Others might be more skeptical. For example, one businessman client I am currently seeing in my private practice had told me that he did not see the value of spending so much time becoming "emotionally available, as you say." But he decided to try the ideas anyway. What he has recently been describing to me is that not only is he a better father and husband (the qualities he had been seeking to improve), but he is also better at his job as a CEO of a highly recognized corporation. He found that his skills of emotional availability have helped him in the workplace. Being more sensitive toward employees, structuring of their efforts, nonintrusive in his suggestions and actions but available and connected, and nonhostile and better emotionally regulated when interacting with them, has helped him keep a great team of players at work. He has built quite a reputation as a nice boss!

Another client—a sixty-year-old female—is, with her husband, now raising her three grandchildren. Her son married a woman overseas while stationed in Europe and had three children with her in five years. With too many cultural and religious issues separating them, the young couple eventually divorced, but not before the biological mother was addicted to street drugs and began to seriously neglect the children. The grandmother stepped in to raise the children, lest they be taken into foster care. She is now raising the children and needs the skills of emotional availability. She recalls having "missed that" when she was raising her two boys in the context of an early bad marriage and is now seeing her grandparenting as a "second chance." Although very busy as a businesswoman, she is grateful that she has a stable family life and financial circumstances that enable them to have more time for nurturing her grandchildren.

Research evidence sees benefits in the area of learning and other aspects of development. In fact, a Harvard University study indicated that emotional connection with one's parents also could be a protective factor against disease. This large study followed a group of individuals over many decades. It discovered that those from loving homes were healthier at middle age, even when factors such as smoking were taken into account. I have seen many patients, students, and participants in research who have recounted stories of depression and/or substance use precipitated by emotional upheaval or even emotional vacancy in relationships.

As a clinician with a private practice, as a professor in interaction with my students, and as a researcher interviewing hundreds of families over sixteen years, I have been impressed by the power of parental emotional availability to help keep families afloat. I've also been struck by the power of emotional *un*availability to create problems even when parents try hard in other ways (paying tuition for private school or college, rarely leaving children with baby-sitters, supervising numerous playdates, and so on). The functional aspects of parent-child relationships are sometimes so time-consuming that parents might not feel they have the energy for emotional connection. Yet when parents recall their own families of origin, they rarely remember the functional aspects of family life; instead, they focus on the family's emotional life (or lack thereof). They seem to appreciate the provision of these functional resources but are affected most by the emotional.

I have placed a great deal of emphasis on the caregiver in this book because caregivers are empowered to make the difference in their relationships with children. Although the concept of emotional availability and security started with research on parents and children, and indeed, most of the research has been on mothers and most of the research has been done with two-parent families, these emotional availability skills are relevant for fathers from two-parent families, single dads, single mothers, grandparents, foster parents, day-care providers, teachers, and all those who work with children. Further, this work has far-reaching implications and extends beyond those who work with children.

Will you know that the principles outlined here are working for you and your child? The proof is in your child when he or she is more responsive to you and comes to you—as a baby, he or she physically moves toward you as well as moves away to explore, as in a full circle, and then the circle starts again; as an older child and adolescent, your son or daughter comes to you with problems and shares joys with you, and there is a greater amount of the pleasure than of the distress—he or she seems to be enjoying life in a confident and secure way.

Many adults relate more easily to older, verbal children than to babies. It is possible for adults to read the signals of babies and to read their view of a relationship and appreciate that babies can tell us so much about how they feel, once we begin to observe and read their signs and communications. Understanding whether they feel secure with us is one of the nicest communications, because just about everything else is built upon that foundation of security.

You are connected to your child for life—and it's up to you to determine the quality of that connection. When you focus on being emotionally available to your child and work to create a rich, strong, loving bond throughout childhood and adolescence, the rewards are not only immeasurable, they will last beyond your lifetime. Your child's happiness and ability to live a fulfilled life are the true legacies of emotional availability. Your loving, supportive, emotionally available relationship is the best inheritance you can offer your precious child.

However, we are connected not only to our children but the wider world in which we all live. It is unfortunate that one of the first clear signs of becoming a global society has meant that our children experience growing up in an insecure and sometimes traumatizing world—even if they are secure with us and we have been emotionally available to them.

Although there can be no clear "formula" for the prevention and intervention of insecurities in general, I have been inspired by the anthropological work of R. Rohner, who has studied many societies. In his detailed research, he has uncovered the fascinating fact that societies have "personalities"—some being cool and distant, others being warm and gregarious, and so on. He further has documented a link between the child-rearing practices of specific societies and the type of personality typically seen in these societies. For example, in cultures where the general child-rearing practices are harsh, rejecting, and full of shaming, the adults are distant, cool, and rejecting in their relationships as well. In contrast, where child-rearing practices are characterized by warmth, support, and caring, adults in that culture have relationships that are kind and caring. Such links to the wider world lend credence to my belief in the importance of parenting in every society.

Many world leaders, both historically and currently, have been raised under abusive conditions. How can they then lead nations toward peace and positive connections when all they have known is brutality, the threat of violence, and relational ruptures within their own childhoods? The field of psychohistory deals with this very issue—of how abusive childhoods have bearing on the brutality of world leaders, how feeling unloved can lead to international terrorism. Studies of prisoners also document unhappy childhoods and their feelings of not being cared for by their parents.

The reason we should think in terms of communities is that research has documented that children need "one supportive figure" in their lives to become happy individuals. Although it is always wonderful to have more supportive figures, it appears that even one—one parent, uncle, teacher, or friend—can make the difference between an individual who has walled himself or herself off from others, unable to feel the pain of a victim, and an individual who can "come back" from adversity.

I would like to think of emotional availability as a responsibility in parent-child relationships as well as relationships in the wider world—between partners, co-workers, in communities, and in the wider world. It is a responsibility that can have far-reaching implications for all of us.

References

CHAPTER 1: PARENTS AND KIDS—CONNECTED FOR LIFE

Children's Defense Fund website, www.childrensdefense.org.

Goleman, D. *Emotional Intelligence.* New York: Bantam Books, 1995.

Maynard, J. "A Mother's Day." *Parenting.* June/July, 1995.

Reik, T. *Of Love and Lust: On the Psychoanalysis of Romantic and Sexual Emotions.* New York: Farrar, Strauss, and Cudahy, 1957.

Remond, C. L. In C. G. Woodson, ed., *The Mind of the Negro as Reflected in Letters Written During the Crisis, 1800–1860.* Washington, DC: The Association for the Study of Negro Life and History, 1926.

Russek, L., and G. Schwartz. Study cited in L. E. Shapiro, *How to Raise a Kid with a High E.Q.: A Parents' Guide to Emotional Intelligence.* New York: Harper-Collins, 1997, p. 28.

Taffel, Ron. *Parenting by Heart: How to Stay Connected to Your Child in a Disconnected World.* New York: Perseus Publishing, 2002.

Toffler, Alvin. *Future Shock.* New York: Bantam Books, 1991.

Whitehead, J. *The Stealing of America.* Westchester, IL: Crossway Books, 1983.

CHAPTER 2: IS YOUR CHILD SECURE WITH YOU?

Ainsworth, M.D.S. *Infancy in Uganda: Infant Care and the Growth of Love.* Baltimore: Johns Hopkins University Press, 1967.

Ainsworth, M.D.S., and S. M. Bell. "Attachment, Exploration, and Separation: Illustrated by the Behavior of One-Year-Olds in a Strange Situation." *Child Development* 41, 1970, 49–67.

———"Some Contemporary Patterns in the Feeding Situation." In A. Ambrose, *Stimulation in Early Infancy.* London: Academic, 1969.

Ainsworth, M.D.S., M. C. Blehar, E. Waters, and S. Wall. *Patterns of Attachment: A Psychological Study of the Strange Situation.* Hillsdale, NJ: Erlbaum, 1978.

Belsky, J., Garduque, L., and E. Hrncir. "Assessing Performance, Competence, and Executive Capacity in Infant Play: Relations to Home Environment and Security of Attachment." *Developmental Psychology,* 20, 1984, 406–417.

Bowlby, J. *Attachment and Loss. Vol. 2. Separation.* New York: Basic, 1973.

———*The Making and Breaking of Affectional Bonds.* London: Tavistock, 1979.

———*Attachment and Loss. Vol. 3. Loss, Sadness, and Depression.* New York: Basic, 1980.

———*Attachment and Loss. Vol. 1. Attachment.* New York: Basic, 1982 (original work published 1969).

——— *A Secure Base.* New York: Basic, 1988.

Bretherton, I., and Waters, E., eds. "Growing Points of Attachment Theory and Research." *Monographs of the Society for Research in Child Development,* 50, 1985, 1–2, Serial No. 209.

Cassidy, J., and L. Berlin. "The Insecure/Ambivalent Pattern of Attachment: Theory and Research." *Child Development,* 65, 1993, 972–991.

Cassidy, J., and R. R. Kobak. "Avoidance and Its Relation to Other Defensive Processes." In J. Belsky and T. Nezworski, eds. *Clinical Implications of Attachment.* Hillsdale, NJ: Erlbaum, 1988.

Grossman, K., K. E. Grossman, G. Spangler, G. Suess, and L. Unzner. "Maternal Sensitivity and Newborns' Orientation Responses as Related to Quality of Attachment in Northern Germany." In I. Bretherton and E. Waters, eds. "Growing Points of Attachment Theory and Research." *Monographs of the Society for Research in Child Development,* 50, 1985, 1–2, Serial No. 209.

Hall, F., S. Pawlby, and S. Wolkind. "Early Life Experience and Later Mothering Behaviors: A Study of Mothers and Their 20-Week-Od-Babies." In D. Shaffer and J. Dunn, eds. *The First Year of Life.* 1979, pp. 153–174.

Sroufe, L. A. "Infant-Caregiver Attachment and Patterns of Adaptation in Preschool: The Roots of Maladaptation and Competence." In M. Perlmutter, ed. "Development and Policy Concerning Children with Special Needs." *Minnesota Symposia on Child Psychology, Vol. 16.* Hillsdale, NJ: Erlbaum, 1983.

Sroufe, L. A., and E. Waters. "Heartrate as a Convergent Measure in Clinical and Developmental Research." *Merrill-Palmer Quarterly,* 23, 1997, 3–28.

CHAPTER 3: THE IMPACT OF YOUR CHILDHOOD ON YOUR CHILD

Biringen, Z., A. Matheny, I. Bretherton, A. Renouf, and M. Sherman. "Maternal Representation of the Self as Parent: Connections with Maternal Sensitivity and Maternal Structuring." *Attachment and Human Development,* 2, 2000, 218–232.

Black, K. A., E. Jaefer, and K. McCartney. "Attachment Models, Peer Interaction Behavior, and Feelings About the Self: Indication of Maladaptation in Dismissing/Preoccupied (Ds/E) Adolescents." In P. M. Crittenden and A. H. Claussen, eds. *The Organization of Attachment Relationships: Maturation, Culture, and Context.* 2000.

Bretherton, I. "Open Communication and Internal Working Models: Their Role in the Development of Attachment Relationships." In R. A. Thompson, ed. *Socioemotional Development (Nebraska Symposium on Motivation).* Lincoln: University of Nebraska Press, 1990.

Broussard, E. R., and M. S. Hartner. "Maternal Perception of the Neonate as Related to Development." *Child Psychiatry and Human Development,* 1, 1971, 16–25.

Campbell, S. B. "Mother-Infant Interaction as a Function of Maternal Ratings of Temperament." *Child Psychiatry and Human Development,* 10, 1979, 67–76.

Fonagy, P., H. Steele, and M. Steele. "Intergenerational Patterns of Attachment: Maternal Representations During Pregnancy and Subsequent Infant-Mother Attachments." *Child Development,* 62, 1991, 210–225.

Grossman, K., E. Fremmer-Bombik, J. Rudolph, and K. E. Grossman. "Maternal Attachment Representations as Related to Patterns of Infant-Mother Attachment and Maternal Care During the First Year." In R. A. Hinde and J. Stevenson-Hinde, eds. *Relationships within Families.* Oxford: Oxford University Press, 1988.

Kobak, R., and A. Sceery. "The Transition to College: Working Models of Attachment, Affect Regulation, and Perceptions of Self and Others." *Child Development,* 59, 1988, 135–146.

Main, M., and J. Solomon. "Discovery of an Insecure Disorganized/Disoriented Attachment Pattern." In T. B. Brazelton and M. W. Yogman, eds. *Affective Development in Infancy.* Norwood, NJ: Ablex, 1986.

Main, M., N. Kaplan, and J. Cassidy. "Security in Infancy, Childhood, and Adulthood: A Move to the Level of Representation." In I. Bretherton and E. Waters, eds. "Growing Points of Attachment Theory and Research." *Monographs of the Society for Research in Child Development,* 50, 1985, 1–2, Serial No. 209.

Van Ijzendoorn, M. H., M. J. Kranenburg, H. A. Zwart-Woudstra, A. M. van Busschbach, and M. W. Lambermon. "Parental Attachment and Children's Socioemotional Development: Some Findings on the Validity of the Adult Attachment Interview in the Netherlands." *International Journal of Behavioral Development,* 14, 1991, 375–394.

CHAPTER 4: THE IMPORTANCE OF EMOTIONAL AVAILABILITY

Aviezar, O., A. Sagi, T. Joels, and Y. Ziv. "Emotional Availability and Attachment Representations in Kibbutz Infants and Their Mothers." *Developmental Psychology,* 35, 1999, 811–821.

Biringen, Z. "Direct Observation of Maternal Sensitivity and Dyadic Interactions in the Home: Relations to Maternal Thinking." *Developmental Psychology,* 26, 1990, 278–284.

Biringen, Z., D. Brown, L. Donaldson, Kremarik S. Green, and G. Lovas. "Adult Attachment Interview: Linkages with Dimensions of Emotional Availability for Mothers and Their Prekindergartners." *Attachment and Human Development,* 2, 2000, 188–202.

Biringen, Z., R. N. Emde, J. J. Campos, and M. I. Appelbaum. "Affective Reorganization in the Infant, the Mother, and the Dyad: The Role of Upright Locomotion and Its Timing." *Child Development,* 66, 1995, 499–514.

Biringen, Z., and J. L. Robinson. "Emotional Availability: A Reconceptualization for Research." *American Journal of Orthopsychiatry,* 61, 1991, 258–271.

Bretherton, I. "Emotional Availability: An Attachment Perspective." *Attachment and Human Development,* 2, 2000, 233–241.

Davies, P. T., and E. M. Cummings. "Marital Conflict and Child Adjustment: An Emotional Security Hypothesis." *Psychological Bulletin,* 116, 1994, 387–411.

Easterbrooks, M. A., G. Biesecker, and K. Lyons-Ruth. "Infancy Predictors of Emotional Availability in Middle Childhood: The Roles of Attachment Security and Maternal Depressive Symptomatology." *Attachment and Human Development,* 2, 2000, 170–187.

Emde, R. N. "Emotional Availability: A Reciprocal Reward System for Infants and Parents with Implications for Prevention of Psychosocial Disorders." In P. M. Taylor, ed. *Parent-Infant Relationships.* Orlando, FL: Grune and Stratton, 1980.

————"Next Steps in Emotional Availability Research." *Attachment and Human Development,* 2, 2000, 242–248.

Emde, R. N. and M. A. Easterbrooks. "Assessing Emotional Availability in Early Development." In D. K. Frankenberg, R. N. Emde, J. W. Sullivan, eds. *Early Identification of Children at Risk: An International Perspective.* New York: Plenum Press, 1985.

Kogan, N., and A. S. Carter "Mother-Infant Reengagement Following the Still-Face: The Role of Maternal Emotional Availability in Infant Affect Regulation." *Infant Behavior and Development,* 19, 1996, 359–370.

Oyen, A., S. Landy, and C. Hilburn-Cogg. "Maternal Attachment and Sensitivity in an At-Risk Sample." *Attachment and Human Development,* 2, 2000, 203–217.

Pipp-Siegel, S., and Z. Biringen. "Assessing the Quality of Relationships Between Parents and Children: The Emotional Availability Scales." *Volta Review,* 100, 2000, 237–279.

Pipp-Siegel, S., N. L. Blair, A. M. Deas, L. J. Pressman, and C. Yoshinaga-Itano. "Touch and Emotional Availability in Hearing and Deaf or Hard of Hearing Toddlers and Their Hearing Mothers." *Volta Review,* 100, 2000, 279–298.

Robinson, J. L., and Z. Biringen. "Gender and Emerging Autonomy in Development." *Journal of Psychoanalytic Inquiry*, 15, 1995, 60–74.

Robinson, J., and C. Little. "Emotional Availablity in Mother-Twin Dyads: Effects on the Organization of Relationships." *Psychiatry*, 57, 1994, 22–31.

Robinson, J. L., R. N. Emde, and J. Korfmacher. "Integrating an Emotional Regulation Perspective in a Program of Prenatal and Early Childhood Home Visitation." *Journal of Community Psychology*, 25, 1997, 59–75.

Robinson, J. L., and L. Glaves. "Supporting Emotion Regulation and Emotional Availability Through Home Visitation." *Zero to Three*, 17, 1996, 31–35.

Sorce, J., and R. N. Emde. "Mother's Presence Is Not Enough: Effect of Emotional Availability on Infant Exploration." *Developmental Psychology*, 6, 1981, 737–745.

Ziv, Y., O. Aviezar, M. Gini, A. Sagi, and N. Koren-Karie. "Emotional Availability in the Mother-Infant Dyad as Related to the Quality of Infant-Mother Attachment Relationship." *Attachment and Human Development*, 2, 2000, 149–169.

CHAPTER 5: THE EIGHT PRINCIPLES OF EMOTIONAL AVAILABILITY

Biringen, Z. "Appendix A: Emotional Availability Scales" (Second Ed.; an abridged Infancy in Early Childhood Version). *Attachment and Human Development*, 2, 2000, 251–255.

Biringen, Z., J. Robinson, and R. N. Emde. "Appendix B: Emotional Availability Scales" (Third Ed.; an abridged Infancy/Early Childhood Version)." *Attachment and Human Development*, 2, 2000, 251–255.

CHAPTER 6: THE TWO SIDES TO EMOTIONAL CONNECTION

Bates, J. E., C. A. Maslin, and K. A. Frankel. "Attachment Security, Mother-Child Interaction, and Temperament as Predictors of Behavior Problems Ratings at Age Three Years." In I. Bretherton and E. Waters, eds. "Growing Points of Attachment Theory and Research." *Monographs of the Society for Research in Child Development*, 50, 1985 1–2, Serial No. 209.

Belsky, J., M. Rovine, and D. G. Taylor. "The Pennsylvania Infant and Family Development Project, 3: The Origins of Individual Differences in Infant-Mother Attachment: Maternal and Infant Contributions." *Child Development*, 55, 1984, 718–728.

Biringen, Z., J. L. Robinson, and R. N. Emde. "Maternal Sensitivity in the Second Year: Gender-Based Relations in the Dyadic Balance of Control." *American Journal of Orthopsychiatry*, 64, 1994, 78–90.

Hetherington, E. M., D. Reiss, and R. Plomin. "*Separate Social World of Siblings: The Impact of Nonshared Environment on Development.*" Hillsdale, NJ: L. Erlbaum, 1994.

Lovas, G. "Gender and Patterns of Emotional Availability Among Parents and Their Toddlers." Paper presented at the Biennial Meetings of the Society for Research in Child Development. Z. Biringen and M. A. Easterbrooks, chairs. "Next Steps in Emotional Availability Research: Diverse Populations, Longitudinal Predictions, and Methodological Inquiry," 2001.

Robinson, J. L., C. Little, and Z. Biringen. "Emotional Communication in Mother-Toddler Relationships: Evidence for Early Gender Differentiation." *Merrill-Palmer Quarterly* 39, 1993, 496–517.

Shamir-Essakow, G. "Attachment, Behavioral Inhibition and Anxiety Problems in Preschool Children." Thesis submitted for the combined degree of Doctor of Philosophy/Master of Clinical Psychology, Department of Psychology (advisor, J. Ungerer), MacQuarie University, Australia, 2002.

Sorce, J., and R. N. Emde. "Mother's Presence Is Not Enough: Effect of Emotional Availability on Infant Exploration." *Developmental Psychology*, 6, 1981, 737–745.

Sroufe, L. A. "Attachment Classification from the Perspective of Infant-Caregiver Relationships and Infant Temperament." *Child Development*, 56, 1985, 1–14.

Swanson, K., L. Beckwith, and J. Howard. "Intrusive Caregiving and Quality of Attachment in Prenatally Drug-Exposed Toddlers and Their Primary Caregivers." *Attachment and Human Development*, 2, 2000, 130–148.

Thompson, C., and P. Cowen. "*Violence: Basic and Clinical Science.* Oxford; Boston: Butterworth-Heinemann in association with the Mental Health Foundation. 1993.

Tronick, E. E., and J. F. Cohn. "Infant-Mother Face-to-Face Interaction: Age and Gender Differences in Coordination." *Child Development,* 60, 1989, 85–92.

Tronick, E., J. Cohn, and E. Shea. "The Transfer of Affect Between Mothers and Infants." In T. B. Brazelton and M. W. Yogman, eds. *Affective Development in Infancy.* Norwood, NJ: Ablex Publishing Corp, 1986.

Tronick, E. Z., H. Als, L. Adamson, S. Wise, and T. B. Brazelton. "The Infant's Response to Entrapment Between Contradictory Messages in Face-to-Face Interaction." *American Academy of Child Psychiatry,* 17, 1978, 1–18.

Valente, E. Jr., and K. A. Dodge. *Evaluation of Prevention Programs for Children.* Washington, DC: U. S. Department of Education, Office of Educational Research and Improvement, Educational Research Information Center, 1997.

Vaughn, B. E., J. Stevenson-Hinde, E. Waters, A. Kotsaftis, G. B. Lefever, A. Shouldice, M. Trudel, and J. Belsky. "Attachment Security and Temperament in Infancy and Early Childhood: Some Conceptual Clarifications." *Development Psychology,* 28, 1992, 463–473.

Vaughn, B. E., B. J. Taraldson, L. Crichton, and B. Egeland. "The Assessment of Infant Temperament: A Critique of the Carey Infant Temperament Questionnaire." *Infant Behavior and Development,* 4, 1981, 1–17.

CHAPTER 7: CREATING EMOTIONAL CONNECTIONS

Cassidy, J. "Emotion Regulation: Influences of Attachment Relationships." In N. Fox, ed. "The Development of Emotion Regulation: Biological and Behavioral Considerations." *Monographs of the Society for Research in Child Development,* 59, 1994, 2–3, Serial No. 240.

Koniak-Griffen, D., I. Verzemnieks, and D. Cahill. "Using Videotape Instruction and Feedback to Improve Adolescents' Mothering Behaviors." *Journal of Adolescent Health,* 13, 1992, 570–575.

Oppenheim, D., N. Koren-Karie, and A. Sagi. "Mother's Empathic Understanding of Their Preschoolers' Internal Experience: Relations with Early Attachment." *International Journal of Behavioral Development,* 2001.

CHAPTER 9: SUPPORTING YOUR CHILD TO HAVE POSITIVE SIBLING AND PEER CONNECTIONS

Arend, R., F. L. Gove, and L. A. Sroiufe. "Continuity of Individual Adaptation from Infancy to Kindergarten: A Predictive Study of Ego-Resiliency and Curiosity in Preschoolers." *Child Development,* 50, 1979, 950–959.

Dodge, K. A. "Attributional Bias in Aggressive Children." In Philip C. Kendall, ed. *Advances in Cognitive-Behavioral Research and Therapy,* Vol. 4, 73–110. Orlando, FL: Academic Press, 1985.

Faber, A., and E. Mazlish. *How to Talk So Kids Will Listen and Listen So Kids Will Talk.* New York: Rawson, Wade Publishers, Inc.

Gottman, J. *Raising an Emotionally Intelligent Child.* New York: Simon & Schuster, 1997.

Greenberg, M. T., and D. Cicchetti. *Attachment in the Preschool Years: Theory, Research, and Intervention.* Chicago: University of Chicago Press, 1990.

Harris, J. R. *The Nurture Assumption: Why Children Turn Out the Way They Do.* New York: Free Press, 1998.

Kagan, J. "Concept of Behavioral Inhibition." In L. A. Schmidt and J. Schulkin, eds. *Extreme Fear, Shyness, and Social Phobia: Biological Mechanisms and Clinical Outcomes.* London: Oxford University Press, 3–13.

Middleton-Moz, J., and M. L. Zawadski. *Bullies: From the Playground to the Boardroom.* Deerfield Beach, FL: Health Communications, Inc., 2002.

Rubin, K. H. *The Friendship Factor.* New York: Viking, 2002.

Sroufe, L. A. *Emotional Development: The Organization of Emotional Life in the Early Years.* Cambridge; New York: Cambridge University Press, 1996.

Waters, E., J. Wippman, and L. A. Sroufe. "Attachment, Positive Affect, and Competence in the Peer Group: Two Studies in Construct Validation." *Child Development,* 50, 1979, 821–829.

Winnicott, D. W. *The Family and Individual Development.* New York: Basic Books, 1965.

CHAPTER 10: PROVIDING EMOTIONAL SUPPORT FOR LEARNING

Barrett, M., and J. Trevitt. *Attachment Behavior and the Schoolchild: An Introduction to Educational Theory.* New York: Tavistock/Routledge, 1991.

Baumrind, D. "Influence of Parenting Style on Adolescent Competence and Substance Use." *Journal of Early Adolescence.* 11, 1991, 56–95.

Cicchetti, D., and D. J. Cohen. *Developmental Psychopathology.* New York: John Wiley and Sons, 1995.

Tofler, I., and T. F. DiGeronimo. *Keeping Your Kids Out Front Withouth Kicking Them From Behind: How to Nurture High-Achieving Athletes, Scholars, and Performing Artists.* San Francisco: Jossey Bass, 2000.

CHAPTER 11: KEEPING THE CONNECTION WHEN IT'S TIME TO TALK ABOUT THE TOUGH ISSUES

Gianetti, C. C., and M. Sugarese. *Cliques.* New York: Broadway Books, 2001.

Krafchick, J., and Z. Biringen. "Parents as Sexuality Educators: The Role of Family Therapists in Coaching Parents." *Journal of Feminist Family Therapy.* 14, 2002 ¾, 57–72.

Rubin, K. H. *The Friendship Factor.* New York: Viking, 2002.

CHAPTER 12: BEING EMOTIONALLY AVAILABLE EVEN IF YOUR CHILD (OR ADOLESCENT) ISN'T

Solomon, J. and C. George. "The Development of Attachment in Separated and Divorced Families." *Attachment and Human Development,* 1, 1999, 2–35.

CHAPTER 13: DUAL-INCOME COUPLES—A NEAT BALANCING ACT

Easterbrooks, M. Ann, and Wendy A. Goldberg. "Security of Toddler-Parent Attachment: Relation to Children's Sociopersonality Functioning During Kindergarten." In Greenberg, Mark T., Cicchetti, Dante, eds, et. al. *Attachment in the Preschool Years: Theory, Research, and Intervention.* The John D. and Catherine T. MacArthur Foundation series on mental health and development. xix, 1990, 221–244.

Gottfried, A.W., and A. E. Gottfried. *Redefining Families: Implications for Children's Development.* Orlando, FL: Academic, 1994.

Lovas, G. "Gender and Patterns of Emotional Availability Among Parents and Their Toddlers." Paper presented at the Biennial Meetings of the Society for Research in Child. Z. Biringen and M. A. Easterbrooks, chairs. "Next Steps in Emotional Availability Research: Diverse Populations, Longitudinal Predictions, and Methodological Inquiry," 2001.

NICHD Early Early Child Care Research Network. "The Effects of Infant Child Care on Infant-Mother Attachment Security: Results of the NICHD Study of Early Child Care." *Child Development,* 68, 1997, 860–879.

CHAPTER 14: EMOTIONAL NEEDS OF FOSTER AND ADOPTED CHILDREN AS WELL AS CHILDREN WITH SPECIAL NEEDS

Chisholm, K. "Attachment in Children Adopted from Romanian Orphanages: Two Case Studies." In P. M. Crittenden and A. H. Claussen, eds. *The Organization of Attachment Relationships: Maturation, Culture, and Context.* 2000: 171, 189. Cambridge, New York: Cambridge University Press.

Gil, E. *Play in Family Therapy.* New York: Guilford, Press, 1994.

Hinshaw, S. *Attention Deficits and Hyperactivity in Children.* Thousand Oaks: Sage Publications, 1994.

Jacobsen, T., and V. Hofman. "Children's Attachment Representations: Longitudinal Relations to School Behavior and Academic Competency in Middle Childhood and Adolescence." *Developmental Psychology,* 33, 1997, 703–710.

Lis, S. "Characteristics of Attachment Behavior in Institution-Reared Children." In P. M. Crittenden and A. H. Claussen, eds. *The Organization of Attachment Relationships: Maturation, Culture, and Context.* 2000: 141–170, 2000. Cambridge, New York: Cambridge University Press

Marvin, R. S., and R. C. Pianta. "Mothers' Reactions to Their Child's Diagnosis: Relations with Security of Attachment." *Journal of Clinical Child Psychology,* 25, 1996, 436–445.

Perry, B. "Incubated in Terror: Neuro-Developmental Factors in the Cycle of Violence?" In J. Osofsky, ed. *Children in a Violent Society* (pp. 124–149). New York: Guilford, 1997.

CHAPTER 15: SUPPORTING YOUR CHILD DURING YOUR DIVORCE AND REMARRIAGE

Bowlby, J. *A Secure Base: Parent-Child Attachment and Healthy Human Development.* New York: Basic Books, 1988.

Emery, R. E. *Marriage, Divorce, and Children's Adjustment.* Newbury Park, CA: Sage, 1988.

Hetherington, E., and W. G. Clingempeel. "Coping with Marital Transitions." *Monographs of the Society for Research in Child Development,* 57, 1992, 227.

Johnston, J. "Role Diffusion and Role Reversal: Structural Variations in Divorced Families and Children's Functioning." *Family Relations,* 39, 1990, 406–413.

Johnston, J., M. Kline, and J. M. Tschann. "Ongoing Postdivorce Conflicts: Effects on Children of Joint Custody and Frequent Access." *American Journal of Orthopsychiatry,* 59, 1989 576–592.

Kline, M., J. M. Tschann, and J. S. Wallerstein. "Children's Adjustment in Joint and Sole Physical Custody Families." *Developmental Psychology,* 25, 1989, 430–438.

Main, M., and J. Cassidy. "Categories of Response to Reunions with the Parent at Age Six: Predictable from Infant Attachment Classifications and Stable Over a One-Month Period." *Developmental Psychology,* 24, 1988, 415–526.

Main, M., and E. Hesse. "Parents' Unresolved Traumatic Experiences Are Related to Infant Disorganized Attachment Status: Is Frightened and/or Frightening Parental Behavior the Linking Mechanism?" In M. T. Greenberg, D. Cicchetti, and E. M. Cummings, eds. *Attachment in the Preschool Years.* Chicago: University of Chicago Press, 1990.

Pressman, L. J., S. Pipp-Siegel, C. Yoshinaga-Itano, L. Kubicek, and R. N. Emde. "A Comparison of Links Between Emotional Availability and Language Gain in Young Children with and without Hearing Loss. *Volta Review,* 100, 2000, 251–278.

Sroufe, L. A., and J. Fleeson. "Attachment and the Construction of Relationships." In W. Hartup and Z. Rubin, eds. *Relationships and Development.* Hillsdale, NJ: Erlbaum, 1986.

————"The Coherence of Relationships." In R. A. Hinde and J. Stevenson-Hinde, eds. *Relationships Within Families: Mutual Influences.* Oxford: Clarendon, 1988.

Teti, D. M., and K. E. Ablard. "Security of Attachment and Infant-Sibling Relationships: A Laboratory Study." *Child Development,* 60, 1989, 1519–1528.

Tronick, E. Z., S. Winn, and G. A. Morelli. "Multiple Caretaking in the Context of Human Evolution: Why Don't the Efe Know the Western Prescription to Child Care?" In M. Reite and T. Field, eds. *The Psychology of Attachment and Separation.* San Diego: Academic, 1985.

Van Ijzendoorn, M. H., and P. M. Kroonenberg. "Cross-Cultural Patterns of Attachment: A Meta-Analysis of the Strange Situation." *Child Development,* 59, 1988, 147–156.

Van Ijzendoorn, M. H., F. Juffer, and M.G.C. Duyvesteyn. "Breaking the Intergenerational Cycle of Insecure Attachment: A Review of the Effects of Attachment-Based Interventions on Maternal Sensitivity and Infant Security." *Journal of Child Psychology and Psychiatry,* 36, 1995, 225–248.

Wallerstein, J., and J. Kelly. *Surviving the Breakup: How Children and Parents Cope with Divorce.* New York: Basic, 1980.

Weiss, R. S. "The Attachment Bond in Childhood and Adulthood." In C. M. Parkes, J. Stevenson-Hinde, and P. Marris, eds. *Attachment Across the Life Cycle.* London: Routledge, 1991.

Woodward, L., D. M. Ferguson, and J. Belsky. "Timing of Parental Separation and Attachment to Parents in Adolescence: Results of a Prospective Study from Birth to Age 16." *Journal of Marriage and the Family,* 62, 2000, 162–174.

Zimmerman, L., and L. McDonald. "Emotional Availability in Infants' Relationships with Multiple Caregivers." *American Journal of Orthopsychiatry.* 65, 1995, 147–152.

CHAPTER 16: KEEPING THE CONNECTION IN TIMES OF CRISIS

Allen, J. *Traumatic Relationships and Serious Mental Disorders.* New York: John Wiley and Sons, 2001.

CONCLUSION

Rohner, R. P. *They Love Me, They Love Me Not.* New Haven, CT: HRAF, 1975.

———*The Warmth Dimension.* Beverly Hills: Sage Publications, 1975.

Van Ijzendoorn, M. H., S. Goldberg, P. M. Kroonenberg, and O. J. Frenkel. "The Relative Effects of Maternal and Child Problems on the Quality of Attachment: A Meta-Analysis of Attachment in Clinical Samples." *Child Development,* 63, 1992, 840–885.

Recommended Reading

Bluestein, J. *Creating Emotionally Safe Schools.* Deerfield Beach, FL: Health Communications, Inc., 2001.

Brooks, R. and S. Goldstein. *Raising Resilient Children.* New York: Contemporary Books, 2001.

Cytryn, L. and D. McKnew. *Growing Up Sad.* New York: W. W. Norton & Company, 1996.

Faber, A. and E. Mazlish. *How To Talk So Kids Will Listen and Listen So Kids Will Talk.* New York: Rawson, Wade Publishers, Inc.

Goleman, D. *Emotional Intelligence: Why It Can Matter More than IQ.* New York: Bantam Books, 1995.

Gottman, J. *Raising an Emotionally Intelligent Child.* New York: Simon & Schuster, 1997.

Hendrix, H. and H. Hunt. *Giving the Love That Heals: A Guide for Parents.* New York: Pocket Books, 1997.

Middleton-Moz, J. and M. L. Zawadski. *Bullies: From the Playground to the Boardroom.* Deerfield Beach, FL: Health Communications, Inc., 2002.

Rubin, K. H. *The Friendship Factor: Helping Our Children Navigate Their Social World—and Why It Matters for Their Success and Happiness.* New York: Viking, 2002.

Seligman, M.E.P. *The Optimistic Child.* Boston, MA: Houghton Mifflin Co., 1995.

Stepp, L. S. *Our Last Best Shot: Guiding Our Children Through Early Adolescence.* New York: Riverhead Books, 2000.

Tofler, I. and T. F. Di Geronimo. *Keeping Your Kids Out Front Without Kicking Them From Behind: How to Nurture High-Achieving Athletes, Scholars, and Performing Artists.* San Francisco: Jossey Bass, 2000.

Index

About the Author

Zeynep Biringen is an associate professor at Colorado State University and a practicing clinical child psychologist. She is the author of numerous research articles on attachment of infants and young children to their parents, emotional availability, and the importance of transition times for children and families. She is well recognized in both national and international scientific communities for her research on parent-child relationships. She conducts one or two international training workshops per year on teaching professionals and researchers how to assess "emotional availability," and she also organizes workshops for parents on improving their own emotional availability with their children. She is the mother of a ten-year-old girl and lives with her daughter and husband in Colorado.